ADVANCE PRAISE FOR

ECOpreneuring

There is gold in going green, and the same drive to make a buck that created global warming can now be harnessed to slow the carbon-based pollution that is overheating the planet. *ECOpreneuring* shows how we can harness our country's entrepreneurial spirit to avert global catastrophe and profit from doing so.

— ROBERT F. KENNEDY, JR.

Inspiring commonsense wisdom! John and Lisa show us how they have built a business while living the life they love. While most of us dream of making a living out of our deepest purpose, this pioneer American family has achieved their mission: to live well, independently while sustaining and restoring the Earth. As writers and innkeepers, they also teach their guests the spiritual art of ethical living. Keep this guide handy to survive whatever the future brings.

— HAZEL HENDERSON, author of *Ethical Markets: Growing The Green Economy*

As our massive environmental challenges yield an array of entrepreneurial opportunities, Free Agent Nation is turning green. *ECOpreneuring* is the ultimate how-to book for starting your business, shaping your legacy, and maybe even saving our planet.

— DANIEL H. PINK, bestselling author of *A Whole New Mind* and *Free Agent Nation*

This practical book does nothing less than redefine free enterprise, away from "the freedom of large corporations to do anything they want to people and planet in pursuit of profit," to "the freedom of everyone to BE enterprising." If you have ever considered starting a business with social and environmental goals, do yourself a favor and read this book.

— KEVIN DANAHER, Co-founder Global Exchange and Green Festivals, and coauthor of *Building the Green Economy: Success Stories from the Grassroots*

Why waste time on business school? If you've ever dreamed of saving the planet through your own business, this book provides everything you need to get started — product ideas, finance opportunities, resources galore, and market-savvy advice. Its inspirational stories are guaranteed to get you to rethink and reintegrate, top to bottom, your personal, political, and professional ideals.

— MICHAEL SHUMAN, author of *The Small-Mart Revolution: How Local Businesses Are Beating the Global Competition*

Inspiring, well researched and easy to read, Ivanko and Kivirist show us that operating a mission-based business benefits communities, preserves resources, and strengthens profits. *ECOpreneuring* will have you cheering for green business everywhere — and might just convince you to start or join one yourself.

— ALISA GRAVITZ, Executive Director of Co-op America

In the carefully crafted pages of *ECOpreneuring*, Kivirist and Ivanko weave together a perspective that can transform how you think about work — and a more sustainable life. Their timely book is jam-packed with the necessary details to sort out what it means to live simply and sustainably in an economy that fosters life, not depletes it. As it turns out, beyond a certain point, there's an inverse relationship between financial wealth and personal well-being. *ECOpreneuring* illuminates a radically different approach both working and living.

— WANDA URBANSKA, host of "Simple Living with Wanda Urbanska"

Lisa Kivirist and John Ivanko prove that working for your passions and with meaning pays dividends in more ways than one. Doing so can change the world. As practical as it is inspirational, *ECOpreneuring* is for anyone who wants to make their green dream business come true. So find a mentor, invest in the future and read this perspective-changing and unconventional business book. It might even retire the staid notion of what many people call "work". No one said work had to be drudgery.

— BRIAN KURTH, founder and CEO of Vocation Vacations

ECOpreneuring opens minds — and doors. It is a delightful, informative read that really reflects the authors' living wisdom.

— MELISSA EVERETT, author of *Making a Living While Making a Difference: Conscious Careers for an Era of Interdependence*

ECOpreneuring

[Putting
Purpose
and the
Planet
before
Profits]

*John Ivanko
& Lisa Kivirist*

NEW SOCIETY PUBLISHERS

CATALOGING IN PUBLICATION DATA:
A catalog record for this publication is available from
the National Library of Canada.

Cover design by Diane McIntosh.
Images: iStock and John Ivanko

Printed in Canada.
First printing April 2008.

Paperback ISBN: 978-0-86571-605-6

Inquiries regarding requests to reprint all or part of *ECOpreneuring*
should be addressed to New Society Publishers at the address below.

To order directly from the publishers, please call toll-free (North America)
1-800-567-6772, or order online at www.newsociety.com

Any other inquiries can be directed by mail to:

New Society Publishers
P.O. Box 189, Gabriola Island, BC V0R 1X0, Canada
(250) 247-9737

New Society Publishers' mission is to publish books that contribute in fundamental ways to
building an ecologically sustainable and just society, and to do so with the least possible impact
on the environment, in a manner that models this vision. We are committed to doing this not
just through education, but through action. This book is one step toward ending global deforestation and climate change. It is printed on acid-free paper that is Forest Stewardship
Council-certified **100% post-consumer recycled** (100% old growth forest-free), processed
chlorine free, and printed with vegetable-based low-VOC inks, with covers produced using
FSC-certified stock. Additionally, New Society purchases carbon offsets based on an annual
carbon audit, operating with a carbon-neutral footprint. For further information, or to browse
our full list of books and purchase securely, visit our website at: www.newsociety.com

NEW SOCIETY PUBLISHERS
www.newsociety.com

Recycled
Supporting responsible use
of forest resources
FSC
www.fsc.org Cert no. SW-COC-1271
© 1996 Forest Stewardship Council
100%

Dedication

To Jack V. Matson — for inspiring us to embrace failure and providing the
necessary organic nutrients for our Earth Mission.

To ecopreneurs of just about every kind that we've met along the way —
thanks for your inspiration.

Disclaimer

Just for the Record

THIS BOOK IS DESIGNED and every effort was made to provide accurate information. It's sold with the understanding that the publisher and authors are not engaged in rendering legal, accounting or other professional services. Each person's legal or financial situation is unique and in the application of the law to the facts with the fair and reasonable interpretation of them. Any action pursued related to the contents of this book should be undertaken with the counsel and advice of a trained legal, tax, investment and accounting professional. Because of the risk that is involved with an investment of any kind, neither the publisher nor the authors assume liability for any losses that may be sustained by the use of the advice described in this book, and any such liability is hereby expressly disclaimed. If legal or other professional assistance is required, the services of a professional should be sought, especially since some of the information could, and likely will, change because it relates to governmental tax law and its interpretation thereof.

Adapted from a declaration jointly adopted by the American Bar Association and a committee of publishers.

Table of Contents

The time is right for ecopreneurs to experience the numerous advantages of operating a business, often focusing on solving the problems facing society. They thrive in the Multiple Economies of Ecopreneurship. Non-profit organizations are also businesses.

Ecopreneurs embark on their quest to ride the Four Horsemen of Opportunity — global warming, ecological collapse, peak oil and debt. Their small businesses play an important role in the American economy.

Definitions, qualities, guidelines and certification programs for sustainable business. How to go beyond business, keeping elements of your life sustainable and thriving with a whole pie purpose.

Ways to shift your perspective about jobs and entrepreneurship, from spending to achieve a standard of living to making a quality life. By creating lives that provide meaning and purpose, ecopreneurs experience social and economic benefits.

Acknowledgments

THE SEEDS FOR *ECOpreneuring: Putting Purpose and the Planet Before Profits* germinated from one common request we kept receiving from our workshop attendees, B & B guests and readers of *Rural Renaissance: Renewing the Quest for the Good Life*: Provide more details on how to start a small green business. Give me practical, helpful information to start my own eco-venture, crafting a livelihood where I can pursue my passions while stewarding the Earth. We are grateful to all of you for inspiring us in our livelihood that blends creative expression, education and celebrating our planet's abundance.

As always, we thank the dedicated folks at New Society Publishers for their continual support and vision, especially Chris and Judith Plant, our editors, Ingrid Witvoet and Judith Brand, and the marketing dynamos, Ginny Miller and EJ Hurst. We still haven't located Gabriola Island, BC, on the map — the headquarters of New Society Publishers — yet the synergy between us remains strong. Thank you for your efforts to move the publishing industry into new, sustainable realms. We remain honored to be part of your team. Our heartfelt appreciation extends to Bill McKibben, who passionately sets the stage for this book, and in every way champions the environment and our communities.

Thanks, also, to our web of friends who continually provide us with feedback, inspiration and positive energy, especially Steve Apfelbaum, Ken and Ann Avery, Scott Coleman, Elizabeth Goreham, Jan Joannides, Dr. Jack Matson, Ron Nielsen, Brett Olson, Mary and Rick Stanek, Cheryl Toth, Matt Urban, Phil and Judy Welty and our local kindred spirited community, especially the Carus, Hankley, Krieger and Vestin families. Deep appreciation to Dr. Jack Matson and Mark and Lechia Davis who generously volunteered to read the initial manuscript draft. Thank you to the individuals who warmly shared their insights for the ecopreneurial profiles featured in this book: David Anderson, Brett and Tawnee Dufur, Priya

Haji, Eric Henry, Jan Joannides, Peter Nicholson, Brett Olson, Chris and Judith Plant and David Van Seters.

It goes without saying that without the guidance, support and resources of numerous non-profit organizations and like-minded businesses, we wouldn't be here today. The following are a few of the many (too numerous to name them all): Renewing the Countryside, The Midwest Renewable Energy Association, Co-op America, Equal Exchange, CROPP/Organic Valley Family of Farms, Travel Green Wisconsin, the Midwest Organic & Sustainable Education Service (MOSES), Willy Street Co-op, Wisconsin Focus on Energy, *Hobby Farms* and *Hobby Farm Home* magazines, *Natural Home* magazine, Illinois Renewable Energy Association, I-Renew, E Magazine, Southern Energy and Environment Expo, SolWest Fair, Wisconsin Trails, *Mother Earth News*, Alliant Energy's Second Nature program, Michael Fields Agricultural Institute, Ecospeakers, Foresight Design, the International Ecotourism Society, the Food and Society Fellows Program, the Thomas Jefferson Agricultural Institute and the W. K. Kellogg Foundation.

This book, like just about all our endeavors, evolves and blossoms as a family project. We are grateful for the loving grandparent support of Aelita and Walt Kivirist and Susan Ivanko, all eager to hang with Liam while Mom and Dad peck away at the computer. Thanks to Liam Ivanko Kivirist for his perpetual enthusiasm and abiding curiosity. We gave him the name "Liam," Gaelic for "great protector," as inspiration for us to keep learning, experimenting and reimagining a more ecologically abundant and socially just tomorrow.

Foreword

RECENT YEARS HAVE SEEN many new coinages as we've begun to realize just how badly we've gone astray and where the answers might lie: "carbon footprint," say, or "localvore." Eco-preneuring is a particularly interesting one, because you're not immediately sure whether the "eco" stands for economy or ecology—whether it stands for green or for green.

As it turns out, either will do—that's the good news here. But only if they're linked, linked tightly.

Our ecological problem stems largely, I think, from the way we think about our economic life. The only thing we've asked of the economy is that it get bigger—that's been our sole criteria for success. And since we're smart people and good at accomplishing what we set out to do, it's gotten bigger. And bigger. And bigger still. By now it's casting a long shadow across the planet, and we've reached the point where sheer expansion seems increasingly unlikely. Consider: if the Chinese come to own cars at the same rate that Americans do, the current 800 millions autos on planet earth will be joined by 1.1 billion in China alone. And then there's India, where Tata just started selling a $2,500 coupe. It can't be done—not enough steel, not enough rubber, not enough gas, and definitely not enough atmosphere to store the effluents.

One of the biggest ironies of our growth model is that we're coming to realize that it has failed to make our society particularly satisfied—indeed, the number of Americans who say they're very happy with their lives was higher in 1956 than it is today, though the standard of living has trebled over that half century.

And yet we clearly need an economic life. We all like to eat, and we all like many of the other pleasures of our time.

What to do? The answer, I think, is to ask more of our economic life than we do at the moment. We need to demand not just growth (in fact, we're probably already oversized). We need to ask also that the economy provide some chance at durability, and that it provide some shot at real satisfaction.

Government policy will help with these goals (western Europeans use half as much energy per capita, and are more contented with their lives by every measure). But so will individual thinking and action of the kind outlined in this fine book. We can begin to build strong local economies that support durable communities, the kind of communities equipped to deal with the dangers this century will bring. But the key word is community—for too long, we've viewed economic life as a battle between individuals for more. Eco-preneuring needs to be a collaboration between people for better. That's where the future lies!

> — Bill McKibben is the author of many books, most recently a collection called *The Bill McKibben Reader*. He is also an organizer of the international global warming campaign 350.org

Introduction

I came to Inn Serendipity expecting a bed and breakfast — I discovered something more. Lisa and John, you created your own eco-zip code here. From the organic breakfast ingredients traveling 100 feet from the garden to my plate to electricity generated from the wind turbine to passionate discussions around last night's campfire, your efforts break the status quo, cookie-cutter business model. Everything integrates under a green umbrella of having both purpose and profit, spiked with creative, innovative zest for living.

— Elizabeth, written in the
Inn Serendipity Bed & Breakfast guest book

OUR JOB TITLE DOESN'T FIT ON A TWO-BY-THREE-INCH BUSINESS CARD. In fact, our diversified business could be its own zip code: an award-winning bed and breakfast; a creative services consulting company; book authors and freelance writers; an electricity utility, harvesting power from the wind and sun; an organic farm producing vegetables, fruit and herbs; a micro biofuels processing facility, transforming waste fryer oil into biodiesel to use in the backup heating system in the greenhouse. We're experimenting with growing tropical plants in our strawbale greenhouse and care for our son without hiring someone to help. Some enterprises generate revenue; others save on expenses, all with a mindset of wanting to make this world a better place.

Our micro business super-sizes our quality of life, not our bank account. Sitting under the starry Wisconsin sky around a campfire shared with guests, we serve up a bowl of warm apple crisp while the wind turbine blades spin atop the tower in the field. Conversations among our guests flow between peak oil to preserving

JOHN IVANKO

Inn Serendipity Bed & Breakfast with solar thermal system, allowing guests to take showers with water heated by the sun.

pea pods, covering everything in between. Our six-year-old son, Liam, breaks in with a refrain on his kid-sized accordion.

We're the CEOs — Chief Environmental Officers — of our business, responsible for the "success" of our operations and its environmental and social impacts. Mostly, we eat what we grow, use what energy we generate ourselves and create the meaningful work we desire. In other words, success is relative to our worldview and based on what we value and find meaning in. Rather than make money from working at a job, we put our limited funds to work for us to serve what we call our Earth Mission, the purpose for which we're here on Earth. We define our business qualitatively, not quantitatively.

Earned income in the form of wages is over-rated. Our limited funds generate passive and portfolio income; we invest in income-producing assets, not splurging on stuff we really don't need. We try to be conservers, not consumers. As a place-based operation, only we can offer exactly what we sell, our interpretation of the B & B experience. Rather than franchising in the financial sense, we've put most of our business plan and operations on the Internet, right down to the electric diagrams of our renewable energy systems in a *Home Power* magazine article — and write books about what we've done so others can achieve their own version of the good life. Rather than trying to achieve more meaning through spiritual or personal development alone, we — like millions of others — are turning to for-profit and non-profit businesses to make a difference.

ECOpreneuring: Putting Purpose and the Planet before Profits buries the staid notion that "doing business" and "doing good" can't blend — as if one must come at the expense of the other. This book stems from our experiences and those of hundreds of other green entrepreneurs we've met from coast to coast at energy fairs and green conferences or roasted marshmallows with around our campfire when they came our way as B & B guests. Others we have interviewed for magazine articles or partnered with on various consulting projects and events. Some ecopreneurs have taken junk bicycle parts and turned them into unique picture frames and bottle openers. Others have opened up eBay stores in the middle of nowhere Montana, running wine tastings on the side. Each has a story to tell; many do exactly that right on their package, website or blog. Each of us, in our own ways, sidestepped the stereotype ingrained by society that the coveted end goal of business remains never-ending growth and financial riches beyond our wildest dreams.

There are millions of small business owners and more on the way when about 77 million baby boomers start "retiring," half of them starting the dream business they've always wanted. One entrepreneur, Brian Kurth, started Vocation Vacations to offer others an opportunity to turn their passions into a career (vocationvacations.com). Forget the gold watch when you work in a company for more than 30 years. How about losing the watch? Now that's freedom.

No one seems to know exactly how many small business owners, entrepreneurs or free agents there are. While definitions run the gamut, the vast majority of small businesses are very small businesses. Dan Pink, author of *Free Agent Nation*, estimates free agents account for about 1 in every 4 workers. The US Small Business Administration (sba.gov) estimates that there are 4.5 million small businesses with 9 or fewer employees. Like us, you might be among the 15 million full-time or part-time small office/home office entrepreneurs, or SOHOs. Or maybe you're among the 75 percent of all US businesses with only one person at the helm, typically self-employed with no one else on the payroll. Amazingly, the US Census Bureau doesn't even bother including these so-called personal entrepreneurs in much of their statistical analysis because they comprise less than five percent of business tax receipts. For personal entrepreneurs, you don't even need a cloaking device; you're practically invisible.

Perhaps you picked up this book yearning for something more than a paycheck or growing weary of a paycheck without a purpose. You want your work to be more about leaving a legacy than making someone else rich or working for their dream, not yours. Bored, you want to do something you feel passionate about that also gives back to our world, makes it a better place. You want more time with your family, growing tired of living with the nagging threat of your job being outsourced or company being acquired (and you being pink-slipped or transferred somewhere away from friends or family).

Or perhaps you want more than commuting to the office in a hybrid car or donating time or money to a charity. Welcome to the emerging social sector, or "citizen sector," of our economy, embodied in the not-for-profit organization that, instead of rewarding shareholders with dividends, devotes resources to solve and serve social, ecological or community issues too often neglected, if not created, by big business, big government and free market globalization. Writes David Bornstein in *How to Change the World: Social Entrepreneurs and the Power of New Ideas*, "Social entrepreneurs are demonstrating new approaches to many social ills and new models to create wealth, promote social well-being and restore the environment." The number of non-profit organizations has skyrocketed over the last three decades, with little likelihood of diminishing.

Today our family thrives on less than what one of us made 15 years ago at the ad agency. Our quality of life has grown exponentially, despite the fact that our financial income on paper declined. There are tricks to the trade that many millionaires — and most of our millionaire politicians — use that allow us to make a life without having to become wage slaves. We agree; it's almost impossible to be amongst the working or middle class and get ahead. We've discovered a different way to bend the ends that never seem to meet, instead forming a circle, where assets generate income and liabilities are minimized. Working with passion and for the Earth is the core of our daily existence. Our diversified enterprises blend and cross back and forth into for-profit and non-profit sectors of the economy, as well as serving or partnering with, at times and very selectively, governmental agencies and big business.

Creativity blooms as we freely hopscotch between a buffet of projects, from running the two guest rooms at Inn Serendipity, writing and photographing for a magazine article for *Mother Earth News* or *Natural Home*, authoring books (some ending up award-winning), consulting on marketing projects for various non-profit organizations as subcontractors, tending our organic growing fields, speaking at conferences, and home-schooling our young son, Liam. Both our lifestyle and livelihood blend and reflect our values, like eliminating our contribution to global warming, eating healthy and local, forming community and renewing the Earth.

While hanging out our shingle and becoming a small business owner is nothing new, mindfully serving the planet through what and how our business operates is. Today's "ecopreneurs" recognize that profit, while a necessity in our world of mortgages and motors, is not enough. We keep a holistic outlook on the big green picture: How can we do well, make a difference and make a living? How can we take advantage of existing small business structures and incentives to benefit both our business and the planet? Running a small business provides freedom to independently control inputs and outputs, from the projects and clients we may work for to the 100 percent post-consumer-waste recycled paper we put in our printer.

We've suffered too long from Free Market Economy Dementia: a state of suspended belief in the free market despite the existence of an alternative reality: ecological destruction, concentration of financial wealth in fewer hands and diminished happiness, community life and family cohesiveness. Free market capitalism fails to optimize societal benefit when companies provide needed products or services at prices "consumers" are prepared to pay. The free market cannot grow infinitely, because we can't find substitutions for everything when there's nothing left on Earth. It's not the economy but the ecology that matters. For lots of reasons, as discussed in this book, no economy can be sustainable in the long term without a balanced, prosperous ecological system and at least some sense of social equity.

A swelling movement of multifaceted innovators — seeking meaning over money, satisfaction over status and preserving the planet over growing profits — have emerged because Free Market Economy Dementia has been treated by an awareness of the reality that if we don't start solving our planetary problems soon, we will face what Keynesian economic theory calls diminishing economic returns — with declines in our quality of life, condition of our natural environment, and, perhaps, human civilization itself. In fact, the non-profit organization Redefining Progress offers compelling evidence that, for many, hard times have already arrived.

We engage in and facilitate a lot of thinking around our campfires and breakfast tables these days. Thinking is the hardest work of all — related to cultivating your Earth Mission — and ecopreneurs do a lot of it. The deeply emotional and personal questions that guests pepper us with — and we openly encourage — reveal that we have many kindred spirits on this journey:

> **Question:** How much sustainable living experience did you have before you made the move from Chicago corporate advertising jobs to running a diversified business as entrepreneurs?
> **Answer:** Not much. We grew up in mainstream, white-bread, suburban, commute-to-a-job lifestyle. We found that passion and enthusiasm go a long way in discovering self-education options.

> **Question:** Did your family get it when you kissed off paychecks?

Answer: Never have and never will. But other kindred spirits provided support and inspiration along the way, leading us to ardently believe we could both do good and craft a livelihood full of meaning and enough money to meet financial responsibilities.

Question: Can you really live on income less than $20,000 a year (mostly passive rental income)? Do you have health insurance? Do you need to keep tight records of business miles, receipts and income?

Answer: A complex yes. Understanding and taking advantage of existing small business legal structures and tax incentives so that we do things correctly, smartly and cost-effectively helps define our personal version of "the good life." We live lean and green and, more importantly, tremendously satisfied. While we do work hard for spells at a time, we strive to also work wisely, generating revenues to support our dreams, our business and the environment.

Our first joint book, *Rural Renaissance: Renewing the Quest for the Good Life*, narrates our personal experiences of moving from urban lifestyles to an organic farm, offering essays about sustainable living, energy conservation, green design, natural building, renewable energy and organic growing. Our narratives balanced

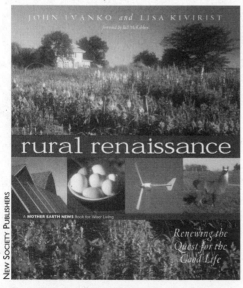

Rural Renaissance *book cover.*

Edible Earth *book cover.*

with practical resources solve the puzzle of how we managed to prosper without destroying the planet, generate revenues without destroying natural capital or exploiting people, and create a wonderful life filled with meaningful relationships, work and experiences.

Following *Rural Renaissance*, our cookbook *Edible Earth: Savoring the Good Life with Vegetarian Recipes from Inn Serendipity* explains how important local and sustainable food systems are to our collective national security and why eating lower on the food chain is better for your health, the environment and your budget. *Edible Earth* explains, through recipes, how we transformed our relationship with food and eating, acknowledging the central role it plays in our life. By eating through our pantry and refrigerator, by selectively purchasing only what we can use, we can avoid wasting over $600 worth of food thrown out each year, the national average. Waste is a concept that defines the industrial era of factories, mass production, free market economy and economies of scale. But waste equals pollution. The elimination of waste redefines our ecological sensibility for the 21st century and is one of the building blocks used by ecopreneurs.

Are You an Ecopreneur?

Is this the job ad you are considering — or perhaps you already applied for this job and got it (like we did for a few years working for an advertising agency in Chicago):

> Join our team and work in a cubicle with no fresh air or a window for 35 years on projects you could care less about for one or more bosses who care more about organizational growth and the bottom line than your growth and happiness (let alone earning enough to pay the increasing bills). Put off doing what you love until, at age 65, you can retire to eke out an existence on half your earned income, attempting to try to physically do some of the things you always wanted to do. By the way, when you retire, the pensions we promised may not be available. Ditto for the healthcare coverage.

Or do you share a personal backpack of dreams like our guests around the campfire do, yearning for a way to feel like the way you spend the majority of your awake hours, energy and talent add up to more than just a paycheck to pay the bills, putting faith in institutions that many not be solvent in 30 years. Stock options are worthless if the company that issued them files for Chapter 11 bankruptcy.

Perhaps you share a vision like the following:

> "My passion is to start a bookstore and coffeehouse, a welcoming local spot that builds community and connections."

"I'd love to work for myself, live in the mountains, do freelance writing and teach yoga."

"I want to do something that involves my family and helps teach my kids that there's more to life than money, like making a difference and leaving a legacy."

"I want to help people, be independent and make a difference in this world, I just don't know where to start, and I'm scared of leaving a company paycheck behind."

Everyone can follow their dreams. Everyone has them. No more specialized training is needed than what you've already experienced up to now. A change of perspective, a new approach to money and wealth and the necessary hard-thinking work of pruning your passions and forming your Earth Mission, your life purpose and business plan are the necessary ingredients.

Adapting to a World of Increased Variability and Instability

We live in an abundant yet fragile world, with regular waves of wounding natural events such as the Southeast Asian tsunami in 2004 or Hurricane Katrina's devastation of 2005. Hundred-year and 500-year events are happening within decades of each other. Every year, new record highs or lows are being set across the globe. Downpours swell to floods. Droughts lead to massive wildfires. Oceans are becoming scarce of fish, or filled with vast dead zones of pollution.

Despite our gains in productivity and innovation, the fuel mileage of the average car in the United States today is the same as Henry Ford's Model T, about 25 miles per gallon. We have so much food that we're getting sick and growing obese eating it. Competitive eating contests have emerged as a new sport. We're wired, but lonely. Some have great wealth, but are starved for time. This book will delve into this Paradox of Progress from the perspective that technology alone will not solve the ecological and social problems that now face humanity.

Human impacts on a global level have led us to arrive at the period of geological time on Earth called the Anthropocene, coined in 2000 by scientist Paul Crutzen, winner of the Nobel Prize. The Anthropocene reflects how pervasive our impacts have been on climate and ecosystems from both carbon dioxide emissions and other pollutants and poor land-use practices like deforestation or urban sprawl that's engulfing some of our best agricultural lands.

Added to ecological instability are additional human impacts, in what we present in chapter 2 as the Four Horsemen of Opportunity — climate change, ecological collapse, peak oil and our indebted nation — representing business problem-solving opportunities, not signs of the Apocalypse. The dangers that our technological innovations may present to us and the rest of Earth's ecosystems are symbolized and painfully felt by citizens and ecosystems around the world near the Bhopal chemical plant explosion (1984), Three Mile Island nuclear accident (1979), Chernobyl nuclear reactor meltdown in Russia (1986), Exxon Valdez oil spill in Alaska (1989) and the September 11 terrorist attacks (2001), just to name a few of the growing number of human-caused disasters or tragedies. Such events remind us of the frailty of both our lives and our world.

ECOpreneuring promotes the idea of using small business as a powerful, positive tool for social and ecological change. By transforming our lives from one of reliance on others for paychecks and meaning to crafting our own livelihood and legacy by doing our part to better this world, empowerment erupts and change occurs. Think of "ecopreneur" as a subset of "entrepreneur," a business with a mission-driven mindset using creative tactics under the green umbrella to protect the planet.

While *ECOpreneuring* will touch on many of the key facets of operating a business, this is not another cookie-cutter business book. Running a business and doing good can and should go hand in hand. Traditional business concepts such as improving productivity, reducing costs, minimizing waste (or putting other's waste to use in your business), attracting and retaining empowered employees or subcontracting to other like-minded companies or free agents eager to help meet your needs, marketing your business and securing access to affordable capital can all be approached from the perspective of sustainability. Reflecting that innovation and creativity are all but linear processes, the very concept of sustainability is fluid, evolving with new perspectives and breakthroughs.

The only constant is change. As a growing number of books, experts, governments and scientists warn, change will become more variable, intense and extreme. Ecopreneurs are at the forefront of this wave and can better adapt quickly to adversity and opportunity.

How This Book Is Organized

ECOpreneuring aims to change the way you perceive money, the role of business in solving some of today's most pressing problems, and the responsibility we must seize to reclaim the commons of commerce and cooperatively restore our planet in peril. *ECOpreneuring* starts off with general trends and perspectives and progressively becomes more detailed and practical, so that by the end of the book, you'll be able to write your own business plan and reimagine a more ecologically sound and socially responsible life, living your dream and leaving a legacy.

Think of this book as a guide, a resource, a "greenprint" for generating your own livelihood that provides passion and satisfaction in leaving our world a better place. It's a guidebook for a GBA — Green Business Administration degree.

Three main sections of the book will guide your journey:

- climate for change
- green business administration (GBA)
- web of relationships

Woven into the fiber of this book, in between the tips on business structure and mileage deductions, are profiles and short examples of small business ecopreneurs and social ecopreneurs working in the non-profit sector who prioritize purpose over profits and community over building market share. We drew these case studies as a cross-section sample from our discussions and interviews with hundreds of ecopreneurs across the country over the past decade. Sidebars provide the practical details and resources for you to create your dream business.

This book is not about making lots of money, though some ecopreneurs will achieve (some already have) significant financial returns because the ideas they implement and businesses they create find a ripe market today. *Ecopreneuring* helps you craft a livelihood to support your values, quality of life and your pursuit of happiness. Money is but a tool to those ends, not the end goal. And ecopreneurial businesses are the types of enterprises that will emerge as the culturally defining institutions in the 21st century: small, human scaled, ecologically and socially responsible, and local.

We envision a nation of ecopreneurs, much like Thomas Jefferson may have believed in a prosperous nation of yeoman farmers, harnessing the freedom of the free market and pioneering spirit but tempered by the local, social and ecological economies that have long made America great. We can change the world, one business at a time.

Part One

Climate for Change

Chapter 1

The 21st Century of Small, Local and Ecopreneurial

You Need a Thneed
I meant no harm. I most truly did not.
But I had to grow bigger. So bigger I got.
I biggered my factory. I biggered my roads.
I biggered my wagons. I biggered the loads
Of the Thneeds I shipped out. I was shipping them forth
To the South! To the East! To the West! To the North!
I went right on biggering...selling more Thneeds.
And I biggered my money, which everyone needs.

— Dr. Seuss, *The Lorax*

COMMERCE HAS BEEN AROUND since humans first traded goats for corn. Farmers and tradespeople, our yeoman entrepreneurs, grew and produced foods or provided needed services in communities while earning a living selling to neighbors. Practically all businesses were small, family-scaled enterprises that provided a livelihood while being based on natural resources and in the communities they served. Agrarian economies first transformed human relationships with the land, allowing us to stay put, plant seeds, harvest the bounty and build communities, rather than roaming the countryside hunting and gathering. While money may have been exchanged, so, too, were bartered items, gifts and services, usually based on natural resources.

The invention of the steam engine — enabling one machine to do the work of 500 horses, what we now refer to as "500 horsepower" — transformed our ability to produce things at incredible speeds. Industrialization boomed, creating wealth by transforming natural and human capital into products or services, often with little consideration as to the ethical, ecological or social consequences. What made this miracle of production possible? Coal. Burning it covered the most industrious communities with a cloud of pollution.

This age of industrialization could turn everything and everyone into a factory for production. Economies of scale guided the quest for profit maximization by increasingly large corporations that ignored the impacts of their businesses on the world around them. All but a few keen observers of the natural world failed to recognize the invaluable and necessary "free" services nature provided to sustain itself and humanity. Instead, our planet served as both a supermarket of materials and labor and a receptacle for waste.

Business ECOnomics

From this period of rapid industrialization emerged the global economy during the 20th century, based on access to relatively inexpensive sources for energy, especially oil and gas, to move products around the world or burn for heat. Placed-based companies morphed into huge multinational corporations, with operations spread throughout the world to produce products as cheaply as possible, exploiting labor and natural resources. By the end of the 1900s, governmental policies and subsidies rewarding super-sized farms or enterprises allowed these companies to prosper at the expense of American taxpayers. By the end of the century, some corporations thrived on owning almost no tangible assets at all, outsourcing their manufacturing to Asian companies. Their "value" is reflected in the intangible assets of brand, reputation, patents, management and goodwill. Thanks to outsourcing and subcontracting, one global shoe company owns less than ten percent of all its tangible assets, yet reaps most of the profits. As discussed by Andrew Savitz and Karl Weber in *The Triple Bottom Line*, for an average Fortune 500 company, as much as 75 percent of their assets are intangible.

The increasingly industrialized global market economy found a perfect developmental dance partner during the 20th century: cheap oil. Based on the widely heralded triumph of the market economy over the planned economy after the collapse of Soviet-style communism, industrialism accelerated, rooting itself in far off "undeveloped" countries where labor, land and resources were cheap or with few or limited ecological or social legal entanglements that might make doing business more costly. Milton Friedman, an economist from the University of Chicago, earned widespread acclaim for his ability to set the record straight on the purpose of business: the only social responsibility for business is to engage in activities to increase profits or maximize shareholder value.

The prosperity that ensued, however, is increasingly recognized as illusory, resulting in the formidable challenges of possible ecological collapse, global warming and social decline with a growing number of super rich and an expanding number of entrapped poor. About two billion of the planet's inhabitants eke out an existence on less than $2 per day, often making the products we wear, eat or use; the late Milton Friedman was never one of them.

> An active propaganda machinery controlled by the world's largest corporations constantly reassures us that consumerism is the path to happiness, governmental restraint of market excess is the cause of our distress, and economic globalization is both a historical inevitability and a boon to the human species.
>
> — David Korten, *When Corporations Rule the World*

As a nation, we're suffering from Free Market Economy Dementia — a state of suspended belief in free market capitalism despite the existence of an alternative reality of ecological destruction, concentration of financial wealth in fewer hands and diminished happiness, community life and family cohesiveness. And it's spreading like cancer to China and India. How can the free market capitalist system that allows 5 percent of the planet's citizens (living in the United States) to use 25 percent of the planet's resources and produce 40 percent of the planet's waste and pollution be considered a successful economic model? The belief that the free market is self-regulating couldn't be further from the truth. The World Trade Organization and various international trade agreements, such as the North American Free Trade Agreement (NAFTA), seek to transform the Earth into one big shopping mall. The present "free market" is neither free nor rational. Our first view of the Earth from space should have revolutionized our perspective for caring for what is a very finite life support system. It didn't.

> The market works to the benefit of the whole of society when it includes all costs and benefits. Only when the market accurately reflects the replacement costs of a resource (a virgin forest or salmon or Arctic oil) and the social costs of its consumption (tobacco being the most obvious) will society begin to respond to the market in a rational way.
>
> — Paul Hawken, *The Ecology of Commerce: A Declaration of Sustainability*

Corporation as "Person"

The construct of the corporation is not new. Most of the wealthy merchants and investor class of the colonial period formed corporations to deflect risk and shield their investments in the ships they dispatched to the New World, to exploit the riches — or minimize their losses if a ship was lost at sea. If the ship sunk, only their investment in it perished, not all of their assets. If the ship returned with gold and silver, the corporation would disburse it generously — only among the shareholders. By the late 1880s, corporations in the US were conveyed legal rights and protection of a "person" independent of shareholders and workers. Now what happens in the corporation stays in the corporation.

Despite the rise in large corporations and their interconnections with government and public policy, small private enterprises have prospered in humble ways, providing a livelihood to its owners and sustaining their local communities. While some large corporations were successful in gobbling up some small businesses or running them out of Main Street communities, many have steadfastly held their ground, reinventing commerce in ways big business could never compete, own or acquire. Small is emerging as the new big as more people become aware of the global and local challenges now facing us. They launch enterprising ventures that reflect the emerging role of business as the catalyst for change. We're redefining free enterprise to mean that every person can be enterprising, not just large multinational corporations that stake claim to freely move anywhere to do business any way they so desire. As this book proposes in chapters 6 and 7, small business owners can work smarter as incorporated or limited liability companies to improve their bottom line while achieving their social and environmental priorities in a reimagined living economy with conserving customers, not consumers.

Serving Conserving Customers, Not Consumers

With awareness building about our far-reaching and global impacts, we're changing how we live, work and play — becoming conservers, not consumers. Instead of borrowing from the future or burning through resources, reducing the possibilities for future generations, ecopreneurs are seeking to thrive in a restorative economy that's life giving, leaving the world a better place. It's a change in consciousness not merely a change in shopping habits. Ecopreneurial businesses, by how they operate and what products or services they offer, foster this conserver behavior. Ironically, many so-called conservatives are more concerned about conserving their present way of life and the status quo, refusing to pay attention to the changing world around them.

At our small-scale Inn Serendipity, created from a four-square farmhouse on five and half acres, our guests can relax, savor a local breakfast with most of the organic ingredients harvested from a hundred feet from our back door and drive away knowing that their carbon dioxide emissions were carbon off-set through our

Small Is Big

According to Paul Hawken, author of *The Ecology of Commerce*, the visionary business book that helped transform how many think about the role of business in relationship to the environment, the 21st century is the century for the small business. In *The Ecology of Commerce*, Hawken argues that companies of the future will exist for the purpose of restoring society, rather than in various ways divorced from or at the expense of society. These companies are repairing ecosystems, improving health and well-being, providing meaningful work, rebuilding communities and protecting the environment. Ecopreneurs thrive in what's been called the "honey bee economy" by living off solar income. Honey bees help flowers in their community when they make their honey by pollinating them. Both plants and bees prosper during the transaction. Sunlight — falling on Earth with infinite supply — supplies the economy with plentiful energy.

> The movers and shakers on our planet aren't the billionaires and the generals — they are the incredible number of people around the world filled with love for neighbor and for the earth who are resisting, remaking, restoring, renewing, revitalizing.
>
> — Bill McKibben

The increasingly small companies are steadfastly creating a web of mostly place-based prosperity, yielding greater peace and security for all. Re-energized

participation in the non-profit Trees for the Future Trees for Travel program. The revenues we generate from our business enterprises, besides meeting any financial obligations, are devoted to the good work of improving soil quality, producing more renewable energy than we use and contributing in various ways to helping others who wish to launch their own enterprise or live in a more sustainable way. Our profits fund our purpose, rather than the purpose of our business being solely to make profits.

10 kW Bergey wind turbine at Inn Serendipity, allowing the business to be a net producer of electricity.

enterprising business owners help democratize and decentralize commerce by bringing it back to serving the community in which it roosts. Some of these small businesses aspire to grow better, not bigger.

At Inn Serendipity, we strive to be the best related to our social and ecological priorities in terms of our modest two-room bed and breakfast. Because of our size, we've discovered we can be more focused, flexible, adaptable, innovative and friendly (campfires and breakfast conversations often last for hours). Plus we have more fun. As we've discovered through the hundreds of interviews and conversations with entrepreneurs who are trying to do "the right thing," the larger many businesses grow, the more challenging it is to operate in ways that achieve social and ecological goals.

This is not to say that all businesses will stay small; there remain some business models that unavoidably demand largesse to accommodate the complexity or scope of the task at hand, like assembling hybrid cars or manufacturing solar cells. But fewer Americans are working in these industries, and even fewer are likely to in the future, thanks to the expanding role technology plays in these industries.

Of the nearly 26 million business firms in the US, about 97 percent have fewer than 20 employees according to the US Small Business Administration. These small businesses account for about half of the non-farm Domestic National Product, or GDP, and generated 60 to 80 percent of the net new jobs

Starting and Staying Small

Recognizing a competitive advantage, many small businesses essay to remain small. Sometimes called personal entrepreneurs or lifestyle entrepreneurs, these owners carefully manage their enterprise to achieve optimal efficiencies in whatever niche market they serve. Many organizations lend support, including the following:

- National Federation for Independent Business (NFIB)
  Conducting research and conducting advocacy on behalf of small business, the membership-based NFIB promotes and protects the right of their members to own, operate and grow their businesses and includes numerous tools and tips. www.nfib.org

- SOHO America
  Helping owners working in the small office/home office environment, this membership-based organization covers marketing, finance, legal, start-up and technology issues. www.soho.org

- Kauffman eVenturing
  Created by the non-profit Ewing Marion Kauffman Foundation, this website provides

over the past decade. While big businesses fired, laid off, downsized and out-sourced jobs, in part, to squeeze more profits for shareholders, small businesses added employment.

Entrepreneurial trends are difficult to track. The US Small Business Administration estimates that there are about 4.5 million small businesses with 9 or fewer employees. About three-quarters of all business firms have no employee payroll at all because they're set up as self-employed persons operating unincorporated businesses. According to the Association for Enterprise Opportunity (microenterpriseworks.org), there are more than 23 million microenterprises (a business with five or fewer employees) in the US, representing 18 percent of all private employment and 87 percent of all businesses. Like us, you might be among the 15 million full-time or part-time small office/home office entrepreneurs, or SOHOs.

Identified by Dan Pink in *Free Agent Nation*, there are about 33 million free agents in America. These "job-hopping, tech-savvy, fulfillment seeking, self-reliant, independent" workers represent about 16.5 million soloists, 3.5 million temporary workers (temps) and 13 million microbusinesses that include construction contractors, real estate agents, nannies, direct sales ventures (e.g., Shaklee, shaklee.com), services subcontractors and accountants. Operating as a microbusiness, or what Pink refers to as a "nanocorp" with three employees or less, is both a personal preference and competitive advantage, allowing the owners to downsize to

articles, research and tools to assist entrepreneurs with a growth-oriented world-view. www.eventuring.org

- US Business Advisor
  Discover the plethora of information from numerous federal agencies that regulate or assist small businesses, including securing grants, start-up guides and legal requirements. www.business.gov

- *Fast Company* magazine
  While emphasizing technology, Fast Company is a website and blog with resource guides and general information related to small and medium-sized businesses. www.fastcompany.com

- BizStats
  Free research and analysis for small businesses, including what the profit margins might be for your potential product or sales per square foot for retail stores; helpful when starting up your operations and determining cash flow and potential sales. www.bizstats.com

provide incredible adaptability, innovation and creativity. Our sub-chapter S Corporation is a nanocorp committed to ecological restoration and social change while turning a modest profit.

According to Mark Hendricks in *Not Just a Living*, as much as 90 percent of the roughly 20 million American small business owners seem to be motivated more by lifestyle than money. His summary of market research completed by Warrillow & Co. suggest three types of small business owners: mountain climbers, entrepreneurs driven by sales and profits; freedom fighters, owners who seek independence and complete control over the who, what, where and when of their work; and craftspeople, businesspeople dedicated to excelling at their chosen craft. Warrillow's research found that the craftspeople represent 60 percent of all entrepreneurs, followed by freedom fighters (30 percent) and mountain climbers (only 10 percent). Besides having less of a focus on money, lifestyle entrepreneurs rarely operate for the benefit of outside investors.

What's a Business?

Affecting every part of our society, a business offers products or services that customers may need, at a price that they're willing to pay and that provide a profit to the owner or shareholders. Commerce has long been the engine of social change, an innovative force in the transformation of who we are, what we care about and what we drive, live in, wear and eat.

A business is governed by the legal requirements set forth both by the federal government and state in which it was formed. Businesses can be organized as either for-profit or non-profit organizations. There are various classifications of businesses based on their size, form or locality. Astonishingly, the Bureau of Labor Statistics still classifies employment in two categories — farm or non-farm — yet fewer than two percent of Americans farm today.

Working Hard for the Money

The main requirement of a for-profit business is to make profits, at least once every three years says the US Internal Revenue Service (IRS). No requirement specifies how much profit must be made, just some. That's the big difference between a hobby, where generating revenue is not the primary goal of the activity, and a business. The non-profit business, formed as a special type of corporation depending on its purpose, uses revenues collected to fund its mission, whether it's saving open space or planting trees around the world to help mitigate the effects of global warming, provide nature-enhancing livelihoods and prevent soil erosion.

As we'll explain throughout this book, we approach our passions — writing, photography, hosting people and desiring to restore the planet — not as hobbies, but as business enterprises. You can blog on the Internet about growing in your garden, or you can write articles about growing food organically in your garden for *Hobby Farm Home* magazine and blog for GreenOptions.com. One's a hobby; one's a business and provides income from writing about something you love.

There are numerous advantages of operating a business for yourself, in terms of tax savings, control over how natural or human resources are used (or misused)

Company Career versus Ecopreneurial Life

The following contrasts a company career with a life as an ecopreneur.

Company Career	Ecopreneurial Life
J-O-B	**Right livelihood**
• identity fits on a 2"x3" card	• diversity of work opportunities
• seniority defines achievement	• ethical work: restores and nourishes the planet
• job description	• knowledge worker
Employee	**Owner - Proprietor**
• paycheck (W-2)	• business revenues
Career	**Concepts, relationships**
• ladder structure	• unstructured, flexible, fluid
Culture of control	**Diversity is stability**
• comformity	• in the marketplace, workforce, nature
• uniformity	• agile, reorganizing, adaptive, resilient
Globalization	**Localization and bioregionalism**
• planet is market	• locally based, but can serve global customers
• everyone is a consumer	• serving conservers, not consumers
• no locus of control, un-rooted	• native, place-based, rooted
Operate under "principles of sustainability"	**Practices of sustainability**
• guidelines, principles	• practices and actions matter most
• greenwash, deception, secrecy	• transparency, accountability, walking the talk
Reactive	**Pro-active**
• change when forced to	• innovative, creative, opportunity-focused
	• state of continual voluntary improvement
"Security"	**Self-reliance, independence, interdependence**
• company will care	• community, customers, social networks will care

and the freedom to pursue your passions without your boss looking over your shoulder. If you grow weary of climbing the ladder, own it. If you don't like the kind of companies that are offering you a job, then make your own in your vision of what it means to tread lightly on the planet.

Ever work for a company and become frustrated or appalled by the waste or inefficiencies you witness on a regular basis and your inability to enact changes to end the waste — even if it also saved the company or organization money at the same time? Ecopreneurs, often by their small, human or family-scaled operations, take the reins and seize control in ways larger organizations fail to even recognize. At Inn Serendipity, on an annual basis we reuse, recycle, reclaim and restore more than we dispose of in our two 35 gallon garbage cans. Piles of tile and grout, old furnaces, wood, children's toys, insulation scraps — all destined for landfills — are in productive, if not also quirky, use in our business today. Our strawbale greenhouse is partially built with the waste stream of our community.

Today information, knowledge and innovation are the harbingers of wealth creation in a world increasingly pressing up against environmental, social and resource limitations or issues created by the previous laissez-faire market-driven economic growth. Once the stronghold for guiding positive changes related to the environment or addressing social issues, federal and some state governments have lost their way, effectiveness and courage to take these issues on. Rather than setting forward-thinking policies, politicians are caving in to re-election concerns or the unprecedented influence of special interest groups, many funded by powerful multinational corporations. The present value of money

JOHN IVANKO

Inn Serendipity strawbale greenhouse.

overrides consideration given to issues that face future generations. Increasingly, citizens are ahead of the policy-makers, voting with their dollars and actions (not words).

Many universities and colleges, too, have become bogged down in the same muck of bureaucracy and complacency that few can even tout a campus that's anywhere close to green, powered onsite with renewable energy, or with dorm cafeterias that feature food grown or raised by area farmers. Few teach personal finance, how to buy your first home or, more importantly, help us discover our life purpose or passions. It's mostly about learning what it takes to get a job.

Ecopreneurship

Entrepreneurs are problem-solvers, possessing an ability to see what was there all along then bringing it to market in new ways. These entrepreneurs become eco-preneurs when their spirit, boldness, courage and determination not only transform the landscape but coalescence into a movement to transform global problems into opportunities for restoration and healing.

Ecopreneurs take a penchant for innovation and problem-solving, applying it to meaningful purpose. Ecopreneurs emblazen the regreening of Earth, restoring degraded land, cleaning the air, building healthy and safe homes, devising clean, renewable energy sources, offering prevention oriented alternatives to treatment-focused healthcare and helping preserve or restore the ecological and cultural wonders of the planet by changing the way we experience travel, just to name a few.

While many entrepreneurs may be motivated, at least in part, to the mantra of "greed is great" on their journey to becoming a millionaire, growing numbers of ecopreneurs are adopting a different course, focusing on solving the problems facing society through the businesses they create, greening their bottom line. Many are redefining their wealth, as we have, not by the size of their bank account or square footage of their home. Wealth is defined by life's tangibles: health, wellness, meaningful work, vibrant community life and family.

There are many ways in which entrepreneurs and ecopreneurs are similar. Both embrace failure and are idea driven, innovative, creative, risk tolerant, flexible, adaptable, freedom minded and independent. However, ecopreneurs go beyond organic, beyond compliance to laws and regulations (or redefine them), beyond consumerism, beyond minimum wages and beyond the free market economy to conduct business.

Successful ecopreneurs change their perspective about money. Instead of working for money, our money works for our aspirations, dreams and hopes for what we want to see the world become — our Earth Mission. Money is an intangible, a tool for change. We invest in the future, not save for it.

Are You an Ecopreneur?

- Are you more interested in what you do and with whom you work than how much you make?
- Does community, environmental and social issues drive what you focus on with respect to your livelihood or volunteer time?
- Do you view your experiences, growing and diverse knowledge base and unique skill sets as the primary value you can offer clients, customers or workplace?
- Do you think the late Nobel Laureate economist Milton Friedman ate too many Big Macs after he argued — much to the chagrin of the massive multinational corporations and millionaire politicians — that "the only social responsibility of business is to make profits"?
- Do you focus your life pursuits on helping others or restoring, enhancing or preserving the environment?
- Are you more concerned about achieving balance in your life, seeking quality of life that doesn't adversely impact the Earth or exploit people?
- Do you readily try new ideas, explore new ways of doing things or adopt new practices or use new products or services that reflect your values?
- Are you mindfully aware of your direct and indirect impacts on life on Earth, and accept responsibility that results in you being actively engaged as a steward of limited resources for the benefit of all life, not just for the present generations but for future generations as well?
- Is work a reflection of your passions and values, deeply fulfilling and providing meaning and purpose, or merely the focus for paying the bills, building personal wealth and funding your retirement?

Earth Mission

Your Earth Mission is the overarching springboard from which your business, livelihood and life launch forward that respects nature and fosters socially just relationships with all life. Wealth without purpose is poverty. Ecopreneurs create enterprises that are ecologically restorative, socially responsive and just and that measure their success in how they build community wealth in a living economy.

While entrepreneurs make their money work for them through the businesses they create, or assets they accumulate, ecopreneurs use their businesses to implement their Earth Mission. If you're earning a living now, perhaps working for a company or organization, then becoming an ecopreneur will revolutionize how you think about money, your livelihood, your life.

Entrepreneur versus Ecopreneur

The following depicts the many differences between an entrepreneur and ecopreneur.

Entrepreneur	Ecopreneur
Values Money	*Values Life*
• I wanna be rich	• passion, purpose, meaning, fulfillment through work
Return on Investment (ROI)	*Return on Environment (ROE)*
• capitalist model, based on scarcity	• nature's model, based on abundance
• depleting natural resources	• enhancing or restoring natural resources
Free trade	*Fair Trade*
• extractive, exploitation	• cooperative, socially responsible, just
Externalize environmental/ social costs	*Internalize and imbed costs in business*
Following regulations	*Setting (voluntary) standards beyond regulations*
• meet governmental regulations	• recognize responsibility, take action
	• innovation opportunities
Stakeholders = stockholders	*Stakeholders = everyone and everything*
• financial results driven	• consider nature, community, future generations
Technology will triumph	*Technology is a tool*
• technology will save the day	• appropriate, individualized, one of many options
Super-size me	*Human-scale, micro-size, small-mart*
• bigger is better	• small is beautiful, less complex, adaptable
• ride the Titanic	• paddle a kayak

Multiple Economies of Ecopreneurship

ECOnomics involves operating in more than the free market economy, the one we commonly think about when buying or selling goods or services. Often depending on their scale, many ecopreneurs with smaller operations thrive in the following economies as well.

Barter Economy

Why pay cash (or charge on credit) for something if you don't need to? Exchanging services or time satisfies needs without draining the bank account. Fruits and vegetables freely flow from our farm; in return, we've received our wooden bed and breakfast sign and clothes for our son, Liam. The barter economy often erupts serendipitously, like when a friend who received some of our vegetables presents Liam with a three-string guitar he made himself. Despite the fact that such informal, community-based bartering has existed for centuries, IRS tax law states that you are required to file a Form 1099-B (i.e., declare as income on which you must pay taxes) if you have more than 100 barter transactions a year. As much as we relish barter, that would be a noble goal to reach.

Household Economy

Self-reliance is underrated, thanks, in part, to companies that advertise solutions to all our problems and needs — for a price. We're surrounded by farms and farmland where we live, yet few residents grow their own food in kitchen gardens. While most Americans can grow at least some food in a container or small plot to offset their food expenses, few realize the sense of empowerment and satisfaction from harvesting their own meals or meeting, as we do, about 70 percent of our food needs 100 feet from our back door. Rather than outsourcing our daycare for our son, we created a work-at-home situation where we could care for him, a means that also optimized our satisfaction as parents.

Collecting and Reuse Economy

America could very well be called the land of opportunity to waste our abundance. From forests filled with wildlife and lakes teeming with fish to piles of discarded tile, bricks and other building materials, reusing, salvaging and, in myriad other ways, transforming someone's trash into treasure provides a cost-effective vector for ecopreneurs to out-compete larger companies while saving money and boosting their bottom line. Working with neighbors, we transform waste fryer oil from area restaurants into biodiesel to use in our backup heating system in the greenhouse. Using freecycle.org, isharestuff.org, and craigslist.org, we pick up things we need and clear out unwanted items, all for free.

Volunteer Economy

From donating time at a homeless shelter to contributing food to a food bank, without the volunteer economy, many non-profits would be out of business, both financially and operationally. While many equate time with money, citizens who freely exchange time or services support what many consider some of the most desirable and prosperous communities, vibrant with civic life with activities and community services. Ecopreneurs can be on the giving and receiving end of mentorships and informal guidance from social and business contacts.

Cooperative Economy

We're members of more than six cooperatively owned businesses, including the nation's largest retail food cooperative, Willy Street Cooperative in Madison, a regional sustainable forestry cooperative, Kickapoo Woods Cooperative, and a community land trust, the Mississippi Valley Conservancy. Common ownership in these mission-driven organizations offer opportunities for us to better steward resources and work together to achieve collective goals, accomplishing more as a group than we could as individuals.

Harvest Economy

Every day, enough sunlight falls on the planet to meet all our energy needs, with some to spare. Instead, most of its citizens burn fossil fuels that end up polluting and destroying the planet. Ecopreneurs search out opportunities in a harvest economy that are often tax free, climate neutral and better for the environment. We harvest so much wind and solar energy that we receive net annual payments from our utility company for our surplus electricity generation. Our electronic "storefront" on the Internet — harvesting page views and with the potential to reach millions of people — costs about as much monthly as a taxi ride in downtown Chicago. It uses a "free network" to grow a business in a way that's almost impossible to do with the corporate-controlled TV or radio air waves.

By operating in these other economies, ecopreneurs short-circuit expenses and boost their bottom lines. The savings flowing from our business are harnessed to work for our Earth Mission.

The Social Sector's Thriving Enterprise

> Social Entrepreneur:
> Society's change agent: pioneer of innovations that benefit
> humanity.
>
> — Skoll Foundation

The entrepreneurial spirit increasingly infuses the so-called social or civic sector of the economy. Innovative organizations, many with a grassroots and ecopreneurial spirit, serve needs previously met by governmental and faith-based organizations. Composed of values and mission-driven people working cooperatively to achieve goals that they're unable to accomplish as individuals, these organizations represent an emerging people power pushing for change, filling the gap left by a failing national government guided more by large corporate interests and money interests than the citizens it is meant to serve. The growth of the social sector has led to the creation of focused social entrepreneurship organizations, like Ashoka, devoted to developing the profession of social entrepreneurship. David Bornstein's inspiring book, *How to Change the World: Social Entrepreneurs and the Power of New Ideas*, puts a face to the movement that many universities are just recently beginning to discover.

Too often, non-profit organizations receive a bad rap, stereotyped as inefficient, solely volunteer-based groups that lose money operationally for the sake of doing good. This is an unfortunate image, as non-profits are simply an alternative form of corporate structure in which, among other requirements, profits generated go back into the organization to support its mission, not into the pockets of owners or shareholders. Further fueled by the ability to accept grant and donation monies, a well-run non-profit organization can be a potential powerhouse for entrepreneurial efforts within the social sector. Non-profits often use contractors and subcontractors to bring outside perspectives to the organization. Practically all of our marketing consulting projects and speaking events have been as contractors for non-profit groups. Foresight Design Initiative, a Chicago-based non-profit, and its founder, Peter Nicholson, serve as inspiring examples of how the non-profit realm can provide an ideal playing field for the ecopreneur.

Foresight Design Initiative

Executive and Creative Director: Peter Nicholson
Place: Chicago, Illinois
Earth Mission: "My goal is to lead an interesting and fulfilled life; to do work that creates important value and is filled with meaningful relationships. Saving the world isn't so much a primary objective, but rather an appropriately secondary one."
www.foresightdesign.org

Figure out what you love to do. Then just do it — under a green umbrella. By focusing on the process, rather than the product, Peter Nicholson serves as ecopreneuring inspiration, founding the premiere non-profit organization serving sustainable education in Chicago, Foresight Design Initiative, based around his passion for design.

"For me, design is manipulating variables for a desired outcome, which in this case is improving our urban quality of life without sacrificing the needs of future generations," explains Peter. "The variables could be anything from words to graphics to economic influences. I'm fascinated with how we could use design to empower people, to improve human conditions holistically. I'm often dismayed by the abundant examples of how poor design hinders us." Today, Peter serves as Executive and Creative Director of Foresight Design Initiative, providing him a palette for sustainable design expression.

Peter's career roots go back to a foundation in music, essaying initially to be a concert cellist. "When I realized I didn't have the talent for professional music, I parlayed my music background into arts administration," explains Peter. Blending music and entrepreneurship, his first venture included launching a classical orchestra in New York City. "I felt classical music was staid and stuck in the 19th century, losing a whole new potential audience. With this new group, we aimed to blow the lid off same old same old and designed fresh, hip graphics and style for every element."

Enticed by design, Peter enrolled in a design graduate program but left after a year, realizing he had garnered the tools he needed, and took his education into his own hands. A residency in Europe led him to the O2 Challenge in the Netherlands in 1998, a life-changing, dynamic, hands-on working conference on sustainable design that planted the seeds for Foresight Design Initiative. "I realized that sustainability would not evolve without a broader application of design and found, in the challenge of this pursuit, barriers that were both worthwhile and fulfilling to engage," explains Peter. "Sustainable design, however, was an emerging field; I knew I needed to create the conditions to practice this vocation."

In 2001 Peter started what eventually became Foresight Design Initiative, an organization that embraces design principles to develop more sustainable solutions, of many types, and to foster a greater inclusion of these issues into society. "Green should be the mass market norm, not the high-end alternative," Peter states. Strategic in organizational structure, Foresight Design Initiative is the non-profit subsidiary of a for-profit C Corporation, Design for Society. While the same board of directors serves both organizations, the for-profit umbrella structure leaves open the opportunity to include strictly for-profit ventures in the future.

Such innovative thinking fuels Foresight Design Initiative's hybrid strategy. "We looked at other successful non-profit organizations and quickly realized a diversified stream of multiple income sources would keep this venture financially healthy," explains Peter. Today funding comes from events, corporate and individual memberships and donations (including in-kind), foundation support, "fee for service" for various green design consulting and education projects, and tuition for their seminars and Urban Sustainable Design Studio, an intensive experiential education program in sustainable design.

Innovative thinking, blended with responding to feedback and input, launched a menu of diverse Foresight Design Initiative programs. Serving as a portal of the growing Chicago green scene, the organization hosts Green Drinks, informal social and educational gatherings appealing to a broad range of urbanites interested in sustainability issues. Additional educational programs include workshops, panel discussions and tours addressing a wide breadth of local sustainability issues, including municipal recycling and affordable green homes. Foresight Design Initiative also handles various contract projects such as designing an educational pavilion for the City of Chicago for a large green festival that generates income for the organization. Foresight Design Initiative's latest venture, the Chicago Sustainable Business Alliance, serves as a network for enterprises dedicated to sustainability in their products, services and practices. "We constantly survey and listen to attendees at our events to either refine events or launch new ventures entirely," Peter adds.

Lean and green, Peter operates with an additional couple of full-time staff. "We aim to keep our overhead down by using just 350 square feet of office space, being frugal with the air conditioner and using a car-sharing service when public transportation won't suffice," explains Peter. "We look deceptively small given our handful of staff, but we rely greatly on an extensive, dedicated network of volunteers." Peter readily admits that this volunteer economy built Foresight Design Initiative into the organization it is today. "Our growing volunteer pool reflects the snowballing green movement as more folks want to get involved and connect with others that share the same values."

This diverse web of people related to Foresight Design Initiative remains Peter's ongoing motivation. "I want a life filled with meaningful, inspiring relationships," sums up Peter. "I love the people I work with, staff, volunteers and colleagues. Today I had two impromptu and amazing conversations with different people. That can't be measured in a paycheck. It's priceless."

As government funding and other forms of "soft" grant-based funding continues to wane, innovative non-profits have created for-profit enterprises that generate unrestricted funds for the organization and its programs. These new hybrid organizations are separated for tax purposes, but they're bending the very way many think about non-profit organizations where innovation, creativity and accountability are central to how these organizations operate.

> Social entrepreneurs are not content just to give a fish or teach how to fish. They will not rest until they have revolutionized the fishing industry.
>
> — Bill Drayton, CEO, chair and founder of Ashoka

There are publishing ventures like the Global Fund for Children Books, which provides a steady revenue stream of royalties from multicultural children's books published in partnership with Charlesbridge Publishers to support the work of the Global Fund for Children (globalfundforchildren.org). Other non-profit organizations are creating enterprises with foundation and governmental grants, then establishing innovative business models to generate self-sustaining revenues for the business, which pass through to the non-profit as the sole stock-holding entity.

The New Bottom Line: Making Things Better

Small businesses, and increasingly green businesses, are already providing viable livelihoods to millions of families in America. You'll find these ecopreneurs selling at farmers' markets, launching non-profit organizations, tinkering with their

Launching a Non-profit Organization

The following non-profit organizations have come about to serve people interested in starting, working in or managing non-profit organizations.

- The Foundation Center
  This is the leading authority in the US on philanthropy, connecting non-profits and the grant-makers supporting them to tools they can use and information they can trust. The Center maintains a comprehensive database on US grant-makers and their grants. It also operates research, education and training programs designed to advance philanthropy at every level.
  www.foundationcenter.org

- Idealist.org
  This organization connects people, ideas and resources to change the world.
  www.idealist.org

- Skoll Foundation
  The foundation advances systemic change to benefit communities around the world by investing in, connecting and celebrating social entrepreneurs and supporting social entrepreneurs through grants, research and resources.
  www.skollfoundation.org

green technology businesses at a community incubator, consulting for non-profit organizations out of a spare bedroom "home office" in their suburban home and operating a bed and breakfast completely powered by renewable energy, like we do.

The global stage has been set for invaluable contributions that ecopreneurs will be making in the coming decades. Restoration and preservation of the very life-support systems on which we depend will be fused with the next generation of environmental and social entrepreneurs who, through their innovative and creative talents, will shine a green light on new ways to work, live and play.

Resetting the scales of commerce, ecopreneurs replace the global consumption craze with new, personal and localized models of business that heal the planet while sustaining our livelihood. In the land of plenty, there's no reason to complain about lack of forward progress in Washington DC or protest rising gas prices. We have plenty of opportunity to make things better and improve our quality of life, now and for future generations. It's not what you say but what you do that matters.

In the next chapter, we'll explore the many ecopreneur opportunities and better define just how big the small business sector is in our economy.

Chapter 2

Restorative Opportunities

DOOM AND GLOOM. The "long emergency." The end of time. There's a small but vociferous movement possessing a worldview that embraces the possibility of Armageddon — a climatic battle between good and evil mentioned in the Book of Revelation in the Bible — or of our civilization heading for some very rough times with suburban America completely collapsing. For some, present-day floods, wildfires, widespread disease and wars are signs of our civilization crumbling. For others, the suburbs will become the ghettos of tomorrow. Some will be saved; others will have a life much tougher than they ever imagined. This is not the depressing final word, but a positive call to action for ecopreneurs. The prophecy of the Apocalypse — with its Four Horsemen representing pestilence, war, famine and death — holds meaning only for those of a particular faith with some rather variable interpretations.

Ecopreneurs, in seeking the hopeful and acting for positive change, are embarking on their quest to ride what we've come to call the Four Horsemen of Opportunity: global warming, ecological collapse, peak oil and debt. In a proactive way, ecopreneurs are finding ways to turn down the heat, replant the forests, crush our dependence on non-renewable and polluting sources of energy, transform waste into wealth, re-establish more secure, safe and bioregional food systems and break the financial sector's stranglehold on our life. In fact, there's also a new movement among various faiths to care for God's creation, a sense of ecological stewardship as a fundamental human responsibility. As many are discovering, those companies and organizations that do not embrace change for the betterment of the environment or fellow humankind will meet the same fate as the dinosaurs. In fact, some already have.

The Four Horsemen of Opportunity

The following four major trends are transforming what types of businesses will survive and, more importantly, thrive while helping solve the many complex issues facing humankind and the planet. The Stone Age didn't end because they ran out of stones. Noah didn't get to work on his Ark after the rain started falling. Ecopreneurs anticipate and embrace changes, leading the transformation of the very economy that created the problems.

Global Warming or Climate Change

Call it what you will, global warming or climate change is heating up to be among the most transformative trends in the 21st century. Thanks to continued scientific exploration, the Intergovernmental Panel on Climate Change (IPCC), composed of the leading global scientists, has reached a consensus that the rising temperatures around the world and changing climate can be directly attributed to human activity. By burning fossil fuels like oil and coal, we add carbon dioxide emissions to the atmosphere, resulting in the greenhouse effect, essentially warming the planet as a result of the trapped gases. Al Gore's *An Inconvenient Truth*, the award-winning documentary on global warming, synthesizes complex information in such a way that even the skeptics might reconsider their stance on the issue — if they care enough about the future of all life on Earth.

The impacts of global warming — increased intensity of storms, increased frequency of hurricanes and tornadoes, extended periods of drought, extreme heat waves, torrential rain downfalls — are likely to get more pronounced as we move further into this century, contributing to other weather-related events like prolific wildfires, widespread outbreaks of disease, loss of food security or extreme water shortages. The global reinsurance company SwissRe has found that losses from natural disasters are doubling about every decade. Some Americans have already found themselves forced to move to places where they can afford, or still get, property insurance.

Global warming is not just about the rising average planetary temperature, but what effects it has on weather patterns, atmospheric conditions and ocean currents. It's creating increased variability and unpredictability in weather. Historical averages are becoming history in terms of predicting future climate conditions. Global warming fosters increasingly severe weather events along with far-reaching impacts like rising oceans or receding freshwater lake levels. If we don't already, we'll all be feeling the effects beyond the longer growing season in our gardens or "weird" and "wacky" weather events. Weird weather will become the new normal, difficult to predict and often extreme.

Ecopreneurs are rising to the challenge to mitigate or solve some of the many issues that contribute to global warming. Some companies are processing biofuels, like biodiesel, that cut down on carbon dioxide and other greenhouse gas emissions. Others are using electric or hybrid vehicles or developing communities and neighborhoods that rely on bicycles and footpaths for residents to get around.

Businesses are changing how they operate in efforts to become carbon neutral, seeking to stabilize carbon dioxide levels globally by offsetting or reducing the amount of emissions from their operations to net zero on an annual basis.

In less than a decade, we've transformed our fossil-fuel-based farm and business into one that is carbon neutral, if not carbon negative, thanks to tree-planting efforts, organic and largely unmechanized cultivation of agricultural crops, production and burning of biodiesel instead of petroleum-based diesel fuel, and surplus electricity generation from wind and sun. Our small scale allows us to maximize our return on environment (ROE) by reducing carbon dioxide emissions.

Ecopreneurial organizations — by how and where they operate and what goods or services they offer — reduce their vulnerability to increasing variability in the climate and weather patterns. Instead of opening up their businesses along threatened coastal or low-lying areas like southern Florida, they select locales that are less vulnerable to the impacts of climate change. Many power themselves with energy they generate onsite or in their community, helping decentralize the energy grid while boosting local self-reliance and maximizing their control over variable and fixed costs in their business. Many foster business-to-business green networks to help shield themselves from practices by companies that choose to ignore climate change as a fundamental variable in how they do business.

Ecological Collapse and the Sixth Great Extinction

How many eggs can we carry with two hands? The answer is simple. What you can carry is based on your size, strength and coordination: carrying capacity. That same concept is what defines our existence on Earth. The plants, water, wildlife, minerals — or in totality, nature — provide various services, in essence, for free. But every living ecosystem around the world is in decline, in many ways magnified by the play between global warming and destructive land use practices ranging from deforestation to sprawl and how we're using nature as a receptacle for our waste and pollution. While heralding the return of healthy populations of bald eagles as a conservation success story, we're overlooking the accelerating loss of millions of other plant and animal species, many of which we know little or nothing about. The next period of the "great extinction" has begun. Since 1992 the number of acres of rainforest, just one of the many diverse ecosystems on the planet, has dropped by 50 percent, at a rate of about a football-field-sized parcel a second. More than 20 percent of the world's oxygen is produced in the Amazon rainforest alone.

According to the Millennium Ecosystem Assessment produced by the United Nations, "over the past 50 years, humans have changed ecosystems more rapidly and extensively than in any comparable period of time in human history." No surprise. Since 1960 our population has doubled and the economic output, the measure of goods and services, increased six times. In some parts of the world, rainforests are destroyed for growing crops or pasturing animals; in others, rich croplands are replaced by tidy subdivisions. These free ecological services are starting to cost us, and soon, food, water, fiber and timber will cost a

Neutralizing Greenhouse Gas Emissions with Carbon Offsets

Trees absorb carbon dioxide from the atmosphere, storing the carbon in the wood for the life of the tree. Renewable energy credits (RECs) reduce the amount of carbon dioxide and other greenhouse gas emissions when fossil fuels like oil, gas or coal would have been otherwise burned, emitting greenhouse gases into the atmosphere. For every kilowatt hour of electricity generated from renewable energy sources like wind turbines, photovoltaic systems or from methane capture on farms, one kilowatt hour less of energy would need to be generated by burning fossil fuels. Sequestering carbon dioxide by planting trees, supporting renewable energy projects or simply documenting energy conservation measures with energy efficient products that set your company apart from the emissions that result from your competitors each contribute in different ways to helping reduce or eliminate your business's contribution to global warming.

For years many European countries — having adopted the Kyoto Protocol amendment to the United Nations Framework Convention on Climate Change that assigns mandatory emission limitations for the reduction of greenhouse gas emissions — created an entire industry of trading carbon dioxide credits among the business community. In North America, neutralizing your carbon dioxide emissions through participation in carbon-offset programs offered by non-profit and for-profit organizations has become commonplace, albeit voluntary. Cap-and-trade carbon emission schemes like those in Europe will eventually be commonplace in the US too.

For now, there are numerous ways for ecopreneurial businesses to be carbon neutral. Some businesses may even become carbon negative or carbon free, sequestering more carbon dioxide than they emit through their operations in their efforts to distinguish themselves in the green marketplace and distance themselves from competitors. A wide assortment of carbon dioxide calculators are available online to assist in determining your emissions from transportation (i.e., automobile and airline travel), heating and cooling and various other aspects of your business operations. Some may be certified or verified through Green-e, Chicago Climate Exchange or Environmental Resources Trust.

Some of the many purveyors of such carbon sequestering programs include:

whole lot more. Some of the regulating services provided by nature, like buffer wetlands that once existed near New Orleans that helped manage floods, are practically gone. These services also affect climate, waste, disease and water supply. Nutrient cycling, photosynthesis and soil formation, along with social services

- Carbonfund.org Foundation
  This non-profit organization makes it easy and affordable for any individual, business or organization to eliminate their carbon emissions, hastening the transformation to a clean energy and technology future through various carbon-offset programs. www.carbonfund.org
- Trees for the Future
  This non-profit assists in planting trees in developing countries around the world, helping to restore ecological integrity, fostering community enterprises and providing carbon off-setting certificate programs for businesses like Global Cooling and Trees for Travel. www.treesftf.org
- Native Energy
  This non-profit organization offers renewable energy credits with WindBuilders (100 percent wind) or RemooableEnergy (100 percent farm methane capture). www.nativeenergy.com
- Solar Electric Light Fund (SELF)
  This non-profit organization promotes, develops and facilitates solar rural electrification and energy self-sufficiency in developing countries, installing solar photovoltaic (solar electric) systems that displace the use of kerosene or diesel fuel, thus helping reduce carbon dioxide emissions. www.self.org
- TerraPass Inc.
  This for-profit company develops and markets economically viable products that combat global warming by mitigating human-made environmental emissions, investing in renewable energy systems to off-set carbon emissions. www.terrapass.com
- Tree Canada Foundation
  This Canadian non-profit organization partners with local volunteers to improve our quality of life by planting and caring for trees that allow businesses to offset carbon emissions. www.treecanada.ca

In terms of addressing climate change through selecting appropriate technology that helps cut energy use, The Carbon Buster's Home Energy Handbook: Slowing Climate Change and Saving Money by Godo Stoyke is packed with pragmatic tips for home energy use. It's immediately relevant to most small businesses, since the majority of them are home-based.

like the sweeping vistas or recreational opportunities, are all tied to nature —
even if we don't account for them in our national (or global) ledger.

To make this point about the carrying capacity, Mathis Wagernagel and
William Rees developed the ecological footprint, quantifying the amount of
water and land the human population needs to support itself based on our current level of technology. In their book *Our Ecological Footprint: Reducing Human
Impact on the Earth* and on the Redefining Progress non-profit website (myfoot-
print.org), they examine our use of resources in the context of the reality that
most Americans need more than 4.5 planets to support our present lifestyle. Add
to this the rapid expansion of some developing countries like China and India,
and we have a recipe without enough ingredients to bake a cake — Free Market
Economy Dementia allows it to continue.

An awareness of invaluable and limited availability of natural capital led to a
new approach to business that seeks to conserve energy, eliminate waste and
mimic ecological processes for products or services, perhaps at times even orient-
ing the economy toward a service economy where products made with natural
materials are reused indefinitely in various ways rather than ending up in a landfill. *Biomimicry* (biomimicry.net) by Janine Benyus and *Natural Capitalism*
(natcap.org) by Paul Hawken, Amory Lovins and Hunter Lovins both capture
the future possibilities of harnessing and preserving nature's abundance.

In *Biomimicry*, Benyus lays out how to use nature as a model, mentor and
measure for business. Nature is the ultimate innovator; humans are the best imi-
tators. We get our camouflage from frogs, turtlenecks from turtles and Velcro
from burdock. In *Natural Capitalism*, capitalism as we know it is transformed by
four principles for business that allow it to make money, serve customers and
solve environmental problems: "radically increased resource productivity,
redesigning industry on biological models with closed loops and zero waste;
shifting from the sale of goods to the provision of services; and the reinvesting of
the natural capital that is the basis of future prosperity." For example, Healthy
Ponds AquaSpheres, from Bioverse (bioverse.com), is just one of thousands of
new products that harnesses nature's way to solving problems. Rather than
dumping heavy-metal-laden chemicals into ponds to keep them healthy and
clear, Bioverse has devised a proprietary natural bacteria and enzyme mixture to
break down excess nutrients which leads to sludge buildup and algae. Even the
"plastics" used to contain the bacteria are made from corn instead of petroleum.

Increasingly, ecopreneurial businesses and aspiring sustainable communities
are also evaluating their operations based on The Natural Step framework (nat-
uralstep.org) first developed in Sweden by Karl-Henrik Robért and being
adopted around the world. It offers the following systems conditions for sustainability: concentrations from society or extracted from the Earth must not be

systematically increasing in nature or be degraded by physical means, and people are not subject to conditions undermining their ability to meet their needs.

Both The Natural Step and the ecological footprint are tools available for ecopreneurs to guide and evaluate the management of their business and evaluate the products or services it offers. The Biomimicry Institute (biomimicryinstitute.org) and the Natural Capital Institute (naturalcapitalinstitute.org) offer resources to help ecopreneurs brainstorm how their ideas can harness nature's abundance — and restore it too.

Peak Oil

Call it the bell curve for barrels of oil. Peak oil is the tip of the bell curve, a point in time when global production of crude oil — the raw material needed to make gasoline, diesel fuel and plastics — tops out, after which production enters into decline. Experts vary as to when, exactly, we'll reach peak; some experts suggest it's already happened.

What if oil, which was only $10 a barrel in 1998, were $100 a barrel today — and $300 a barrel in ten years? Impossible? From 1996 to 2007, the price of a barrel of oil grew at an unprecedented rate of 600 percent, from $10/barrel to $70/barrel. In a time of increasingly expensive energy, the most ecopreneurial businesses will minimize or eliminate transportation costs or recognize the business opportunity to generate the energy needed by the business as a part of how the business operates.

While the oil wells will not go dry overnight or even over the next half century, gas prices and just about everything else in a global economy will get a lot more expensive because the oil supply is diminishing and the cost of getting to what remains is becoming more expensive. This reality will transform how we approach transportation, and because of its pervasiveness in our culture and economy, it will change how — and where — we do business.

Indebted Nation

We're living among a nation of purchasing patriots. But the wealthiest of nations, we're not. In less than 50 years, the US went from being the world's largest creditor to its biggest debtor. We're drowning in red ink and seemingly heading toward bankruptcy, not just governmental debt, but corporate and individual household debt as well. The total debt in the US, including household, business, financial and government sectors, is estimated at $32 trillion. This translates to about $115,000 for every woman, man and child (and growing). For the first time since the Great Depression, Americans have a dis-savings rate.

For those who live within or below their means, the credit crunch will be less painful, though unavoidably felt as foreclosures and personal bankruptcies reach friends, neighbors and customers. Some people will thrive as they always have in more self-reliant communities and neighborhoods that value relationships over money in the Multiple Economies of Ecopreneurship, operating in ways that don't require currency.

> Abundance isn't a matter of acquiring how much money you desire; it's a matter of being happy with how much you presently have.
>
> — Ernie J. Zelinski, *The Joy of Not Working*

Some ecopreneurs will launch businesses that provide life coaching and social services to those people struggling to adjust to the new reality of expensive energy or community turmoil. Other ecopreneurs, because they have mastered fiscal responsibility, will simply scale back their operations without significantly diminishing their quality of life. Chapters 6 and 7 dive into an ecopreneur's approach to money, assets and debt.

Cynical Nation

For lots of reasons explored in these pages, many Americans have grown weary and distrustful of our politicians, CEOs and even institutions long considered to provide the moral high ground and source for life guidance and progressive thinking. From the accounting shenanigans at Enron to the seemingly never-ending parade of scandals in Washington DC, the bigness of the corporations, government and other institutions has created an environment where big bad things erupt and continue to do so. It's not hard to observe people putting more energy into complaining about something than fixing it. We throw up our hands, uttering "lesser of evils" statements, and become cynical, detached and disenfran-chised. Why is it that important decisions must be made by powerful elites or interpreted for us by "experts"?

Scale does matter. Accountability and transparency are difficult when com-panies, organizations or institutions are spread out to the far reaches of Earth. Devolution, human-scaling business or organizations and retaking control of our local community are sweeping across the country. A new generation of entrepre-neurs — many of whom are lean, green and local — are rising to the challenges, recognizing opportunities in the problems that face humanity and the ecological systems on which we all depend. Call these entrepreneurs "ecopreneurs," even though as a group they're as diverse as their perspectives are on how to live well with purposeful businesses that walk their talk.

Cynicism, negativism or fundamentalism aren't the only ways to cope. Many emerging ecopreneurs, forming both for-profit and non-profit organizations, are choosing to organize or reorganize themselves into niche businesses. Instead of treating everyone everywhere as one "consumer" and viewing natural and human capital as strictly an input for industrial production, ecopreneurs are transforming ideas into solutions to many planetary woes without destroying the planet or exploiting its citizens (or customers and clients) in the process.

Redemocratizing and Decentralizing Commerce

Technology has, indeed, changed society, and with nanotechnology looming on the horizon, much of our intellectual life (or medical histories) could soon fit into our pockets. Powerful home computers and a web of high-speed interconnectivity through the Internet have forged a networked community of people — and potential business customers. Suddenly we can own an Internet domain name just like big business and big government. In fact, a small business can do more with less than ever before, transforming what it means to open up a storefront or offer a product or service.

The publisher of this book, New Society Publishers, sits on a western Canadian island so remote we have yet to find it on the map. Their network of designers, editors and artists are linked together seamlessly through the Internet. Another approach and showcasing the power of local, our *Edible Earth* cookbook from Paradigm Press, produced on ancient forest-free, 100 percent post-consumer-waste, recycled paper sourced from a company in the Midwest, was printed by New Life Press in Monroe, Wisconsin, just down the road from us, with a population just over 10,000. Technology in the printing and recycling industries along with powerful computers matched with knowledge and know-how can change what's possible.

New Society Publishers

Chris and Judith Plant have long been the visionary beacons for one of the most progressive and forward-thinking publishers on the planet. Their New Society Publishers has emerged as the leading activist publisher, walking the talk their books advocate. More than 25 new titles a year contribute in fundamental ways to building an ecologically sustainable and just society, and do so with the least possible impact on the environment. Besides printing all their books devoted to various sustainability topics on 100 percent post-consumer-waste, recycled, ancient-forest-friendly paper since 2001,

Co-Publishers Chris and Judith Plant
Place: Gabriola Island, British Columbia, Canada
Earth Mission: "Working towards living in community within the gifts and limitations of a particular place. This 'bioregional' view of the world is one that never fails to inspire us."
Website: www.newsociety.com

they're the first North American publisher to be carbon neutral, recognizing that climate change can be solved through more responsible business practices.

"Publishing was the means by which we could act as a catalyst, helping many people to bring their ideas and experiences to an increasingly wider audience," explains Judith Plant, who shares the publisher responsibilities with her husband, Chris Plant. They started in the publishing industry as the publishers of both *The New Catalyst*, a bioregional journal addressing local issues from the context of global environmental and social justice movements, and Judith's first book, *Healing the Wounds: The Promise of Ecofeminism*, published by New Society Publishers, then a non-profit collective based in Philadelphia under the umbrella of the Movement for a New Society.

After time together with the Nisga'a First Nations peoples of Northern British Columbia, Chris and Judith and their three children joined an intentional community in the southern interior of British Columbia in the early 1980s. During this time they published *The New Catalyst* while living off-grid, growing most of their own food and home-schooling their children. With the opportunity to partner with their friends and colleagues at New Society Publishers in Philadelphia and technology being what it was in 1989, Chris and Judith made the decision to move to Gabriola Island, one of the beautiful Southern Gulf Islands of British Columbia, where they could plug into the grid allowing for fax machines, telephone lines — all necessary to the publishing industry and unavailable from their remote mountain commune. On Gabriola Island, they planted some seeds of their own on ten acres that would change their impact on both the peaceful small community and planet forever. In 1996, thanks to the financial backing of an angel investor who cared as much about the bioregional and sustainability movements as they did, they purchased the world rights for the existing titles from New Society Publishers in Philadelphia that at the time was planning to shutter their operations. Sharing their values and vision, they recreated a model for what the publishing industry could be; by 2001 they were publishing books without cutting down a single new tree for paper.

Chris and Judith formed a new limited liability company, keeping the New Society Publishers name but shifting its publishing focus from non-violent social change to sustainability themes that now include conscientious commerce, ecological design, environment and the economy, education and parenting, gardening and cooking, globalization, natural building, peak oil and renewable energy. Most books are published primarily for the North American market, with 80 percent of their total sales coming from the United States, though distribution includes the United Kingdom, New Zealand, Australia and South Africa.

Thanks to the power of computers, Internet and telecommunications, the company — while proudly dedicated to the local community (the company is one of the larger employers on an island of 4,000 people) — fosters creative working relationships with ten employees and numerous subcontractors who serve as editors, proofreaders, layout artists and cover designers, many of whom work from home offices scattered throughout North America. Technology, mindfully applied, has allowed New Society Publishers to cultivate an interconnected collaboration of dispersed creative individuals. "We have adopted this structure because it allows people to work in the midst of their ongoing lives. Families first, work second," explains Judith, reflecting one of the original priorities she and Chris set forth when first recreating New Society Publishers. Their staff receives six weeks paid vacation and extended healthcare benefits as well as bonuses whenever possible.

"As partners in life and business, our relationship has had to succeed in terms of mutual respect and trust," adds Judith about working with her husband. She's quick to point out that they do work in separate offices. "This gives us space, a precious commodity for those who do everything together," she happily beams. While Judith and Chris shoulder the financial and administrative aspects of the business, they extend numerous decision-making responsibilities for the business and book project development to their creative staff who share their values and commitment to the planet.

By going carbon neutral and printing on ancient-forest friendly, post-consumer recycled paper, New Society Publishers continues to change with the changing times. Many titles are now offered in electronic book form. Such commitment to social and ecological values boosts New Society Publishers' bottom line. "These initiatives have given us, our staff and our authors confidence that a difference can be made and that there is some sort of honor in the world of business," shares Judith, relating to their company's carbon-neutral operations and use of recycled paper for their books.

Unlike those of larger publishing houses, New Society Publishers' more than 150 authors play a central role in bringing each book to market, providing input and direction on the cover and design of their books, while initiating their own marketing efforts. "We feel that each book project is like a birthing process with many midwives along the way, but the 'baby' is the author's, New Society Publishers is the agent." Their authors are driven by their passion for change, not royalties.

Sidestepping anything that resembles retirement for these activist entrepreneurs, Chris and Judith intend to foster the continued growth and evolution of the company, continuing to turn over the day-to-day operations to seasoned staffers who have been with the company for years — and who are also their neighbors. They've rededicated themselves to reaching out to both their local community, through donations to their Community Kitchen that provides food to area residents, and those who might struggle to find Gabriola on a globe by heading to Green Festivals and renewable energy and sustainable living fairs, sustainability conferences and green expos. They're constantly taking the pulse of the planet, shepherding new books that improve the health and well-being of all life on Earth.

"We're keeping the channels of communication open between New Society Publishers and the various movements for social and environmental change, responding to the issues of the day by building up the list with books that put tools into people's hands to truly build a more just and sustainable world," says Judith.

Commerce has gone full circle, returning to small businesses as much potential presence on the Internet as any other organization, regardless of size. Like the early European markets that formed around the town square or central cathedral, the Internet is full of small communities constantly being organized around values, purposes, missions. To a large degree, our lives can become unmediated by the media thanks to blogs, independent news portals and e-zines, like treehugger.com. Print magazines like *In Business* (inbusiness.org) or *E/The Environmental Magazine* (emagazine.com), PBS programs like *Ethical Markets* (ethicalmarkets.com) hosted by Simran Sethi and *Simple Living* (simplelivingtv.net) with Wanda Urbanska, and on the radio, Betsy Rosenberg's *EcoTalk Radio* (airamerica.com/ecotalk), American Public Media's Marketplace (marketplace. publicradio.org), or Amy Goodman's *Democracy Now* (democracynow.org) keep us on the cusp of new green innovations and the marketplace.

The opportunity for small business in the democratized global electronic network can provide handsome returns for a nominal investment of time, resources or expertise. The hybrid global-local market that results from this, in addition to the agility most small businesses possess, becomes a key advantage for small-time operators looking to reach customers anywhere in the world. Deliveries of their products, like any transaction from any other business, are made by FedEx, UPS or the postal service, door to door and — as Amory Lovins determined through extensive research at the non-profit organization, Rocky Mountain Institute (rmi.org) — in a more efficient and less ecologically damaging way than if you would open a bricks-and-mortar store in a suburban or urban strip mall. The ground-breaking Rocky Mountain Institute is all about creating

Glocalization: The Hybrid Global-Local Economy

Making an effort to prioritize a locally based economy within a global market is occurring throughout the country in the form of farmers' markets, food cooperatives, alternative currency initiatives and exchanges like freecycle.org. While it's unlikely that a photovoltaic or wind turbine system manufacturing plant might be based in your community, the goods and services you might need on a daily basis, like food, clothing or telecommunication services, would be. Thinking globally and acting locally has never resonated so clearly with more of us realizing that even the most basic local decisions, like how we meet our energy needs, has global implications in terms of climate change.

The power of computers and electronic links of the Internet have transformed where and how business can be conducted. Magazines are now published from high-rise urban apartments, and your accountant might be at the end of a cul-de-sac in abundance by design by achieving greater productivity from energy and resources — one of the hallmarks of ecopreneurial businesses.

This century already bears ripe fruit from the blossoming of sustainable and green business. Businesses — mostly small and medium-sized — are seizing the opportunity to rapidly jump-start enterprises devoted to solve myriad environmental and social problems, problems once addressed by government programs or institutions. Green is good.

The Citizen Engine Powering the Ecopreneurial Era

Powerful social trends have fanned the fires of would-be ecopreneurs in America. Suddenly, a nation of nine-to-fivers has given way to a spirited bunch of innovators, searching for a new way to work, live and continue their pursuit of happiness. The following are among the largest trends that may propel ecopreneurship.

Big Business Busters

Is anyone really worth $5,000 per hour? That's what some CEOs are earning, up over 300 percent from the 1950s, not even including pensions, fringe benefits (like a company car or jet) and deferred income or stock options. Meanwhile, perhaps thanks to your colleagues in the next building who work in mergers and acquisitions, you realize you're only a day away from a pink slip or required transfer. For many in the dwindling middle class, your salary raises have not even kept up with inflation.

Working for a big corporation is not what it used to be. Once, you could devote much of your life energy to meeting the needs of a large employer and your suburban neighborhood. Existing in a paradoxical way, the global and local economies will be dueling it out over the coming years as rising energy prices and other pressures transform both how we do business and where. Increasingly, your customers may be only a mouse click away on the Internet, making e-commerce one of the biggest markets ever tapped and in a way that has leveled the playing field with big business. This reality has spawned the hybrid global-local economy.

Authenticity plays a vital role in distinguishing the local economy. Ecopreneurs value place-based attributes and seek to preserve them, attributes like the flavors, culture and people that make an area unique and special. Eating seasonally, landscaping with native plants and community involvement form priorities. When necessities are not available locally, a special effort is made to source the item involving Fair Trade or by considering a host of other sustainable practices.

look to a retirement filled with a comfortable pension, adequate healthcare and a relatively comfortable quality of life. Once. Due to rising medical costs and increased pressures on profitability and growth in company share price, these same lifetime employees, many now retired — are witnessing first-hand how the single-minded pursuit of profits in a free market economy is whittling away their healthcare, pension and anticipated quality of life. Some Fortune 500 companies have discovered that Chapter 11 bankruptcy protection lets them shed their underfunded pension commitments for their retirees onto the federal Pension Benefit Guarantee Corporation (presently underfunded as well).

Reacting to the troubling trends, more corporate employees are busting out and cashing in to a new business where they can make the calls. They're discovering greater security by securing themselves through their own business.

Business Balancers, Choosing a Lifestyle Business

"It's not about the money," say many ecopreneurs, regardless of whether they operate a non-profit fundraising consulting business or a website design firm. It's about creating a lifestyle that sustains the planet while providing a way of life that's filled with happiness, personal satisfaction, meaning and the time to do the things they want to do. It's about living life on your terms, not those dictated by society, your boss or your parents.

Many have skipped out on the two-income job trap, before the handcuffs clasped down. These ecopreneurs carefully select lifestyle businesses that maximize control and flexibility so they can raise their family, care for an elderly parent, spend more time with friends, support non-profit organizations, serve in public office or contribute in myriad ways to their community. For some, running on the stairmaster to try and strike it rich was what almost killed them, destroyed a marriage, left them with regrets or provided them poor health. They learned fast and, as a result, are business balancers now.

As we explore in *Rural Renaissance*, there is a net US population migration into rural areas, especially those with beautiful scenery, numerous amenities and an attractive quality of life. This migration is echoed by Peter Wolf in *Hot Towns: The Future of the Fastest Growing Communities in America* who describes this national migration — the fifth in American history — as starting in the 1970s and resulting in millions of people moving into areas with scenic beauty, recreational opportunities, relatively clean air and water and fewer social problems.

In many cases, the information knowledge-based ecopreneurs could easily be classified as members of what Richard Florida refers to as the "creative class" in his book *The Creative Class*, people who prioritize place-based attributes over access to highways or tax breaks for where they want to open up shop. Or they migrate as Paul Ray and Sherry Ruth Anderson's "cultural creatives," individuals who share an ecological worldview, from their book, *The Cultural Creatives: How 50 Million People Are Changing the World* — explored in chapter 8 on marketing. In many ways, you might be splitting definitional hairs when trying to distinguish small business owners from ecopreneurs, free agents, the creative class and cultural creatives. These individuals escape easy classification — in part, because of their diversity.

Business Is Booming for the Boomers

"We're not going to suddenly take up golf and shuffleboard," admits one recently retired boomer who moved with his wife to Appleton, Wisconsin, to be closer to his daughter and family, cashing out of their California property when the money was great. He runs a four-room bed and breakfast they purchased turnkey, immaculate and smartly decorated with a Tuscany theme.

The 78 million baby boomers, born between 1946 and 1964, are emerging as America's leading entrepreneur class — with cash. Boomer businesses transform a passion into an enterprise, launch a dream business or give back to society in ways that share their years of experience and knowledge. Some businesses generate needed income to cover healthcare costs and shrinking pensions from corporations that have stiffed them. According to research by AARP, more than 5 million Americans over 50 are self-employed, accounting for 40 percent of the self-employed workforce.

Shattering the Glass Ceiling: Women

Almost half of the American workforce are women. Tiring of the glass ceilings that separate themselves from economic, development and growth opportunities that disproportionately get offered to still male-dominated workplaces of many corporations — especially the largest ones — women are setting out on their own and setting up their own shop, consultancy or enterprise.

With double-digit growth, women entrepreneurs — especially Asian American and African American women — now number more than 6 million, accounting for about 28 percent ownership of non-farm firms, according to the US Small Business Administration.

Diversity and Diversified

While board rooms at many Fortune 500 corporations often look much alike — disconcertingly white, white-collared and male — the offices and operations of ecopreneurs defy definition and are practically impossible to quantify accurately. Ecopreneurs tend to be a diversified bunch in terms of age, race and educational backgrounds. According to Steve King, co-author of the Intuit Future of Small Business Report from the Institute for the Future (iftf.org), "Leading small and personal businesses will be a group of Americans, including young adults — even teens, women, immigrants and aging baby boomers."

From farmhouse offices to garage laboratories, ecopreneurs have entirely new workstyles and business networks. Catch them at Green Drinks events (greendrinks.org), participating in the Burning Man gathering (burningman.com) or at a Green Festival, Bioneers Conference (bioneers.org) and renewable energy and sustainable living fairs. Send them an e-mail and expect a personal reply. Some happily work on the weekends, while others focus on getting the work done in only three days a week. Some ecopreneurs own a suit and tie, while others fancy organic cotton or hemp T-shirts and shorts when heading to work (sometimes in a room in their own home).

Besides coming from diverse ethnic, cultural and even mixed-race backgrounds, ecopreneurs thrive in a diversified livelihood and lifestyle. For some, there is rarely a typical day. Some own two (or more) properties, homes or other real estate holdings, of which they might rent out what they don't reside in or use themselves. Millionaires, they're often not. These wise property owners have focused their prudent investment strategies on income-producing assets rather than betting on the whims and often whimsical stock market gyrations. Some ecopreneurs have so many different irons in the fire that should one or two projects disappear, say resulting from an act of terrorism or unforeseen severe weather event, their livelihood can still sustain itself from the other, unrelated projects they might have in their portfolio.

Climate of Change

We live in tumultuous, rapidly changing, technology- and information-overdosed times. With an international war on terror with no clearly defined enemy (or resolution), a competitive addiction to various energy sources, and a pressing climate change that has already begun to transform how we live, what we grow, where we travel and, even, where we can live — we, like many, are starting to wake up to the reality that we cannot continue living as we do. The free market economy cannot sustain its unlimited growth, with or without governmental intervention, or begin its correction without trillions of dollars being lost in the process.

Despite our civilization of plenty enjoyed by many in America, a lot of us find ourselves searching for stability and sanity in an unbalanced world. But millions of ecopreneurs have found a resolution to their search in the form of a small business.

The next chapter will examine the concept of sustainability, both in business and life.

Chapter 3

Sustainable Business

B OTH OF US CAME OF AGE IN THE LATE 1980S when yuppies ruled, Gordon Gekko epitomized success and shoulder pads were way too big. Fortunately, we quickly lost the bad fashion and big hair. As we plugged through our 20s during the economic boom of the 1990s, our notion of success evolved beyond dollar signs. Call it an early mid-life crisis, but as we saw our supervisors at the ad agency eat daily take-out from Styrofoam clamshells at their desk, play office politics and live more at work than at home with their spouse and kids, we gazed into life's crystal ball and didn't like where we saw ourselves heading.

> "The first rule of sustainability is to align with natural forces, or at least not try to defy them."
>
> — Paul Hawken

Flash forward to today, where geckos hawk car insurance: you get paid when you crash your car. Celebrities sport hybrid cars. Global warming earns network lead-story status. Former yuppies bond in the Fair Trade, organic coffee kiosk at a brand new Whole Foods Market. The organic food aisle continues to grow faster than any other section of the supermarket. This spark of mainstream interest makes the timing ripe for tides to permanently turn, ready for sustainable business growth with visions richer than just profit, and for entrepreneurs with an ecological edge to prosper beyond paychecks.

What Is a Sustainable Business?

The word "sustainable" pops up in various contexts of doing good for the planet and causes academics to devote years to analysis and study. The word is thrown around by think tanks when promoting "clean coal" or nuclear power, and by politicians defending the need for continuous growth in jobs and the economy. "Sustainable living" describes efforts to live in ways that are ecologically and socially responsi-ble, from choosing biodegradable cleaners for your home to the type of car you drive. In *Rural Renaissance*, largely devoted to the practices and pragmatics of sus-tainable living, we suggest a definition that emphasizes the self-reliant, local community while recognizing the responsibility we have as global citizens.

Sustainable living balances the economic, ecological and social needs of all life with that of our own, while enhancing those possibilities for future generations. Sustainable living values diversity, creativity and passion; it's not about growth of property, wealth or stuff. Rather it's about creating livable communities and fos-tering greater social and economic equity, while preserving and restoring the ecosystems we depend on for our very survival. Our goals as individuals, global citizens and business owners are to plant more trees than we've used, help culti-vate a bioregional and sustainable food system that is more secure for us and our community, completely offset the carbon dioxide emissions caused by our energy use, live a fossil-fuel-free life and feed the flames of our imagination. We have our lifetime to do it. While there are limits to growth (this planet can only sustain so many people), there's no limit to development of a better way of living, one filled with creativity, adventure, security, nature and meaning.

Much of our journey — in our small business, journalistic pursuits, travels around the world and interviews with hundreds of fellow travelers, business own-ers and global citizens, both young and old alike — has been spent discovering solutions and ideas capturing what sustainable living could be. Our adaptive approach listens to our intuition and instincts while mindfully considering the vast amount of information, scientific research and personal experiences available. There isn't one way or even a best way to approach sustainable living and run-ning a sustainable business, since personal circumstances, location, climate and financial considerations are different for each of us. No one can write the rule book for running a sustainable business, since it would be outdated before it was even printed. An undercurrent throughout this book is that life and business are moving faster than we can keep up. Change and evolution are the only constants.

As we look at Webster's definition of the word "sustainable," there's much to be desired: *sus·tain·a·ble, adj.* 1. able to be maintained. 2. exploiting natural resources without destroying the ecological balance of a particular area.

If marriages are meant to be sustainable, it's no wonder they're ending in divorces. Ecopreneurs take sustainability beyond treading water. We aspire to continuously push the envelope to do better, with less negative impact on Earth while fostering more positive, restorative changes. Sustainable businesses aren't a cog in the wheel of capitalist progress, turning nature and labor into private wealth for a select few. They're catalysts for ecological change using the power of commerce to transform how we live on Earth. In many ways, the concept of permaculture design, first developed by Bill Mollison and David Holmgren in Australia, offers a simple way to view your business, expressed as an ethic: care for the Earth and all life; care for people everywhere; and share the surplus and avoid waste and pollution.

A growing number of businesses, however, approach sustainability personally from their perspective on how their priorities fit under the following key qualities of a sustainable business.

Practices Before Profit: Focus on the Triple Bottom Line

Traditionally, economics focuses on one clear bottom line: profit. Income minus expenses equals profit, that Willie Wonka golden ticket to all the sugar-coated answers to financial fulfillment. But a growing number of us realize cash profit is illusory, a sugar rush that quickly melts and leaves us empty. Sitting on a golden nest egg means nothing if we needed to sell our soul, divorce our values, destroy our relationships and squander our time on Earth.

First coined by John Elkington and articulated in his book, *Cannibals with Forks: The Triple Bottom Line of the 21st Century*, the triple bottom line doesn't drop the idea that businesses should earn a profit. It adds that businesses should do so in ways that take into account environmental and social performance in addition to financial performance. It requires a strong and efficient organization, perhaps even more so. Not only do you need to make a profit, you need funds and resources to reach beyond where mainstream business stops. A triple bottom line means expanding the spectrum of values and criteria for measuring business success to include: the planet, people and profits.

Bottom Line: Planet

Whatever your business, its impact on the environment must be not only assessed but addressed, ideally leaving a situation better than when you started. Sustainable businesses can, and should, aspire to not merely mitigate or minimize their impacts on the environment, but in the very way they operate their business, it should make the planet healthier, community more prosperous, air clearer and bring greater economic and social justice. It's the fundamental role of business to restore, heal, enhance or nurture the living systems on which we depend. Bottom line, does the mission of the business contribute to making this world a better place, not just line your pocket with more money?

A business's impact may take on different shades of green, depending on its owners' passions, abilities and resources. It's difficult to judge a non-profit global warming educational organization as a "better" business for the planet than a family-owned restaurant featuring local foods, or for that matter, launch a business that your heart may not fully be in because on paper it stacks up as the "right" thing to do. Adopting a planet bottom-line mission that transforms a conventional

Shades of Green

Various perspectives and priorities exist under the umbrella of sustainable business, depending on one's location, resources and experience. Rather than judge and label one business "greener" than another, Shades of Green appreciates differences and encourages us all to do what we can to better the planet through our work.

Depending on the industry, the best-practices bar of green business will be different. From a climate change perspective, is getting on a jet with your family to fly to an exemplary ecotourism lodge in the Caribbean better than driving a couple of hours to an indoor water park in Wisconsin in the winter? Discussed later in this chapter, numerous benchmarks and certification programs exist, with more on the way. Ecopreneurs and the companies they pilot will forever be improving and evolving the businesses far beyond regulations, exceeding national benchmarks and certifying their products or services. These innovative businesses will reimagine entirely new ways to operate or create products or services that are part of the restoration and living economy, perhaps, even, opting out of the free market money economy altogether through localized currency not even based on the US dollar, like Madison Hours (madisonhours.org) or Ithaca Hours (ithacahours.com).

business can be as important to helping the planet as starting out green from the get go.

A planet bottom line continually examines inputs and outputs, addressing the materials we use and how we use them as well as minimizing waste. Ecopreneurs recognize and incorporate ecological limits into their business models. As in nature, limits create opportunities and demand innovation. For some of the smaller businesses, by keeping small and human scaled, we can readily control inputs and outputs, prioritizing clean water, air and energy sources while minimizing if not eliminating waste. With Inn Serendipity, we empower ourselves to financially value and take the time to make these decisions — from what type of bananas we blend in our B & B smoothies (ideally organic and Fair Trade certified) to using green energy. We participate in the "Second Nature" green energy program with our local utility, Alliant Energy, purchasing green energy to offset what we can't produce ourselves during certain times of the year.

Bottom Line: People

People play a fundamental role in the ecopreneur's business philosophy, realizing four different groups of people have their own sets of needs and priorities. Many ecopreneurs we've interviewed talk about stakeholders, not stockholders. They generate profits by caring for their stakeholders, not trying to crush competing businesses. They're more concerned with nurturing their community, customers and employees, if they have them. The following are the four groups of stakeholders.

Customers

Cultivating caring customers drives ecopreneurial business success. Ecopreneurs view their customers much more as kindred spirits, sharing Earth-based values and priorities. Customer service, product quality and guaranteed services or products are crucial to their business success. Addressed further in chapter 8 on marketing, valuing customer communication translates to showcasing honesty, integrity and transparency. A respectful challenge banters between customers and sustainable businesses, much deeper and more personal than in typical customer interactions. Ecopreneurs expect to be scrutinized by their customers, and likewise, our customers expect candid, honest replies. Customers challenge ecopreneurs with questions like: Do you carry envelopes made with post-consumer waste? Can I get this in hemp? How do you offset your greenhouse gas emissions? Where are your ingredients sourced from? These questions keep our business constantly moving forward toward higher goals and expectations. On the flip side, at Inn Serendipity we must be honest that our guest rooms don't feature air conditioning or TVs.

Workers

If your small business hires staff, it should pay a fair "living wage," a minimum hourly wage that would afford a reasonable standard of living, often far above the legally mandated minimum wage. A triple-bottom-line approach to staff takes into account benefits such as healthcare, profit sharing, ongoing training and openly addressing employee needs as they arise, such as eldercare and childcare. Employee health goes beyond insurance co-payments and looks at issues such as the quality of the physical work environment. For example, many green businesses pride themselves on their green and natural building practices, using no-VOC (volatile organic compounds) paint on the office walls, which translates into no harmful out-gassing, incorporating daylighting into the buildings or providing complimentary meals.

For some businesses that find they wish to expand, they follow the 150 Rule, limiting the number of employees or contractors to 150 or less. According to anthropologist Robin Dunbar, our ability to maintain meaningful relationships within organizations and keep the business moving in the same direction tends to top out at about 150 people. Beyond that, communication tends to break down, the business starts to resemble a slow-moving glacier and odd things start happening in cubicles.

Challenge the stereotype that "big" equals "better;" you don't need to grow large to be exceptional. Stand prepared, however, since this concept goes against what the media, chamber of commerce, community development corporation or perhaps your hometown business leaders might see as "more-based" quantitative standards of excellence: creating more jobs, selling more stuff, building more warehouse space. Other businesses will potentially receive local accolades or the regional "entrepreneur of the year" plaque, while your business may earn a reputation of "interesting," a polite term for "weird." Delight in your oddity. Dance to the tune of a different drummer, inspired by a rhythm of doing good, not just contributing to the quantitative obsession. When it comes down to it, qualitative measures mean more. For proof, just think about the top ten most meaningful and important things in your life. They probably can't be quantified in dollars and cents.

Keeping business small inspires personal attention to detail when it comes to caring for your staff and subcontractors. For example, there is such a thing as a free lunch at Wildrose Farm Organics in Breezy Point, Minnesota. Owners Chuck and Karen Knierim provide a free, healthy lunch for the dozen seamstresses of their organic clothing line using organic vegetables from their garden and eggs from free-range chickens (wildrosefarm.com).

Vendors and Suppliers

How a sustainable business chooses and interacts with vendors and suppliers, so-called business-to-business transactions, that provide the supplies and services the business needs to run is one way ecopreneurs are helping grow and magnify our impacts. We seek out like-minded vendors with whom to do business. Co-op America's Green Pages (greenpages.com) is often our first stop to look for products our business might need, since it lists thousands of socially and environmentally responsible businesses.

A growing number of small businesses are perhaps inspired by the Amish and their collaborative sense of community and shared economic prosperity. Rather than working alone, many Amish provide goods or services to each other, working together on projects that on the surface may benefit only one farmer, but on the whole end up benefiting the entire community. As author Bill McKibben writes about in *Deep Economy*, there's greater comfort and security from community membership than individual ownership. This idea is reflected in the business-to-business commerce mushrooming on the Internet and in small businesses, especially the nanocorps, or new forms of interlinked commercial websites, like Sohodojo.com.

The growing Fair Trade movement increasingly helps with purchasing decisions, particularly for food such as coffee imported from developing countries, with labeling certification programs providing greater accountability, enabling you to ensure that the farmer is paid fairly. Fair Trade practices value fair payment for the product, investment in local people and communities, environmental stability and gender equity. Fair Trade trumps free trade in the present free market global economy, since the latter often exploits people and resources to achieve higher financial returns, an idea showcased by World of Good, launched by Priya Haji and Siddharth Sanghvi. The non-profit TransFair USA (transfairusa.org) offers information and a company directory for all Fair Trade certified products, including coffee, tea, herbs and fruits or vegetables.

World of Good

Fostering an economy based on social and economic justice, World of Good, launched by co-founders Priya Haji and Siddharth Sanghvi — just after they graduated from University of California Berkeley Business School — features unique gifts and handcrafts from artisan communities around the world. By selling through an ever-expanding distribution network of retailers nationwide, they are building a whole new economy based on Fair Trade. Ten percent of their profits get funneled to their sister non-profit organization, The World of Good Development Organization, which helps support artisan communities and works to strengthen international fair wage standards.

"Our aim is to make it easy to help customers make a good choice — not to buy more, but to buy differently," explains Priya. "They can expect

Co-partners: Priya Haji, CEO, Co-founder with Siddharth Sanghvi
Place: Emeryville, California
Earth Mission: "Empower people in the US to realize that they have power to influence the global economy through their purchasing choices. Specifically, by influencing the way that our multinational companies source in countries around the world through Fair Trade and other people-positive initiatives, we can change the lives of millions of women in order for them to live, be sustainable and self-determined and improve the conditions of poverty faced by their children."
Website: worldofgood.com

quality, convenience and style — yet the products can be made in a way that actually helps the people who make them. Right now, our products are women's accessories and housewares. As World of Good grows, our aim is to make the choice for people-positive products easy to find in every category of daily life. We want every human-made product to be a tool of relationship and empowerment for the person who crafted it. Imagine every product not as a material thing but as a bridge of connection and transformation."

Priya's economic vision parallels her innovative approach to structuring her business. World of Good is actually two intertwined yet financially and operationally separate organizations. The for-profit World of Good features beautiful and interesting handcrafted products from artisan communities worldwide. The non-profit World of Good Development Organization focuses on building strategies to substantially improve economic and social conditions for millions of artisans and their families around the world by funding health and education programs. This hybrid for-profit and non-profit brainchild draws inspiration from its founders' global travels and youthful idealism tempered by a pragmatic zest and passion for social enterprise.

"My mom is from India and my dad from Tanzania, and both overcame significant obstacles to be together and come to the United States. I was fortunate to excel in school with the support of my family and friends — and in the process, I developed a passion for understanding how our economy functions: consumer consumption, the trade deficit, international economic development and the challenges of harnessing trade for change. I have traveled around the world to different communities of women who look just like me (Mexico, India, Thailand) and when I looked into their eyes, I connected with the same aspiration for learning, desire for a good life, a healthier community and world. I knew that my own best contribution to the world was to join together with these other amazing women entrepreneurs and build a bigger, life-changing market-access channel."

In order to build this market access, the company sources about 80 percent of its products directly from the artisan groups, mostly women, residing in 34 countries. Like other members of the Fair Trade Federation, World of Good pays a 50 percent deposit on all orders, builds long-term business relationships and provides market and design feedback so that groups remain globally competitive in the Western market. With sales growth in the triple digits each year, in contrast to national giftware growth of only three percent, World of Good is starting to make an impact with respect to making it easier for customers to find ethically sourced products.

"One of the things we realized from the very beginning was that products had to be high quality and fashion forward or customers wouldn't buy them — regardless of the mission," admits Priya. "I am not sure if we have transformed global issues into an opportunity," replies Priya, relating to the Fair Trade movement. "Rather, we have taken the global issue of changing trade practices as a commitment and constraint into our business. Our customers who want to take this constraint and commitment into their own lives form our core consumer group — the people who will guide us, exchange ideas with us, help us creatively build this vision."

Funded by grants and individual donations, the non-profit World of Good Development Organization has also created a revolutionary Web-based tool called the Fair Wage Guide to help strengthen international wage standards. In essence, artisan communities worldwide can calculate a fair wage for their products. "The mission between the organizations is the same: Create a way for customers in the US to make choices that directly alleviate poverty in developing countries around the world," says Priya. "But, the business and the non-profit are intentionally separate because they have very different roles within this common mission. They have independent leadership and work autonomously with collaboration."

Before the Internet, their business model would have been challenging at best. Now co-founder Siddharth Sanghvi takes the lead on technology. "We often work with artisan groups through the Internet, designing products, communicating on micro-finance and managing payments without spending the money to travel there," explains Priya. "We are also able to maintain a live, current catalog on the Internet to support our customers at all times. We work with products that are handmade in limited quantities so the selection is ever-changing, and our technology infrastructure allows us to be flexible at a very low cost. The non-profit's Fair Wage Guide allows us to help artisans do real-time pricing to see how their wages compare at any moment in time in 89 countries with real, current economic data."

Echoing the power not of commerce but of the customers who purchase the products or services companies make, Priya concludes simply: "We do not have to do anything extraordinary. Just change our ordinary purchase choices. It is our choices that can change the lives of millions."

Similar to Fair Trade, a growing movement of companies and organizations are committing to source products from sweatshop-free manufacturing facilities. Sweatshop labor, whether in the form of employing children, women and men in substandard plants for unfair compensation or under inhumane, dangerous or toxic working conditions, contributes to growing social inequity around the planet and, obviously, exploits people for profits. To research products or services, consider using responsibleshopper.org from Co-op America, documenting social and environmental impacts of major corporations while providing opportunities to vote for change with your dollars. Global Exchange, an international human rights organization dedicated to promoting social, economic and environmental justice around the world, devotes numerous resources and information related to a globally fair and just economy (globalexchange.org).

Investors

If your business is large enough to require financial backing from investors, then providing competitive returns on their investment is a must. Most ecopreneur businesses, however, find that socially responsible investors tend to embrace the values and mission of the organization by offering more flexible and financially favorable terms.

Bottom Line: Profit

Profit validates the existence of the business, except now it stands as one element of a supporting trio within the triple-bottom-line approach. Profit can't be overlooked or minimized; failing to generate enough revenue to cover expenses means you won't be around for long. All the "doing good" notions won't cut it if a business fails financially. You can't take advantage of governmental structures designed to enhance small business without showing some profit. The key for some ecopreneurs is how much.

That notion of "some profit" remains a refrain throughout this book: How much is enough? By keeping lean and green, by incorporating profit as one element versus the inclusive end goal, by maximizing deductions and other business incentives keeping green values at heart, profit takes on new meaning. Profit now serves as a tool, not the sole end goal. These businesses have embedded tithe initiatives, whereby 10 to 20 percent of the profits from the enterprise are donated to various charities. For example, 10 percent of our profits, as authors of this book, are donated to the non-profit organization Renewing the Countryside.

Fields of Green

Sustainable businesses can prosper in all industry sectors, but not all businesses can be sustainable. Given our knowledge about the far-reaching impacts of nuclear waste — the reality that this lethally toxic waste product from the production of nuclear power will exist on Earth for more than 10,000 years — or global warming emissions belching from coal-fired power plants, both coal and nuclear power are bedfellows that must be replaced by cleaner and safer options. While the politicians and big businesses might spin their myths otherwise, sustainable businesses harness or use energy from renewable energy sources like wind or solar. Some even make their own home-grown biofuels.

Using the Four Horsemen of Opportunity and dovetailing them with your Earth Mission and personal situation in terms of where you are on life's journey — whether you're just starting out from college or eager to leave a legacy for your grandkids to enjoy or take over running — what types of industries or fields are ripe with possibilities?

Discussed in more detail in chapter 8 as it relates to marketing, the Lifestyles of Health and Sustainability (LOHAS) marketplace consists of five main segments where ecopreneurs would most likely prosper (lohas.com), quantified by research completed by the Natural Marketing Institute (nmisolutions.com). According to the Natural Marketing Institute, approximately 16% percent of the adults in the US, or 35 million people, compose the segment of the marketplace most likely targeted by ecopreneurs. The general segments are as follows:

- Sustainable Economy (green building, renewable energy, resource efficient products, environmental management, socially responsible investing)
- Healthy Lifestyles (organics, nutritional supplements, personal care)
- Ecological Lifestyles (organic and recycled fiber products, ecotourism, ecological home products)

- Alternative Healthcare (health and wellness care, naturopathy and homeopathy, complementary medicine)
- Personal Development (mind, body and spirit products; yoga, spiritual products).

Below are more detailed descriptions of a few of the many emerging businesses and enterprises likely to thrive in a living and restorative economy. So many are sprouting every day that even the mainstream media are covering what's hot in green. As the Four Horsemen of Opportunity might likely collide to create an environment of extreme variability and instability, pressure will be increasingly felt to maintain basic life-support and living systems, like adequate food, shelter, clothing and community cohesion.

Power in Renewable Energy

Biofuels like biodiesel might soon begin to replace our addiction to oil-based fuels while renewable energy generation from the wind, sun and biogas captured from methane in farm operations or landfills will help shift electricity needs away from the highly polluting or wasteful coal-fired and nuclear power plants. Many smaller operations are becoming their own power producers as a part of their business model, reducing their dependency on utilities and oil companies. The non-profit Apollo Alliance for Good Jobs and Clean Energy (apolloalliance.org), a joint project of the Institute for America's Future and the Center on Wisconsin Strategy, seeks to rejuvenate the US economy by creating the next generation of industrial jobs while treating clean energy as an economic and national security mandate to rebuild America.

Pollution Mitigation, Ecological Restoration and Protecting Climate and Ecosystems

Restoring nature and areas that have experienced ecosystem degradation, help-ing mitigate or clean up polluted areas, sequestering carbon dioxide emissions or protecting fragile and endangered ecosystems are all aspects of a rapidly growing industry. This is, in part, because municipalities, companies and land management agencies are finding themselves pressing up against the realities of inappropriate or poor past land use decisions. Started in a farmhouse by Steven Apfelbaum, Applied Ecological Services (appliedeco.com) has grown to become the nation's leading ecological consulting, contracting and restoration firm.

Food for Thought

Sustainable agriculture is the production or harvesting of food or fiber products from nature in a way that enhances and sustains it. From organic food products

to pasture-raised livestock, from little or no use of chemical fertilizers or pesticides to the humane treatment of farm workers, sustainable agriculture addresses
the reality that we are what we eat. The present conventional food system is
unsustainable — given that for every calorie we eat, more than seven calories of
energy go into producing it, not to mention the loss of distinct local flavors and
cuisine.

Clothing Matters

Clothing was listed among Henry David Thoreau's essential human needs (the
others being shelter, food and energy). The market for sweatshop-free and clothing made from natural fibers or recycled products continues to grow. Perhaps
responding to the more general awareness of the amount of chemicals sprayed on
conventional cotton crops — among the most of any agricultural crop in the US
— and the exploitative labor practices in garment manufacturing, the fashion
industry is going green.

Healing and Healthcare

Caring for a rapidly aging population; growing, processing and retailing organic
food; providing preventative and alternative medicine that are supplements or
alternatives to traditional treatment-focused medical care are all on the rise. On
a personal development level, demand for life, career and family coaches is growing as more people explore ways to reconnect with their passions, interests,
partner and dreams. Personal development covers mind, body and spirit products such as CDs, books, tapes, seminars and various spiritual-related products
and services. Yoga studios not only provide personal development on a fitness
level, they also address spiritual and community needs. Representing this quest for
self-inquiry and discovery, enrollment continues to rise at the Omega Institute in
Rhinebeck, NY, and the Esalen Institute in Big Sur, CA, offering such workshops as "Introduction to Spiritual Activism: Cultivating Joy While Changing
the World."

Ecotourism

Spas, retreat facilities, culinary experiences and ecotourism — travel that helps
preserve, protect or restore the natural or cultural areas while providing financial
and other benefits to local communities — are, like the organic food industry,
growing at double-digit rates.

Socially Responsible and Fair Trade Businesses

"Selling for less" when it's made in China at a child-labor sweatshop or offering
products that are, by most standards, supporting oppressive political regimes,

inhumane working conditions or destroying the environment grow less appealing when the true social and ecological costs of products are realized. New socially aware customers are prioritizing their values, no longer purchasing solely on price. People are using the power of the purse to stand up for human rights around the world.

Caring for Community within Communities

Every time an old Victorian home is transformed into a new B & B or an abandoned warehouse is turned into a community center or art gallery, communities are participating in the restoration economy. Rather than paving over and plowing down, ecopreneurs are reimagining new purposes for old buildings, spaces and places. Perhaps as a reaction to suburban sprawl, loss of social neighborhood cohesion and increased congestion in urban areas, more communities are being born or reborn as conservation developments where residential and commercial interests are finally relinked, or formed as eco-municipalities, intentional communities, sometimes with cooperative living arrangements and common land or property ownership arrangements, spawning the need for community facilitators and designers, architects and planners.

Natural Building and Green Design

Besides addressing energy use, how can homes, commercial buildings and any human-created space serve as a model for careful stewardship of water, management of waste and safe air quality and provide a comfortable living or working environment without adversely affecting the planet? From heating and cooling innovations to natural, sustainable flooring materials like bamboo, there's innovative abundance in this industry. Recycling services, reuse warehouses featuring reconditioned items or construction project discards, Internet-based exchange portals like craigslist.org, and ways to transform waste into new products are examples of such business creation.

Greentech or Cleantech

These sustainable technologies are products that are made in ways that use less energy, materials or resources, or eliminate waste and potentially toxic substances or manufacturing processes, discussed in detail by Ron Pernick and Clint Wilder in *The Clean Tech Revolution*. Energy Star (energystar.gov) products, certified by the US Environmental Protection Agency (EPA), help reduce energy use. Eco-efficiency and eco-effective products are addressing rising energy prices and improving the health of our home, business and community. Eco-efficiency makes products better. Many of the breakthroughs address zero-waste manufacturing processes, like the present transformation from incandescent to compact

enLux lighting, producing the world's first LED drop-in replacement for incandescent floodlights.

fluorescent lighting. On the horizon are LEDs, like the super-efficient enLux LEDs (enluxled.com) that we already use in our greenhouse. Eco-effective companies are re-engineering or designing better products — a product that provides the same service but in a totally new way, like the Rehance process of TS Designs, a leading example of a triple-bottom-line business in order to survive and prosper.

T. S. Designs

Co-partners: Eric Henry, President, and Tom Sineath
Place: Burlington, North Carolina
Earth Mission: "Harnessing the power of business sustainability — and the triple-bottom-line business model — in order to change the direction of the American society."
Website: tsdesigns.com

Often stressed ecological systems emerge, evolve and reorganize in the most innovative ways. The same holds true for T. S. Designs, the nation's largest maker of the most sustainably printed T-shirts, that revolutionized the very process of manufacturing. Ironically, their transformation was brought about by the North American Free Trade Agreement (NAFTA), championed by the US government, that nearly destroyed their business when their customers shifted to off-shore sources for cheaper T-shirts.

T. S. Designs, founded by Eric Henry and Tom Sineath, now uses 95 percent American-made organic cotton in their T-shirts. Its patented REHANCE printing process allows them to avoid using plastisol, normally made out of polyvinyl chloride (PVC), thus reducing the harmful ecological impacts of these ubiquitous products. But the company doesn't just make an eco-effective product; it transformed its business model from a focus on profits to operating by a triple bottom line: people, planet and profits. Instead of selling to the Gap and Nike, it now sells to Whole Foods Market and Greenpeace.

"Although Tom and I have always taken care of our employees and tried to make socially and environmentally responsible decisions with our business, our transition to a triple-bottom-line business was not spurred by inspiration, but by desperation," admits Eric, about their transition. "We believe that if you go outside your market to source a product that your market is capable of supplying, that is not sustainable. Unfortunately, this is due to NAFTA's and the World Trade Organization's missions that are driven solely by consumer price and do not consider environmental or quality-of-life costs."

Realizing that Eric and Tom couldn't do it all on their own, T. S. Designs contracted with Sam Moore, a chemist and advisor related to T. S. Designs' evolution into a triple-bottom-line business. It's his breakthrough innovation related to the proprietary REHANCE process that created a competitive advantage for T. S. Designs, in more ways than one. "Sam had the foresight to develop it based on the green chemistry model, which emphasizes the lack of any front-end ingredient of a process whose disposal would be a concern on the back-end," explains Eric, in essence putting into practice the reality that there is "no away" to dispose of waste.

The REHANCE process is water based, with the printing taking place in the fabric, not on it. Most printing commonly uses plastisol made from PVC, hazardous to the environment both in its manufacture and disposal. With REHANCE, toxic aspects of the printing were avoided, while improving the quality of the printing on the T-shirt by eliminating cracking and flaking and improving breathability. Their move to purchase cotton from organic sources addresses the reality that about 25 percent of the world's pesticides are used on cotton. Forced by NAFTA to innovate to survive while adopting a triple-bottom-line approach to business, T. S. Designs emerged with a better product with a lower ecological impact.

Eric believes the triple-bottom-line approach can be used for just about any business. He started the Burlington Biodiesel Co-op at the T. S. Designs plant that now produces more than 200 gallons of biodiesel a week for employees and the community at large with its off-the-grid, green-built, card-swipe B100 biodiesel pump recently installed in partnership with Piedmont Biofuels. Then there are plans for a Company Shops Marketplace Co-op that will reconnect farmers with their community through a grocery store featuring locally grown or raised agricultural products. Like many ecopreneurs, Eric's Earth Mission lands him on various boards for numerous non-profit organizations, including Co-op America and area universities.

"I did not choose the textile industry because of its ability to express my Earth Mission," admits Eric. "My Earth Mission chose me because we were in the textile industry. Our desperate, difficult transition has made us even more aware of the importance of a sustainable business model and has given us a better perspective that allows us to be a leader for the cause."

Customers are still king, regardless of whether big business or big government tries to dictate otherwise. Ultimately, these customers determine the continued success of T. S. Designs and other green businesses, recognizing their own transformation from consumer back to citizen and their role in determining the kind of future they want. "Now that people are becoming aware of the costs of manufacturing other than the price they have to pay, such

Clothing Facts	
Amount Per Shirt	
% Daily Values	
Sweatshop Labor	0%
Pesticides Used	0%
Plastic Prints	0%
Harsh Resins	0%
Certified Organic Cotton	100%
Water Based Inks	100%

tsdesigns.com
printing t-shirts for good™
© 2007

T. S. DESIGNS

T. S. Design Clothing Facts

as environmental and social footprints, we are finding our model to be more rewarding every day," observes Eric. "As more and more people see value in an organic cotton T-shirt made in the United States, we gain customers. It's all about what they consider important to their lives."

"T-shirts and apparel in general has always been a conduit for transmission of ideas and concepts into the marketplace," continues Eric. "Consider Nike's branding of its own apparel; no one buys Nike for the product, they buy it for the message, for the brand. We decided that if Nike and companies like Nike can succeed with nothing but an image, we could easily succeed with our message because the contents of and processes that make our products reflect that message. Our products have both message and substance, something Nike can't achieve with their current model. Our Clothing Facts brand has definitely become the spearhead message that explains and advertises the substance of the products themselves."

Rather than thrive in an economy based upon extractive, exploitative practices or that views nature as a receptacle for waste or strategies for product obsolescence, sustainable businesses reinvent enterprises where, as William McDonough, noted eco-architect and co-author of *Cradle to Cradle*, points out, "There is no away" when you throw something away. Everything goes somewhere.

Sustainable businesses are whole Earth enterprises, enterprises that move beyond offering a "green" product or service to customers. Whole Earth enterprises, depending on the industry, manage water, heating and cooling, lighting, cleaning, purchasing, food preparation, waste, energy and labor as all being central to the operations of their business. If you're a restaurant that makes deliveries, offer the service on bicycle or with a vehicle that's powered by electricity or homemade biodiesel from the waste fryer oil from your restaurant. If you make clothing, how can your business provide living wages to seamstresses, help farmers who raise crops for fiber and use electricity that comes from renewable energy? Even if you can't put up your own photovoltaic or wind turbine system, your business can still buy Renewable Energy Certificates (RECs), or "green tags," (eere.energy.gov/greenpower/index.shtml) or participate in a green energy program with your utility.

At Inn Serendipity, our livelihood is inexorably linked to our food systems, energy systems and living systems. Growing organic food for ourselves and B & B guests, practicing conservation and generating our own energy onsite allows us to care for the Earth, spending incalculable hours restoring soil health, mitigating our carbon emissions or reducing not only our waste stream but that of our community as well by participating in and promoting the reuse and exchange economy. Like raising our own son, these efforts go uncompensated from the perspective of our free market economy and can't be measured in dollars.

Regional Roots

A sustainable business roots locally and is linked to its community for customers and for the goods or services it needs. This means priorities for both generating and spending income from our regional area or bioregion. Our place of business defines what we are, how we are connected to other community businesses and who our customers might be. Exactly how "regional" depends on your living situation, needs and map you

Lisa Kivirist harvesting pea pods at Inn Serendipity.

select. Of course, the Internet and the ability to reach millions at the click of a mouse became an intermediating variable as to how you might define your roots. If a community is in decline or dying, however, sustainable small business cannot succeed, since social and economic purposes are intertwined. Some large corporations tap these situations by exploiting resources or the labor market. But working for minimum wage is not prosperity; it's wage slavery.

For us, being rural, our regional footprint extends more broadly to the Midwest. Our B & B breakfast reputation stems from the idea of a truly local breakfast: most of the ingredients are harvested onsite. When other ingredients are needed, we try to source them as regionally as possible. In our southwest corner of Wisconsin, we fortunately possess a wealth of locally made cheeses that we can buy at a discount directly from Alp & Dell, the retail store at the local Roth Käse cheese factory. Bruno, the Swiss-born store manager and cheesemaker, knows us regulars and tells us if he has an overload of a certain cheese, which we freeze for future use, to sell us at a deeper discount. Likewise, several times a year we load up on organic dairy products at Organic Valley Family of Farms' outlet store in LaFarge (near our cabin). When we need to stock up on bulk pantry ingredients and ethnic items, we pool our shopping list for our next trip an hour north to the Willy Street Co-op in Madison. We are members and enjoy their selection of Fair Trade products. Like the majority of shoppers, we bring reusable canvas shopping bags to the checkout aisle.

While we aim to buy the majority of our purchases at other Midwest businesses, most of our business income also comes from the Midwest. The majority of our B & B guests drive less than three hours to get to the farm. Our consulting clients are based in our region, hiring us for projects ranging from tourism promotion for our local chamber of commerce to a marketing project for a regional conservation organization. Renewing the Countryside, the non-profit organization with which we partner on various creative writing and marketing projects as subcontractors, is based in Minneapolis. All of our writing and consulting projects are managed from a home office.

That's not to say we say no to opportunities outside our bioregion. Rather, we evaluate these options more selectively. Let's say we're invited to speak at an organic farming conference in California mid-winter. We'd evaluate financial compensation (which could come in different forms — such as advance purchase of our books) with travel time and options (remembering to offset our carbon emissions with tree-planting efforts), opportunities to network and learn new things and the ability to travel together as a family and provide new educational outlets for Liam, with whatever else we have going on at that time.

As peak oil hovers on the horizon, the economics of globalization will be forced to change. When American gas prices top $7 a gallon — about the same as Europeans pay now — the Wal-Mart model of cheap imports will oust their advertising icon of a smiley face pirouetting down the aisles slashing prices. By focusing on a local economy, ecopreneurs rise above this downward economic spiral likely to affect most larger companies addicted to the energy needed to move their products halfway around the world.

Growing roots and permanence play important roles in this bioregional focus of sustainable business. If American households committed to an address for a decade or two, instead of the average of seven years, a bigger green vision could emerge showing financial benefits, especially for home-based businesses. Installing a solar hot water heating system starts paying back after an average of 4.5 years. Our wind turbine will pay for itself in about 17 years, assuming electricity rates stay the same — which won't happen. As rates continue to climb, the timeline to profitability shortens. Plus, equipment can be depreciated over its effective lifespan (more on this in chapter 6). Like small-sizing your operations, staying put can also be a competitive advantage.

Planting long-term roots in a community increases interest in local activism, getting involved with development, education or other issues aligned with your values and passion. When our livelihood builds on a local economic base, business and community interests intertwine. While business community involvement is hardly a new concept, ecopreneurs often express such interests from different platforms than the traditional routes of attending Rotary meetings or donating to the United Way. Being the first in one's county to erect a wind turbine paves the way for other community members to go through the process in the future. Some ecopreneurs offer seminars or workshops and host school groups and open houses.

Above all, a local approach showcases the inherent unique characteristics or quality of that area. Homogenization rules in a world where many businesses focus on providing everything 24/7. But a contrasting movement exists where people search for the authentic and personalized. At Inn Serendipity, we've found guests seeking hand-signed artisan pottery mugs, not ones with a Made in China stamp on the bottom. Even our young son

Hand-crafted mugs by Steve and Jane Fry, co-owners of Elk Falls Pottery works, Elk Falls, Kansas.

has proclaimed when well-intentioned grandparents took him to the Rainforest Café, a restaurant designed to simulate a rainforest: "It's all fake." As more people crave and search for the authentic, this market for businesses that prioritize regional roots will increase and become a powerful business force. Petunias don't belong in Phoenix, and strawberries and January's snow don't mix. Showcase cactus in Arizona and gorge on Wisconsin berries in June.

Whole Pie Purpose

Sustainable business looks at the holistic picture of how we live our lives. Doing good for one slice of your life forms a strong start but needs duplication in other aspects of daily life. From tea choices to travel destinations, our daily decisions impact our sustainability quotient. Worthy save-the-planet intentions in your business fizzle if your lifestyle choices head in disparate directions. It can be hard to convince people on the importance of global warming or caring for the poor when you live in a super-sized, 10,000 square-foot house.

Whole Pie Purpose differentiates between "principles" and "practices." It's not about what you say — a noble mission statement on paper — but what you do, how you do it and why it matters. Customers drawn to ecopreneur businesses demand transparency, accountability and tangible practice. How much carbon dioxide has your business sequestered or avoided sending into the atmosphere; that's what counts. For caring corporations, they consider ecological and social costs of doing business into their business plan. How much food comes from area farmers? How does your manufacturing process result in the discharge of waste?

In the philosophy of Whole Pie Purpose, the concept of sustainable business reaches beyond the business plan, deeper than day-to-day business operations. Sustainability Beyond Business (SBB) forms a fundamental paradigm shift of

Guidelines and Certification Programs for Sustainable Businesses

Numerous guidelines and certification programs now exist for green businesses depending on your industry.

Sustainable Business Checklists

Ecological Footprint
Fifteen easy questions estimate how much land and water you need to support your lifestyle. Interesting comparisons against footprint impacts from other areas of the world. www.myfootprint.org

The Natural Step
Various resources and inspiring global examples serve as a guide to help companies, communities and governments onto a more socially and economically sustainable path. www.naturalstep.com

Sustainable Business Networks or Associations

Co-op America Business Network (CABN)
The oldest, largest and most diverse network of socially and environmentally responsible businesses in the US, organized by Co-op America. Participating companies' using business as a tool for social change, are "values-driven," not simply profit-driven. They're socially and environmentally responsible in the way they source, manufacture and market their products and run their offices and factories. They are committed to and employing extraordinary and innovative practices that benefit workers, communities, customers and the environment.
www.coopamerica.org/greenbusiness/network.cfm

Business Alliance for Local Living Economies (BALLE)
An international alliance of more than 50 independently operated local business networks with members dedicated to building local living economies, envisioning a sustainable global economy made up of local living economies that build long-term economic empowerment and prosperity through local business ownership, economic justice, cultural diversity and environmental stewardship.
www.livingeconomies.org

Institute for Local Self-Reliance
A non-profit research and educational organization that provides technical assistance and information on environmentally sound economic development strategies.
www.ilsr.org

Certification Programs

Leadership in Energy and Environmental Design (LEED) for Construction and Home Building

The LEED Green Building Rating System is the national benchmark for high-performance green building, giving building owners the tools they need to have a quantifiable impact on their building site. www.usgbc.org

B Corporation

Stakeholders, not just stockholders. Certified by the non-profit organization B Lab, a company can define themselves as environmentally and socially responsible to its customers or investors by being certified as a beneficial corporation, or B Corporation. Practices reviewed include charitable donations, energy efficiency, democratic decision making and environmental stewardship. www.bcorporation.net

Energy Star

A certification program with over 50 categories of appliances and products that use less energy, save money and help protect the environment. www.energystar.gov

Cradle to Cradle

Reviews environmentally intelligent design of products that consider the entire lifecycle of ecologically safe and healthy materials. www.c2ccertified.com

Forest Stewardship Council

Sets standards for responsible forest management and certifies products from specific woodlands. www.fsc.org

Greenguard Indoor Air Quality

Approves various building and home or office décor products with low volatile organic compounds, or low-VOC. www.greenguard.org

Green Seal

Provides standards and certification for diverse products, including paints, windows, alternative-fuel vehicles and paper. www.greenseal.org

Green Globe

Green Globe is the worldwide benchmark and certification program for the international travel and tourism industry. www.greenglobe.org

Travel Green Wisconsin

An example of a statewide movement promoting sustainable travel, including various checklist criteria for greening and localizing travel-related businesses in Wisconsin, the first state in the nation to introduce such a comprehensive program. www.travelgreenwisconsin.com

Certified Organic (in US by US Department of Agriculture)
USDA's National Organic Program regulates the standards for any farm, wild-crop harvesting or handling operation that wants to sell an agricultural product as organically produced. www.ams.usda.gov/NOP

Scientific Certification Systems
Certifies ecologically preferred products or services like cabinetry, doors, flooring and paints. www.scscertified.com

how to approach a business, career and livelihood. Boundaries between "job" and "life" intertwine and must be nurtured and holistically approached to create a sustainable lifestyle, reaching beyond just business. If your health is off, business is off. If your relationships need priority care, business can't thrive. In a dysfunctional governmental regulatory environment, following the laws are not enough. SBB means leading by example — producing all your energy with renewable energy today, not 20 years from now — self-enforcing your operations and beginning to redefine what being green means through constant refinement, improvement and experimentation.

"The trouble with the rat race is even if you win you're still a rat," wisely comments comedian Lily Tomlin. We found this proved true for us as we pumped our energy — physical, mental and spiritual — into a paycheck job with few true benefits. Lattés lose their buzz after a while. Trapped into believing our worth stood based on possessions, we found ourselves ignoring or taking for granted the various other aspects of wealth that are far greater determinants to our well-being than any pile of cash could ever be.

The Journey Continues

Don't think of sustainable business as a finite end goal. We never checked off "achieved sustainability" on our to-do list and never will. Sustainability remains an ongoing mantra and motivator in the journey. Sustainability is never achievable since it's an evolving journey, as with nature. Sustainability fosters innovation and continual improvement.

This book doesn't proffer a right and wrong approach to business. Rather, it encourages innovation under an umbrella of shared values. This foundation of understanding sustainable business concepts now flows into the next chapter as we make these concepts pragmatic and personal, developing an understanding of the practical dollars and cents behind hanging out your own green business shingle.

Chapter 4

Make a Life, Not Earn a Living

Aᴿᴇ ʏᴏᴜ ᴡᴏʀᴋɪɴɢ ʜᴀʀᴅ, but feel like you're hardly working on anything you care deeply about? Do you find yourself lost in the cubicle maze, dependent on the caffeine drip to keep you going to so many meetings that you need a BlackBerry to keep them straight? Do your raises and promotions never seem to let you pay off the credit card balance, or exit the earn-and-spend culture of consumption? Do you find yourself in a family where you need two income earners just to keep up with the bills? Or are you "retired" or semi-retired but short on cash?

You're not alone. We've interviewed business owners and listened around campfires and at conferences to stories of people searching for and finding different ways of working and living. We worked at an advertising agency long enough to know that our job was going to affect our health, our relationship and the world we've come to love and want to preserve for future generations. They say that recognizing a problem is the first step to solving it.

While the 8 million or so millionaires and billionaires keep getting richer, we remaining 292 million Americans are left to pay the government's mounting bills through our diligent tax payments. We try to achieve the American dream of home ownership and a sense of happiness, despite being left out of the prosperity that has concentrated wealth in even fewer hands, especially over the last two decades. Truth be told, the inflation-adjusted median wage and benefits of average American workers has stagnated or declined for over two decades. Meanwhile, the average pay for major corporate CEOs has increased to more than 300 times the median worker's pay. It's not unusual for Wal-Mart's CEO to earn as much as 900 times the average Wal-Mart worker. Adding to the pain, just about everything got more expensive relative to the rate of increase in wages, from healthcare to a college degree. We're making less in earned wages and median household income, yet spending more.

Some of us don't feel like we've been left out of the boom because we live in larger houses (or perhaps own a second vacation home or condo), drive a new car, manage to pony up at the gas pump or watch movies delivered to our doorstep, viewing them on a high-definition TV. But these signs of wealth are merely illusions for those Americans who cashed out of appreciated stock holdings in the stock market run-up from 1982 to 2000, inherited money from Depression-era grandparents, used their house as an ATM machine by taking out a home equity loan or maxed out their credit cards. It's no wonder we have a negative savings rate nationally.

We'll explore managing debt in more detail in chapter 7 (Money Matters) — turning assets into income-producing enterprises and avoiding debt — since this is essential for both a sustainable business and life. Like the need to live on solar income (not fossil fuel), we thrive on current income, not borrowed future earnings. Becoming an ecopreneur is about creating value from the values you hold deeply, becoming smart about what wealth you have and changing your perspective from a world based on monetary wealth to one based on purpose. Money is a tool for accomplishing your vision of what the world can become through the business or non-profit organization you create.

Creating Value from Your Values

Becoming an ecopreneur is transformational, requiring us to disassociate money with well-being, since having lots of it guarantees neither happiness nor health. Happiness is not getting what you don't have. Rather, it's finding pleasure in what you have right now. Finding meaning in your life, a purposeful vision and Earth Mission drive ecopreneurs to excel, overcome obstacles and express an idea that can possibly transform how we view the world and our place in it. Ecopreneurs create value with their deeply seated personal values of ecological stewardship, social responsibility, community sustainability and compassion for the right for all life to prosper on Earth. Their work enriches their life and the lives of others, often in ways that are non-financial.

The following six approaches define ecopreneurship, embodying your Whole Pie Purpose and Sustainability Beyond Business explored in the previous chapter.

Making a Quality Life, Not Living to Work

Life offers more than a paycheck, corner office and promotional title. In fact, many of us are working ourselves to death. Less than 40 percent of working Americans actually take all the vacation time that they're offered, and many who do have a hard time disconnecting from the office, voicemail and e-mail. Added to this are the hours each week we spend commuting, wasting time and polluting the environment unless you're fortunate to be able to walk or bike to work.

Who we are has become defined by what we own and the company we work for. For many people, their identity is so closely associated with their job that when they stop working, they end up passing away not long afterwards, lacking hobbies, social connections or life purpose. But what it says on a business card says nothing about our passions, interests, talents or aspirations.

A shift in perspective is underway, from desiring a standard of living defined by possessions and financial wealth to a quality of life defined by experiences and genuine well-being. For many people, maintaining their high standard of living contributes to their poor quality of life, not to mention often contributing to the destruction of the planet. True, we must earn enough money each year to afford some of the products or services we need or to meet certain obligations we might have in our society. But some ecopreneurs do so in the context of living below our means. Our annual income ebbs and flows from peaks to valleys, like the changes of the seasons. Throughout the journey, we never lose sight of the real bottom line: our quality of life. Our health, our happiness, our deep connection to the natural world and to our local community are far more important than helping support the continued — and unsustainable — increase in spending and consumption. We have no intention of being the richest person in the cemetery.

When redesigning and reorienting our life, we started experimenting with our own ecologically modeled Diversified Quality of Life Index, measured by various factors including the health of family relationships, enjoyment of work, level of satisfaction with life and opportunity for continued development and community involvement. Community involvement can be immediately local and place-based, or it can be virtual (on the Internet) or temporal (at a Green Festival or renewable energy fair). Involvement can be issue-oriented, like contributions to national or international non-profit organizations. Our currency is composed of joy, happiness, friendship, satisfying self-reliance, peace.

Generating cash flow, while necessary, usually accounts for less than five or six hours of work per day on average, leaving plenty of time for non-financial aspects of our Earth Mission and pursuit of happiness. As it turns out, much of our income-producing work does not command high compensation. We're intrinsically motivated by meaning and accomplishing deeply satisfying projects, like children's books. We place more value on the quality of our work and the types of projects and their ability to serve our Earth Mission than the size of the advance or magnitude of the fee we could extract from clients. We're not extrinsically motivated by money, status or power. Never setting sales goals for our business (not uncommon for many ecopreneurs), we've also never calculated what our hourly wage would have been, for example, working on this book.

Recognizing that not all relationships are healthy, we endeavor to wean ourselves from those that are negative, energy-depleting or competitive, while nurturing those that are restorative, peaceful, energizing, reciprocal and collaborative. We're not afraid to walk away from obligatory or harmful relationships any more than we are to divorce ourselves from our once dependency on the conventional food system.

The Gross National Product (GNP) is the total value of the free market economy's output of goods and services, measured in money. We'd argue that it's measuring a false sense of prosperity. In fact, such atrocities as the September 11 terrorist acts, the Exxon Valdez disaster, violent crimes, divorces, the wars on drugs or terror, and the expanding prison network all contribute to the GNP; however, these hardly add to the well-being of Americans. Not accounted for within GNP is the loss of natural capital: soil, forests, water and wildlife. Nor are the ecological services rendered by the biological processes of nature: the cleansing of water, wetlands buffering coastal areas from storms, sequestering carbon dioxide taken in by trees — all of which foster climate stability.

As if GNP is not enough, add to it the Consumer Confidence Index, an index developed by clever researchers to measure "consumers' expectations" toward employment and other current conditions that, statistically speaking, influence their willingness to keep spending. Since two-thirds of the US economy, as measured by the GNP, is based on Americans spending money on stuff, the Consumer Confidence Index is a barometer of how future spending and consumption will fare.

The Consumer Confidence Index and GNP measure the wrong things. Our health, our happiness, our deep connection to the natural world and our local

Diversified Quality of Life Index

Our Diversified Quality of Life Index (DQLI) is measured by various factors including the health of family relationships, enjoyment of work, physical health and well-being, level of satisfaction with life and opportunity for continued development. Among the essential tenets of DQLI:

- Having a meaningful livelihood that expresses our passion, creativity and soul.
- Ongoing opportunities for life-long learning and experiences.
- Maintaining mental, physical and holistic spiritual health.
- Opportunities for continuous personal, spiritual and creative development.
- Having control over our schedules.
- Building solid, meaningful relationships with our family and friends.
- The satisfaction and joy that comes with greater self-sufficiency.
- Connecting to the interdependent web of life that provides an abundance of diverse perspectives and experiences.

community are far more important than helping support the continued — and unsustainable — increase in spending. Our business life dovetails and intersects with the Multiple Economies of Ecopreneurship in which we thrive, bartering for a granite countertop installation, writing an article in exchange for an advertisement for our book and donating a set of multicultural children's books to help raise funds for the Cystic Fibrosis Foundation, helping the son of a local family friend.

It turns out that our questioning of the GNP is similar to what the nonprofit organization Redefining Progress has been proposing with their Genuine Progress Indicator (GPI), which values things like volunteerism and accounts for loss of natural capital and for the loss of leisure suffered by people working excess hours. According to their scientific methodology, while the GNP has continued to rise, their Genuine Progress Indicator has steadily fallen since the 1970s. Economist Mark Anielski, author of *The Economics of Happiness* developed Genuine Wealth, a practical economic model that helps redefine progress and vastly improves our well-being, based on five capitals: human, social, natural, built and financial.

We're both optimistic and hopeful, in part, because we've seen ways humankind has demonstrated an outpouring of compassion, creativity and cooperation to solve seemingly insurmountable problems. What matters most to us is what has always mattered — love for all life, meaningful social relationships, good health and peace. Our life changes have helped us focus on what's important, meaningful and authentic — meaningless when calculating GNP — and probably interpreted negatively by those calculating the Consumer Confidence Index.

By achieving an increased sense of happiness, we've come to understand that there's a hierarchy of needs. While we journey toward becoming all that we can be, our life, the land and our community life is becoming richer. We're not advocating millions of Americans to take a vow of poverty. Rather, we're inviting everyone to join millions of Americans who are living below their means, downshifting their consumption, sharing instead of hording and simplifying instead of spending more at the mall. Spend less, live more.

Putting Money to Work, Not Working for Money

We should think of paper money, or fiat currency, as nothing but a piece of paper, backed by a sovereign government who issues it. Since 1971 the US dollar, a fiat currency, is no longer backed by gold or any other commodity. If our government needs more, it prints more, which can, and often does, lead to inflation. When the value of money is diluted, it takes more money to buy the same amount of goods or services. There can also be deflation, where less money is available, sometimes spiraling downward into an economic depression. A particular currency can be devalued, which make products or services in one country worth less and therefore more affordable in other countries where their currencies are worth more relative to the devalued currency.

Fortunes have been made and lost over money and the faith we place in it. Despite this, there are many in America who still want to be millionaires. By dedicating your life, and life energy, to working for a company, you garner a salary, plus benefits like health insurance or a pension. What you make from your job will rarely be enough to retire money rich, if that's your plan. For the average American working for a paycheck, May Day — a pagan spring ritual where you dance around a Maypole — marks yet another, less festive occasion. From the first of January until around the first of May, all the money you earn goes to pay your share of income tax to the US government. Kiss those months — that money — goodbye. Life is not a reality TV game show. Money doesn't grow on trees; it's printed on dead trees by the government and backed by nothing, yet most of us spend four months earning cash we'll never see.

The Wealth of Poverty

Poverty is more a state of mind than an economic condition. The truly poor are those who regularly go without food and safe drinking water, lack proper clothing, have no place to live, possess few resources and little hope. Few Americans are poor in this sense, but about two-thirds of the planet's inhabitants are. Ultimately, there can be no ecological and economic sustainability without social justice and economic equity. More than two billion global citizens earn less than $2 a day, a number that despite the benefits touted by globalization proponents seems to be rising. Signs of our global economy's Free Market Economy Dementia headline daily news and help make some marginalized people into terrorists or a few disenfranchised wealthy, well-educated people into powerful and dangerous extremists.

Even many of the financially well off find themselves in one of the following forms of poverty. While lack of money (or fear of not having enough and losing what you have) is most commonly thought of as poverty, many of us find ourselves encountering other forms of poverty in our lives.

Time: We now live in one of the most over-worked, over-scheduled periods in human history, affecting people of any social or economic standing. This time famine inspired the Take Back Your Time Day (timeday.org) every October 24, to preserve our family, health, community and environment by rededicating hours to such rarified pastimes as sharing dinner time with family and friends. Growth of the slow food movement (slowfood.com) echoes the interest in slowing down and savoring the moment around the dinner table.

We followed the advice of our parents, as most children do: get a good education, go to college and get a job — a nice, secure, well-paying one, with great fringe benefits, stock options or profit-sharing. But the bimonthly paychecks — after the government gets its share for income, Social Security and Medicare taxes — aren't enough to keep up with the bills. Even with raises and promotions, many of us feel that we keep getting further in the hole, since the more we earn in earned income, the more it's taxed. The reality is that the system is largely devised this way, not to tax the very rich but to exact a fee on the middle class and poor to keep these wage earners on the treadmaster of a job — or "promising career."

When you're earning wages, you're making money for someone else or, often, something else called a corporation and its shareholders. For your job, you get a paycheck, from which income taxes are withheld to pay for an ever-expanding governmental bureaucracy of the size that even the Romans or Greeks would envy, according to William Bonner and Addison Wiggin in their exhaustive and provocative book, *Empire of Debt: The Rise of an Epic Financial Crisis*. Besides buying a new

Belongingness: Friends and family have been pushed to the edges of our daily experience, or relegated to quality time at the holidays. Many people fill in spare minutes each day watching TV, shopping or surfing the Web — poor substitutes for social interaction and no match for a lengthy conversation over dinner.

Health: Access to affordable and adequate healthcare is quickly becoming a life-or-death decision. Care has become based more on insurance coverage than medical advice, both of which have financial costs for the best care spiraling out of reach for all but the most affluent. Preventative care, whether in the form of a YMCA workout routine or regular stroll around the neighborhood with a good friend, is often an afterthought or pursued only after the onset of a life-threatening illness.

Community: Loneliness fills many who live in some of the largest cities or sprawling suburbs. Community-based interaction and civic involvement has dropped off precipitously over the past several decades, as documented in Robert Putnam's book *Bowling Alone*. Largely missing are the European piazzas or town squares.

If you would attempt to quantify poverty, don't look to the government for answers. Amazingly, the US government still defines poverty based on the cost of feeding a family in the mid-1960s, adjusted thereafter based on the consumer price index and inflation. The cost of healthcare, insurance, housing, energy, transportation and college tuition, many spiraling upward at double-digit rates, are omitted.

car to commute to your job, usually purchased with bank financing, many people acquire a mortgage from another bank to buy a house or condo. Now you have property taxes on top of income and payroll taxes.

So you're earning wages to pay taxes to the government, interest payments to the banks that hold your car loan and house mortgage, and insurance premiums to cover yourself if anything sours. All the while, you help make more money for the company you work for and the shareholders of the business. You're working so you can afford to keep paying the bills to keep your house, your car and your

Why Wages and Consumption Wreck Our Lives

It's practically impossible for a family of three or four to make enough money with only one wage earner receiving the US median annual income of $34,269 to afford a typical middle-class lifestyle. Most families find that both parents must work in order to pay the bills, as depicted below, which do not even include food, energy costs or any lifestyle choices related to travel, clothing and the like. Keep in mind that the federal government fosters taking on debt by providing a disincentive to save and an incentive to borrow: you're taxed on your interest income and can deduct interest charges on your mortgage.

Household Estimated Average Annual Expenses

Items	Household Expenses
Federal income taxes	$16,000
State income taxes	$1,500
Average minimum balance on credit card to Bank 1	$300
Mortgage payment to Bank 2	$10,000
Private mortgage insurance (PMI)	$840
Car loan payment to Bank 3	$5,748
Property taxes	$2,385
Car insurance	$847
House or property insurance	$481
Health insurance (premium, uncovered medical exp.)	$10,880
Total Expenses	$48,981
Median US Salary	$34,269
Net Savings (neg.)	($14,712)*

*requiring a second wage earner

Sources: Adapted from 2005/2006 data found on Bankrate.com, Edmunds.com, Insurance Information Institute, Mortgage Insurance Companies of America, Center on Budget and Policies Priorities, 2006 Parade magazine

life. Meaningful work — working passionately for something you care about — is relegated for those retirement years, increasingly elusive thanks to rising energy, food and healthcare costs. Anyone you know putting off "retiring" because their stock portfolio didn't deliver enough returns for them to feel comfortable enough to try living off interest and dividends? Either they're still working or had to get a job to make ends meet.

It doesn't have to be this way, as many ecopreneurs are discovering. Small business can be a one-way ticket to keep more of the money you earned while

The highest tax rates are on salaried employees, with much lower tax rates applying to dividend, interest and capital gains on real estate holdings that are sold or appreciated publicly traded stock holdings. If you're like about 60 percent of Americans who do not pay off their credit card every month (the average balance is $10,000) but just pay the minimum balance, that $1,500 plasma TV can end up costing more than $2,850 by the time you pay it off. While home ownership has never been higher in the US, about 67 percent of homeowners have a mortgage, according to the US Census Bureau. Seventy percent of Americans have at least one car loan, according to LendingTree.com.

Compellingly explained at length in *The Coming Generational Storm: What You Need to Know About America's Economic Future* by Laurence Kotlikoff and Scott Burns, Social Security is both inefficient and inequitable, especially related to the dependent or survivor provisions. It's beyond the scope of this book to address this in full; suffice to say that both wage earners in a household must contribute to the flat payroll tax (for Social Security and Medicare) of 15.3 percent for the first $90,000 of earned income. But thanks to the Social Security and Medicare system, there is often no long-term financial gain based on the payroll taxes contributed by the second wage earner from the perspective of securing additional Social Security benefits in retirement. A dependent spouse can receive Medicare benefits regardless of any previous contribution and collect Social Security based on the contribution history of the higher income for the other spouse. Rather than having both spouses out working, one spouse (with the lower income) might engage in other non-wage-based activities, perhaps managing the family's investment portfolio, managing a rental property, caring for the children or an elderly family member, growing food in a community garden or reducing household costs in other ways, as discussed in chapter 1.

doing good for the planet. Forming a Limited Liability Company (LLC), C Corporation or S Corporation are among many options to garner the greatest return on your investment in life energy and increase your savings, allowing you to do the things you want to do, not have to do. While most employees must pay federal taxes on earned income at the rate of 28 percent or higher, C Corporations only pay federal taxes at a rate of 15 percent. S Corporations and LLCs pay taxes after legally acceptable tax deductions, not before. Chapter 6 will detail the differences between these and other business structures available to ecopreneurs, and some of their many benefits.

Why Being Your Own Boss Is Better from a Taxation Perspective

As you'll see below, the government gets its share of your earned income before you even see it on your pay stub. In this case a sub-chapter S Corporation pays taxes after business-related expenses are deducted, thus reducing the taxable amount. If you ran your own business in the greatly simplified, home-based nanocorp business example below with very modest revenues, you would therefore be able to keep $7,200 of your hard-earned money versus only $200 if you're an employee.

With more money left over from our work, we can devote our time and resources to our Whole Pie Purpose and activities we care most about, our Earth Mission. While our business activities are kept separate from our personal activities — with plenty of documentation related to our business operations for the Internal Revenue Service (IRS) — we never lose sight of our Whole Pie Purpose. We take turns being with our son, tending the gardens and spending

Individual Wage Earner		Business set up as sub-chapter S Corporation	
Earned Income (wages/salary):	$40,000	Gross Business Revenues:	$40,000
Federal Tax (28% bracket)	-($9,800)		
After Tax Income:	$30,200		$40,000
Expenses:	-($30,000)	Business Expenses:	-($30,000)
Net Income:	$200	Net Revenue	$10,000
		Corporation Federal Tax	-($2,800)
		(S corp. pass-through income in 10% bracket)	
Savings	$200		$7,200

time with friends and family, actively balancing work with other more important aspects of life.

Besides adopting a different approach to our lifestyle by living below our means, we do not earn much in the form of wages, the most highly taxed form of income by the federal government. We sometimes end up paying 15 percent or less tax on interest and earned income from our small business payroll. Dividends and capital gains are taxed at 15 percent. To keep enough cash coming in, we focus on passive and portfolio income from our investments. Passive income flows from various investments in assets that range from rental property to interest-bearing Certificates of Deposit (CDs) and bank accounts. Portfolio income can come from dividends and capital gains realized through ownership of publicly traded stocks, bonds and mutual funds that are in various ways invested in companies that are socially and environmentally responsible.

Because the government constantly tinkers with the tax code, we work with our accountant to be kept abreast of important changes that might impact us or our business. Your business might account for a much larger-scaled operation, but we've found a perfect human scale that allows us to be small but effective and profitable at what we do.

Searching for Meaning, Not Searching for Status or the Right J-O-B

When it comes down to it, most of us believe in something greater than ourselves. Our faith, regardless of the denomination, guides us on our life journey, steering us out of trouble, giving us solace in tough times and reason to celebrate and share when life is good.

Yet, if any of the national studies about our genuine well-being are even half accurate, many of us are unhappy, stressed out and dissatisfied. We've busied ourselves on the ladder to somewhere, hoping to recognize the top floor when we reach it. If we reach it — before we get downsized, outsourced or just crash on Prozac — will it be something that brings joy, peace or fulfillment? Is work the meaning of life? What do you do for a living? Why is this the question most often asked when you first meet someone? Why not? How is your community, your family, your health?

Becoming an ecopreneur fundamentally changes the way we approach sustaining ourselves financially, emotionally, physically and spiritually. Focusing on what you value guides what you do on a daily basis and is reflected in the Buddhist concept of "right livelihood," work that is also ethical. Regardless of what stage of life you're in, right livelihood allows you to work for your passions without destroying the planet. According to the Right Livelihood Award Foundation (rightlivelihood.org), it "reflects a belief that each person should follow an occupation consistent with the principles of honest living, treating with respect other people and the natural world. It means being responsible for the consequences of one's actions, living lightly on the Earth and taking no more than a fair share of its resources."

Understanding the Difference Between Poor Health and Good Healthcare

If good health is important — and it should be for everyone — then a regular exercise routine along with eating right becomes a feature in our sustainable lifestyle, whether you walk around the block, do yoga or work out three times a week at a local YMCA like we do. Remember the last time you had the flu or a lingering cold? Get much done? When we're healthy, we take our good health for granted. Despite what our politicians and healthcare providers might suggest, good healthcare does not necessarily provide good health. Our lifestyle and daily habits contribute to feeling great just about every day of the year.

Some companies provide a good healthcare plan when it comes to physician access and medical coverage. But what does that matter when the stress-filled, unhealthy environment in a cubicle — with no access to the outdoors and fresh air — ends up giving us poor health? The American healthcare system is great — perhaps the best in the world — if we crashed in our car. It's designed for treatment, not prevention. It's a healthcare system based on the poor health of relatively well-off people who can pay (by credit or otherwise) for the services it provides. Perhaps it's no coincidence that the fastest growing segment of the health and wellness movement — among the promising areas for ecopreneurs — is focused on preventative, alternative medicine. A sustainable business, then, provides the means by which the owners can strive to maintain good health.

Recognizing a Wealth of Friends, Family, Community

If time with your spouse, friends, family or community is essential to your happiness and fulfillment, then organize your business to serve those priorities. From incorporating family into your business or selecting various enterprises where you can fold in various lifestyle interests, your enterprise can take relationships to a whole new, integrated level. Some entrepreneurs work with their teenagers to create a business that they, themselves, own. Others, perhaps those with artistic talents like writers or photographers, can include their family on the trip when they're on assignment. When we completed a "Kid Friendly Scotland" article for *Scottish Life* magazine, part of the trip related to the writing assignment could be written off as a business expense, deducted from the income we received for the article and photography. By blending your livelihood, a richer quality of life is possible — one that requires a lot less money.

One aspect of living on less takes the form of self-reliance and self-sufficiency. An almost blind faith exists that large corporations and big government will take care of our needs in America. The free market economy has, in essence, commodified human needs, from water in water bottles to an erection in a pill. We're losing those skills — like growing our own food, building our own shelters, caring for and educating our own children — that make up the very core of our ability to both survive and prosper.

As we set out to build our diversified livelihood, one of our goals was to be directly involved with raising our own child — both of us, directly, meaningfully and joyfully. So rather than choose daycare, we operated our own homecare. While we lost the tax credit deduction from the wages we would have earned had we gotten a job to pay for his care, spending the first years of our son's life together defies any financial accounting.

We also thrive on, and garner deep satisfaction from, working with people and businesses that we can relate to. Friendships aside, however, respect for professionalism needs to be a priority. Our relationship with Renewing the Countryside exemplifies such a blend of business and friendship. We originally hooked up with this Minneapolis-based non-profit organization to partner on

Creating a Workstyle

What is work and what is leisure? Are we ever off the clock or on it? Just as yellow and blue blend on the palette to create green, traditional notions of work and leisure blend in our lives, resulting in a fused livelihood that serves our Earth Mission. Traditional boundaries between work and leisure are meaningless to us, though we document various aspects for the IRS. Is Tiger Woods working when he tees off at a golf tournament? By working at what we love, work is a pleasure. That doesn't mean we never have workdays filled with challenges, trials and headaches. But the benefits of our workstyle far surpass the downsides.

We don't start and stop work at certain times; weekends and weekdays merge. We have no Monday blues or TGIF buildups because we refuse to work on projects we don't care about. By having so few financial needs, we don't need much cash flow to achieve a balanced financial equilibrium. In general, we probably spend more time and creative energy working on projects than we did during our stint at the ad agency. This is our workstyle, our approach to defining how we function best and fall into that state of flow where we are so absorbed in what we're doing that we're oblivious to time passing. Drafting an article, facilitating a workshop discussion, reading to Liam — even picking strawberries; they're all different aspects of how we achieve our workstyle.

educational outreach efforts after our book *Rural Renaissance* came out. The co-founder and executive director, Jan Joannides, fully shares our passions for rural revitalization. Jan and her husband and the organization's co-founder, Brett Olson, share our philosophy of integrating family business under an umbrella mantra of stewarding the Earth. While friendships deepened — as outgrown kids' clothes get exchanged between families — so did our professional ties. We've worked as paid subcontractors with Jan on numerous projects, from writing community development profiles to book marketing projects. Other times we regularly promote the organization at our various presentations and workshops. Jan doesn't push the friendship button to get us to do volunteer work for the organization, and likewise, we always deliver what we're contracted to do in a timely, professional fashion.

Renewing the Countryside

Co-Founders: Jan Joannides and Brett Olson
Place: Minneapolis, Minnesota
Earth Mission: "Creating a connection to one's sense of place and to promote solutions that are working, so that my children and future generations have access to a healthy quality of life."
Websites:
www.renewingthecountryside.org;
www.greenroutes.org

In a world overdosed with negativity, Jan Joannides roots for the opposite underdog, building an organization and livelihood around showcasing the positive side of what's working right. As co-founder of Renewing the Countryside, she created a means to showcase positive examples of rural revitalization while simultaneously serving as an inspiring example of how one's purpose and life can passionately blend.

The seed for Renewing the Countryside stemmed from Jan's master's thesis work in the late 1990s profiling vibrant, diversified Minnesota farms and ranches. "As I interviewed these folks, I became so deeply inspired by their story and commitment to their family farms that I wanted to get these narratives out to the public, since the media often focus just on the negative decline of rural America," explains Jan. Inspired by a similar venture in the Netherlands, she tapped into grant funding to publish *Renewing the Countryside: Minnesota* in 2001, showcasing 44 profiles of successful rural enterprises.

The enthusiastic response to this book led Jan, in partnership with her husband, Brett Olson, to found Renewing the Countryside as a non-profit organization in 2002. Its mission is to strengthen rural areas by championing and supporting rural communities, farmers, artists, entrepreneurs, educators, activists and other people who are renewing the countryside through sustainable and innovative businesses, initiatives and projects. "After all," she says, "rural America is abundant with prospering enterprises as diverse as colors in the rainbow." Brett leads the creative side of the organization, developing innovative public education strategies and campaigns.

Rather than reinventing existing wheels, Renewing the Countryside tapped into the support and resources of a large, established non-profit organization, the Institute for Agriculture and Trade Policy (IATP). Such an arrangement helped jumpstart Renewing the Countryside without needing to worry about overhead and office expenses, which were provided in kind by IATP for awhile. Collaboration and cooperation are often a common refrain among social entrepreneurs and ecopreneurs. "Working within an existing, flourishing venture like IATP gave our organization a tremendous running-start advantage," admits Jan. "Aside from saving on expenses, we have this amazing pool of seasoned experts as mentors working in the same building which gave us a credibility boost."

With the success of the Minnesota book, Renewing the Countryside has worked with other organizations to publish state- or region-specific books and calendars that are tied to public education campaigns. Book projects cover such states as Iowa, Washington and Wisconsin. Eager to expand the reach of the case stories, the organization launched an interactive online story database that can be searched by topic of interest, serving as a premiere means by which people interested in starting a rural business can learn about others' experiences, from artisan potters to businesses powered by the wind and the sun, and rural communities can find strategies for creating a more vibrant, sustainable economy.

As leaders of an agile and innovative organization thriving on new ideas and picking up quickly on trends, Jan and Brett welcome new project opportunities that showcase local foods and ecotourism. One is Green Routes, an informational venture helping Minnesota travelers incorporate their values of preserving natural and cultural resources into their travels through discovering small, unique businesses rooted in local communities. As a leading example nationwide for regionally focused, community-based green travel initiatives, Green Routes has already earned a reputation for its engaging Web-based mapping interface.

With a handful of full-time staff, a flock of interns and a network of independent contractors, Jan credits this entrepreneurial-minded tribe of people with forging the organization's success. "People who work on issues bigger than themselves, who work in ways much more flexible than the mainstream nine-to-five workforce, tend to be much more creative and innovative," Jan comments. "I've learned, however, to hire folks with a blend of shared values and passion with strong skills, such as meeting deadlines and communication skills. Enthusiasm alone won't cut it."

Jan and Brett thrive on blending differing themes with their own quirky, connected workstyle, at times bouncing e-mails back and forth in the same room to keep projects on track. While their organization's focus is on all things rural, they themselves live in a rambling historic house smack in the middle of a hip, urban enclave. "We live the best of both worlds as we like both the city and rural scene," comments Brett. "An advantage of being in the city is that we are able to see the possibilities of making urban-rural connections, something we see as very important as we especially need urban people to be advocates for rural people and rural areas."

Blending also serves as the mantra of their family life, taking an active role in the parenting of their two young children who are often at work-related functions or hanging out at the office. "I never believed that there is just one right way to do something," reflects Jan. "Work can blend with your passions, family and values, especially if you surround yourself with like-minded people. I can take a business phone call outside at the park while watching my kids play just as easily as I could in an office cubicle." Working in partnership in both family and work life adds challenging and rewarding lifestyle elements for this creative duo. "Working together has caused us both to prioritize what's really important and to improve our communication so we say exactly what we mean, especially when we're stressed on deadline, are tired and have hungry kids to feed," Jan explains with a smile. As their husband-wife workstyle tangoes with a shared passion for sustainable rural revitalization, they harvest their own version of the good life, a cocktail of green acres and city living.

For many people during the Great Depression, wealth was not measured by what you had in the bank. Few people had much at the time. Rather, it was measured by the gathering of friends; the cohesiveness, support and love among family members; and people coming together in communities to care for one another. As we describe in *Rural Renaissance*, for many a small town in America, it's still this way. That's what's driving the continued "lifestyle migration" into rural areas, especially by young families and retirees. In fact, many boomer retirees are nicknamed "boomerangs" when they first take early retirement somewhere warmer but return to where their family is when their health turns poor. In times of turmoil or financial crisis, you can't buy friends or family. The ecopreneurs, in how they operate their businesses, know most of their customers by name — often, because they're also their friends.

Magnifying the Butterfly Effect

Remember the last time you got a pebble in your shoe? It bothered you so much that you had to stop and remove it. The same is true for the power of small businesses. An idea exists that the flap of a butterfly's wings in Indonesia may create a series of miniscule changes in the atmosphere that could ultimately cause a tornado to appear in Kansas.

Don't underestimate the power and force that one small business may contribute to a better world. Collectively these millions of businesses are, in fact,

Ecopreneur's Balance Sheet

Philosophically, here's what an ecopreneur's balance sheet might look like:

Assets	Liabilities
Personal health	Poor habits, leading to poor health
Earth mission	Distractions of time, resources
Friends and family	Negative people
Community	Local businesses not owned locally
Customers	Dissatisfied customers
Passive investments (interest, dividends)	Debt
Portfolio investments (royalties)	Financial responsibilities like local taxes
Nominal earned income from business	Insurance
Independence, time, control and flexibility	Lack of organization and determination

redefining how commerce is conducted: ethically, ecologically, socially responsible. Rather than building empires of concentrated wealth controlled by huge corporations or powerful political elites, ecopreneurs are re-establishing local, sustainable, diversified economic communities that are both inspired by and help preserve the richness of the planet.

Breaking Away

Becoming an ecopreneur is hard work. It takes courage to believe in yourself, your Earth Mission. You have plenty of talent to make your green dreams come true. There will be a never-ending cascade of reasons from parents, friends, family, your current employer or our culture — bent on taking the safe, secure way — why you can't be your own boss, earn money for yourself and restore, steward or heal a planet in dire straights.

We're on a fast-moving journey called life, with a guaranteed ending point — called death. How we choose to live this gift of life is based on our ability to navigate through it without losing our soul, destroying what we cherish or exploiting what we love. Eat the strawberry.

It's the paradox of life that to sustain us something else must die. Energy is neither created nor lost, just transformed from kinetic to electric to chemical to many other forms. Nothing lost, nothing gained. A natural equilibrium tapped by ecopreneurs. More and more, we're recognizing that every action, behavior

Eat the Strawberry

A friend visiting the farm recently wore a T-shirt emblazoned with a photo of a big, juicy-looking strawberry and the words "Eat the Strawberry." When asked the origin, he explained that he actually had designed — and sold — the shirt himself, based on spreading the inspiration he drew from the following fable of Buddhist origin.

> A man was jogging through the woods when, all of a sudden, he realized he was being chased by a tiger. Surprised to encounter a tiger, he didn't contemplate why there was a tiger in the woods but rather started running for his life — until he ran up against the edge of a steep cliff. Peering down over the edge, he saw a second hungry tiger waiting for him at the bottom. Unable to run forward or jump down, the man noticed a small branch growing out from the side of the cliff a few feet below where he stood. He jumped and hung on the branch, not knowing what his next move would be but realizing that this way he'd at least be alive. Then he saw two small mice intensely

and choice we make impacts everyone else around the world. It's a small world after all.

We found ourselves rather suddenly planted in a four-square cubicle after graduating college, complete with telephone, computer, Rolodex — and access to all the coffee or soda pop we could drink. Our task: to produce the best advertising in the world, bar none. In exchange, we received a bimonthly paycheck, fringe benefits called health insurance, and the opportunity to learn and contribute to the culture of consumption by helping produce advertising that would help sell more stuff. At our former jobs, we helped promote computer games that would be obsolete in less than four years (and unable to be recycled or reused, thus garbage) or greeting cards for just about the most ridiculous reasons possible. We secured jobs in what would become one of the most insecure careers around.

We needed something to help us discover just how destructive the path was that we were on. Yet none existed. Most of our friends had joined the treadmill just like us and knew nothing better. Some even had big mortgages, car payments and credit-card debt far beyond what they earned each year, living off future earnings, not present.

What is wealth, anyway? Could it be your worth as a human being, not the net worth of your assets as stockbrokers, financial planners or banks like to advise? We've met or interviewed hundreds of people who consider themselves chewing away on the branch, now slowly cracking and about to fall off. Suddenly, the man caught a glimpse of a single bright red, ripe strawberry growing from a rambling vine within his easy reach right above his head. The man picked the strawberry and popped it into his mouth, readily absorbed by the juicy flavors of this ruby treasure. It was the best strawberry he ever ate.

While this man's fate and the tragic ending stands clear, the fable symbolizes the life journey we share. The tigers represent death, and the mice stand for time, two inevitable facets of life that will come eventually to all of us. The strawberry reminds us to live in the moment, to enjoy and savor what is ripe and readily picked when we have that opportunity, not to be sorry over the inevitable that can't be controlled. As ecopreneurs, we remind ourselves to live in the present, take advantage of opportunity and act on our livelihood dreams before the inevitable tigers and mice catch up with us and we're left with regrets. So, eat the strawberry.

wealthy beyond measures, but they're using a different measuring stick. After all, what's the value of good health, where you can mostly do the things you want to do, with a partner, friends or a community with whom you share the journey of life?

The next chapter explores the development of your mission, purpose and strategic goals for your business as they intersect with your life passions, aspirations, values and priorities.

Chapter 5

Cultivating Your Core:
Passions, Purpose and Earth Mission

Hi, ho, hi, ho, it's off to work we go.

— The seven dwarfs in unison.

I owe, I owe, it's off to work I go.

— Anonymous

Passion. We hear that word from the boardroom to the bedroom, encompassing an emotion so powerful that poets and philosophers, songwriters and psychiatrists can't do it justice. Passion stirs you up so much inside that you're blinded to anything else.

Sure, passion seems an apt word choice for love affairs, but what about work? How would you feel if you could feel the same tingle in your toes the next time someone asks you "What do you do?" What would it take to be so wrapped up in a mission and in a project that you dream about it at night and it serves as your espresso jolt wake-up in the morning?

We all have baggage — past experiences and beliefs — that limits our perspective on what — or who — we can be today. Your practical dad's refrain, "A job is work, it's not supposed to be fun," to your grandma's quote about Cousin Jane's last six-figure sales bonus. Or it may be yourself, so used to career tracks and direction bestowed upon you from someone else that you struggle with crystallizing an honest answer to the question: What exactly do you want to do?

Perhaps adults perpetually ask children what they want to be when they grow up because we want to harness some of their enthusiasm, their wild passion for dreams to be fulfilled. Often these childhood visions take diversified directions. Kids can't choose just one thing they are interested in, so why try? Ask our son what he wants to be when he grows up and he'll rattle off, "Farmer, rock star and Jedi Knight."

Passion guides and invigorates your sense of purpose: knowing what it is that you were placed on this Earth to do. With such passion and purpose, confidence blooms, enabling you to take on even more new challenges and projects. Suddenly, you're defining success on your terms, not someone else's. Passions do ebb and flow, evolve and change. So does everything else around us and in nature. If we keep evolving as ecopreneurs, keep learning and encountering challenging situations and people, our passions broaden and deepen. Your Earth Mission is the expression of your passions and purpose. The ideas in this chapter will help crystallize your direction and interests and transition you into the ecopreneur mindset.

Seven Dwarfs Therapy: Hi Ho Humdrum

For many people, finding or discovering your purpose and passions are the toughest part of following your dreams and launching your business. Societal expectations tend to be stacked against allowing us to become the human beings we're meant to be. We're lured by the perception of safety or security, fooled by paychecks and educated into believing that getting a life is about getting a job. Inspired by Snow White's seven dwarfs, we refrain, "I owe, I owe, it's off to work I go." The better the training, the better the job, the more money you'll have, the better your life. Millions of people, regardless of age, but especially those who have progressed through financially prosperous careers, are questioning the very assumptions that led them down life's path to start with.

Why? Because there "Ain't no trick to get rich quick." Snow White's seven dwarfs say so while toiling in a mine, dig, dig, digging for diamonds and gems. Each of them represents personality traits that each of us have, to some degree. We're all one or more of them at least some of the time.

Which of the seven dwarfs best captures a slice of your life?

Doc

Well-intended leader, but whose mind isn't focused on the situation at hand. Spacey in a lovable sort of way, he tries hard to make the best of a situation, but perhaps he was recruited for a job that just wasn't suited for him. Maybe he went down the common path of dwarf expectations, doing what everyone else around him viewed as expected jobs, rather than examining his own strengths, interests and passions. How many doctors are children of doctors?

Sleepy

Peaceful, quiet, silent. Sleepy drifts through the day in another world and oblivious to what's going on around him. This happens when we get so busied by a situation that we lose our connection with the world around us. For about three years, we were sleep walking through life while engrossed in the corporate advertising grind, buzzed on cappuccinos, unobservant to the seasons or our neighbors. We were too busy to notice that the Canada geese were in a never-ending loop around the mesmerizing bright lights of Chicago, eventually dying from starvation. We didn't take notice or assume accountability for the loads of gear and stuff we created marketing plans for, aimed at selling more volume, stuffing more closets and then ending up in a landfill.

Dopey

The more we earn, the more we spend. A dopey — or dare we say, dumb — cycle that when you look at the hard numbers just doesn't make sense. For the first four months, we work for the government to pay our share of income taxes. The next four months we work for the bank to pay our mortgage. The next three months for a different bank to keep up with our credit card minimums. The next two months for our car payment and property taxes for our house or condo. Ignorance may tout itself as bliss, but self-imposing oneself in the Dark Ages of dopey-ness doesn't release us from fiscal responsibility that, if practiced, can yield sanity. By continuing to educate ourselves, growing aware of and taking charge of our situations, reality hits and may sting initially, but long-term we evolve stronger and smarter. Minding your own business can be a great start.

Happy

Like Happy, we tramped (commuted) off to work every day, Monday through Friday and sometimes on the weekend, to extract wealth by selling more stuff, exploiting fellow humans (Dopey cleaned up the unusable jewels) and creating heaps of waste. But we, like Happy, appeared "happy," at least on the outside. At face value, we lived the glossy American Dream with gobs of shiny electronics, hip apartments furnished by the Pottery Barn and trendy take-out cuisine. But scratch the surface and you'd realize behind the happy façade sulked two young professionals lacking connection to what we valued most: health, friends, family, community and nature.

Bashful

Shy, insecure and lacking confidence, Bashful quietly does his job while blending in with the wallpaper. With such an approach, searching for the safe and secure route through life, many people miss out on the opportunities to use their gifts or unique talents to their fullest. Seeking a "comfortable life," they never step out of their comfort zone and take on any challenges. Confidence crumbles like cookies. We exert more energy and cause more stress trying not to rock the boat than departing on a different one. Who knows what Bashful could have been if he broke out of his comfort zone and took a risk.

Grumpy

Letting anger and ignorance snowball inside, Grumpy rightfully earned his name. Fear and insecurity have long been used as a means to rule the masses, make a sale or simply intimidate. We've all encountered Grumpys and, admittedly, perhaps have turned to the Dark Side when our anger got the best of us. From giving the finger to a crazy driver to chewing out the overseas customer service representative on the phone, stress, anger and a sense of helplessness unleashes our inner Grumpy. Still, just as Grumpy's big nose and stubborn demeanor can be turned by the kindness of the very woman he at first detests — Snow White — social connections and community melt anger.

Sneezy

Sneezy apparently said no to drugs, and sneezed for it. But today, we're among the most medicated and drugged-up society ever. Powering our bodies with processed food leads to a rundown body, desperate for extra additives to run on, from Prozac to asthma inhalers. By nurturing our bodies, eating well, exercising and prioritizing care as needed — perhaps homeopathic allergy drops for Sneezy — the potential of our lives erupts and awakens.

As multifaceted and complex people, we need to realize and accept that these varying qualities of the dwarfs emerge from time to time in our lives. But as ecopreneurs, we can rise above them by unearthing our passions, committing to a purposeful life and putting into practice our Earth Mission.

Proclaim Your Passion

Schools don't foster it. Most parents advise against it. Corporations crush it.

There are issues that many people go through life without ever honestly exploring: who you are, what you value, how you behave, what you buy (or don't buy) and what your priorities are. Passion often, unfortunately, ranks as an optional side dish on the buffet of life. If you can find a job that provides the staple meat and potatoes, lucky you. Dessert, or feeling passionate and fulfilled by what you do, adds a nice touch if you can get it — but is definitely not necessary.

We say go for dessert first — identify your passion and build your work, your business, your life around that which makes your toes tingle. A reverse perspective to the normal career path, we realize. It took us almost a decade of soul-searching, global travel and life-changing experiences — both positive and negative — before we started to unearth the human beings we were deep down inside, our core that represented our heartfelt passions, reflected our values and our Earth Mission that guides our life. Partner your passion with small business and satisfaction blooms far richer than just dollars of a paycheck.

Some perspectives on identifying your passion:

Shift Your Thinking

Ecopreneuring stems from a paradigm shift in how we approach a career and how we define livelihood. Like nature, we thrive on interdependence while aspiring to a greater degree of self-reliant independence — the ability to make it on our own in a supportive community. This shatters the prideful image of a generation ago where the "company" would "care" for you and your family after you retired.

Think independent and multidimensional: a Portfolio Perspective. Like a diversified stock portfolio, by having multiple income sources stemming from your passions, your livelihood provides multiple benefits. A Portfolio Perspective also provides the opportunity to integrate and overlap these interests intelligently and strategically, using business deductions effectively (more about this in chapter 7). Such a shift fundamentally alters the historic perspective separating your "job" from your "leisure" activities. Your job earns you money to pay for your leisure interests. What if you love photography or helping people savor healthy and locally grown food? Why not make that part of your livelihood?

Portfolio Perspective:
Look at your life as multidimensional; Different rather than just one paycheck coming from one job, have a range of income-generating sources. Different elements contribute to fulfillment and satisfaction. If one project disappeared, you'd still have others. One interest fuels ideas or business leads in another area.

Another paradigm shift comes from the slick image of big business that society spoon-fed us since childhood. Big is better. Big can do more. No thanks, say many ecopreneurs, embracing the power of small business and realizing the potential in becoming a "Mosquito Business." Debunking the notion that bigger is better, Mosquito Businesses use their leanness and small size to their competitive advantage. Less baggage equals the ability to fly, to quickly — and often more cost-effectively — maneuver to make something happen, often beneath the radar. And if anyone still needs convincing that small can be powerful and effective, try spending the night with a mosquito in your tent.

Tree Your Passions

Trade the visual of career "track" for a "tree." A track gets you from point A to B, "assistant account executive" tracks to "senior account executive." No opportunities for detours. You must choose and stick to one direction. But like a tree, we humans need to stretch and grow in a variety of directions. Some branches grow tall and strong while others may hold back or even wither and crack and die off.

The same process applies to our interests, as we keep diversified while rooted to the same trunk or shared core values and visions.

Look to your past experiences for skill sets and tools to craft your ecopreneur business and lifestyle. Most likely, this next chapter in your life ranks as an "Emerald Encore," not your first job experience but rather a new direction stemming from your past experiences. We bring past experiences, history and personal knowledge to this new chapter in our life that can enhance and strengthen us as ecopreneurs. No need to feel guilty or ashamed about former career paths — say us, two former corporate advertising clones. Instead, look to being an ecopreneur as the opportunity to make an encore, to regain the stage and leave a final, lasting impression that satisfies and makes you proud. The most prized of gems, the emerald gains its value, its uniqueness, from its rarity. Likewise, your Emerald Encore will contribute to your legacy, the lasting positive impact you want to create in this world.

Small Potatoes Urban Delivery

Founder: David Van Seters, president and CEO
Headquarters: Vancouver, British Columbia, Canada (with several locations in US and Canadian cities)
Earth Mission: "Business has become the more powerful group in society. My mission is to harness that power so as to do more than just make a profit by protecting the environment and being socially responsible."
Website: www.spud.ca and www.spud.com

Small Potatoes Urban Delivery, or SPUD, is no ordinary delivery service. First, they promote organic food with free home delivery. Second, they sell food grown or produced by local or regional farmers, whenever possible. Their business model intersects the double-digit growth in organic food and the buy-local movement, while reducing carbon emissions and urban congestion through their resource-efficient delivery service. Topping it off, SPUD harnesses the Internet to offer customers the opportunity to customize their orders with a guarantee of satisfaction.

David Van Seters, SPUD's founder, president and CEO, admits: "We consider ourselves to be in the lifestyle enhancement business. It's not just about simplifying busy lives with home delivery but also enhancing their lives in the broader sense of having a better quality environment and healthier communities." SPUD protects the environment by buying local, organic, minimally packaged and eco-friendly products. It builds community by creating more direct connections between food producers and consumers, while reducing traffic congestion and pollution by delivering groceries on a set route and avoiding private car trips to the grocery store. Finally, they educate customers about important food issues through a weekly newsletter. Even leftover food is donated to food outreach groups and disadvantaged families.

"SPUD allows people to make a significant positive change with virtually no effort," continues David, quite determined to change the world one grocery order at a time. "They just shift their purchases from one source to another, and then not only are they saving time to do better things with their lives, they are automatically reducing food miles, eliminating plastic bags, avoiding pesticides on crops and so on." And their customers care, often joking that they get free karma with every grocery delivery.

The seed for SPUD germinated after David completed a study on the economics of sustainable community food systems. "It was through this work that I became much more aware of the high amount of waste and energy use in the grocery industry, as well as how the design of the system leaves growers and food producers with less than 20 cents of the food dollar."

"So long as we can play a role in helping customers to reduce their food miles, we will continue to grow because we want to have a big social and environmental impact," says David, who launched SPUD with $150,000 of his own money, transforming his livelihood from that of consultant to practicing ecopreneur. Already a profitable $10 million business with over 3,500 deliveries a week, SPUD serves the Canadian cities of Vancouver, Victoria and Calgary as well as the US cities of Seattle, Bellevue and Redmond, Washington. Many more cities are in the works.

"Preventing pollution, rather than just fixing it up after it occurred, is not a scientific or technical issue, it's a management issue," beams David. "When one of our delivery vehicles leaves the warehouse with 100 orders, it eliminates the need for an entire grocery store parking lot of cars to drive to the grocery store and back." Harnessing the power of the Internet, potential customers can calculate how much energy, time and other costs could be saved by switching to SPUD. To further reduce environmental impacts, SPUD is gradually switching its vehicles over to alternative fuels like natural gas and biodiesel.

In the beginning, working with local farmers was challenging. "When we started the business we thought we could just put out the call to local growers and they would produce the crops we needed," explains David. "However, we had multiple farmers showing up on the same day with the same crop or farmers showing up late or showing up with wilted lettuce because they didn't have refrigerated trucks. To overcome this, we partnered with a local distributor who helped organize the farmers and ensure that they delivered a high-quality product on time."

In the summer and varying slightly from city to city, SPUD sources about 80 percent local fruit and vegetables (40 percent in the winter) compared to about 20 percent local content year round at a typical grocery store. Each of SPUD's customers' orders travels an average of less than 745 miles (1,200 kilometers), more than cutting in half the national average of about 1,500 miles (2,400 kilometers). The fewer the food miles, the better SPUD's Return on the Environment (ROE).

Capitalizing on their environmental, social, Internet-leveraged and local foundations, SPUD covets a unique and strong competitive advantage. "We can be competitive with grocery store retailers who offer home delivery because no one buys as locally as we do, and that is what our customers want," says David. In a sense, SPUD provides farmers' market freshness and organic selection to their customers' doorsteps that costs no more than what they would pay at their local grocery store, thanks to the reality that they don't rely on centralized warehouses like most other food retailers do.

Financing SPUD's growth reflects a growing awareness of just how valuable value-driven business models translate to strong earnings even in an industry with marginal two percent profit margins. "We are seeing a strong increase in the number of investors who want to make triple bottom line investments," observes David. "This should create a competitive advantage for social mission businesses in the long run." To spur investment in SPUD's expansion, his company offers convertible debentures — debt which can be converted to stock after one year or rolled over into a new loan. Some investors get out after a few years while others turn their debt into stock of the company.

With no plans to go public — something recognized as a threat to SPUD's values — David is introducing both share ownership and stock options plans for all staff, staff who he credits as a talented and dedicated team who shares his passion for creating a better world.

Spoken of as perhaps the next Bill Gates of organic food delivery, David eyes the future, focusing on progress not perfection. "As long as we are continuing to get better every year, I am happy," he admits. "You are not successful as an entrepreneur unless you are involved in an endeavor that is helping to build a better future for people and the planet. We try to enrich the lives of all the people involved in our business, including suppliers, customers, staff, investors and the communities we serve."

Passion Pruning

Our interests can and will run all over the board, shooting off in what may seem like disparate directions. The key remains to continually focus, narrowing in on and pruning back to your core interests, particularly those that blend passion with income-generation.

Manage the Vine

Like a garden mid-summer, multiple passions can grow wildly to the point that they need a good prune. Passion Pruning keeps us focused as ecopreneurs, working toward our goals but doing so strategically and thoughtfully. By clipping

LISA KIVIRIST/INN SERENDIPITY

John testing out new all-electric CitiCar for local commuting, recharged by a photovoltaic system.

deadweight, the tree will grow stronger. Likewise, by keeping focused on key projects and visions, by keeping small and lean, ecopreneurs flourish as well.

One approach to deciding where and how to prune is to remember income generation. "Think Inc." prioritizes those projects and endeavors that help the bottom line and make your business viable. When Passion Pruning, remember to focus on projects that fall under the "inc" for "income" umbrella. Sometimes a project may literally earn cash: creating natural soaps and selling them online. Sometimes volunteer efforts lead to income-generating projects long-term; evaluate how you spend your time accordingly. Other times a project may save money, fit under your Earth Mission and even add public relations value.

Such was the transportation case with our Inn Serendipity all-electric CitiCar project: restoring a circa 1974 electric car in close collaboration with our neighbors Phil and Judy. It's a vehicle that we can use to make fossil-fuel-free trips to town. Before we had the brakes fixed, the TV cameras had already filmed a segment that included footage of the car for a program on the Hallmark cable channel. The vehicle is recharged using a photovoltaic system, and its batteries serve as an emergency off-grid electricity backup system should the greenhouse lose power in the winter.

Mantras of the Ecopreneur

Under the paradigm shift from "jobs" or "careers" to livelihood and small business, we've come to realize some approaches common among the ecopreneurs we interviewed or met.

Plug in as Needed

Use technology selectively. With overdoses of daily options to keep connected, surrender the never-ending challenge of keeping up with the techno world and choose your necessities wisely. Part of this motivation roots green in that we want to lessen our contribution to the overflowing technology wasteland. With tons of computer peripherals and technology discarded annually, as a society we consume more technology than we can process and dispose of properly.

Confession: we don't have a cellphone or BlackBerry-type device. By today's standards, this makes us borderline Amish, but the cellphone choice reminds us to question what we really do or don't need and choose wisely. When folks call us, they can always leave a message on our answering machine — still have one of those — and we essay to return calls promptly.

With multiple, diversified projects continually on our plate, a paper monthly calendar, the kind our local bank gives out free each year, is the best tracker of commitments for us. With the majority of our writing and B & B income stemming from word-processing computer tasks, our Apple laptop suits us just fine, even if we missed the latest operating system upgrade. In addition to portability, laptops prove to be the greener computer choice since they use 50 to 80 percent less energy than desktop models, depending on the model.

The key remains to objectively and personally evaluate technology and apply only as necessary. Question what types of technology would benefit you, what would truly make life easier and more efficient versus adding another layer of stress and distraction. Having a detailed website for the B & B helps us by allowing potential guests to learn about Inn Serendipity — saving time, printing and mailing resources. We find that the less technology dominates our lives, the more we can be outdoors around the farm, enjoying Liam or working on projects we enjoy. More on technology as it relates to the ecopreneur follows in chapter 9.

Punt

As in football, remember to sometimes punt: kick the ball before it reaches the ground. Don't require perfection in your business in order to be in business. Look for change, progress and steps that you can measure in your forward movement. Many businesses or ideas never became reality because the owners obsessed over the details and never got the business off the ground. Among the financially richest people on the planet, Bill Gates is a great example as the co-founder of a company releasing an imperfect product with every launch of a Microsoft operating system. Who hasn't had their computer crash, a result from software bugs in the system that are fixed with later software updates and patches.

"Great Idea, Let Me Get Back to You"

As a consequence at times of working under the green umbrella, ecopreneurs tend to get asked repeatedly to donate goods, services and speeches and, as a result, time and energy. With value-driven businesses, doing something "because it is the right thing to do" needs to be balanced with the bottom line, nurturing a profitable and viable business. We remain open to all ideas and opportunities, but with the caveat that everything is negotiable and no decision is made right away. Take the time to think about and create a situation that could indeed benefit all involved parties.

The key here remains to ask, get creative and think about expanded opportunities — and potential income streams — taking the time to consider what if, rather than an immediate yes or no.

Detour Roadblocks

Expect to encounter ongoing roadblocks, often from well-intentioned family and friends who think your path as an ecopreneur makes no sense:

- "Get a real job and do some volunteer work on the weekends, if that's what you want."
- "What are you going to do about the mortgage, kids' college fund, or health insurance?"
- "Is this what we paid for you to go to college for?"

While some of these comments may be well intentioned from the giver's perspective, others may stem from a twang of envy: What gives you the right to make such changes while I'm still stuck in my situation? Be prepared for the likely possibility that not everyone may be there for you. Develop what we call "realistic relationship expectations," the idea that some people will be there for you more than others.

For the people roadblocking your dream and goals, the best approach parallels our strategy dealing with summer highway construction: Just go around it. Find another path and avoid toxic naysayers. Not an easy thing to do, especially when the negative comments come from our parents or other people we usually count on for support. We now feel alone at a time when our self-confidence should be standing high. At this point, sidestep and move on. Detour around people or situations that cause you to regress, to feel shaky and question your beliefs. Refocus that energy positively.

Think Seventh Generation

Ecopreneurs question the long-term consequences of their decisions, not just how something will affect today's world but what consequences it holds seven generations from now. Seventh Generation thinking is often attributed to the Great Law of the Iroquois: "In every deliberation we must consider the impact on the seventh generation … even if it requires having skin as thick as the bark of a pine." Seventh Generation thinking not only accepts but creatively thrives on this idea that we need to accept long-term responsibility for what we do today. Anticipate harsh criticism, mockery or complacent disregard from those who don't share your sense of responsibility. Seek solace with those who do.

Creative Make-do

Before buying new, ask yourself, Can we make do with something we already have? Being organized helps with this idea, like keeping office supplies organized, stacking mailing envelopes that can be reused as they come in and cutting up recycled cardboard for mailing flats.

A little homespun creativity goes a long way. When some local retailers offered to carry our cookbook, *Edible Earth*, we needed to provide them with an in-store display. The perfunctory reaction would be to Google "book display holder," order something online made from virgin cardboard or plastic that generically looks like any other holder. Instead, we picked through our stockpile of assorted baskets (mostly trash-picked or saved from various gifts) to find something that fit five cookbooks. We printed a small sign on yellow cardstock, "Cookbook by Local Authors," added color with a red rubber stamp of a tomato, "laminated" the sign with clear packing tape, then mounted the sign with duct tape to an old wooden spoon tied to the basket. The resulting display looked professional but with a quirky, homespun style — an accurate depiction of our business philosophy. And, importantly, we created this display for next to no cost reusing items we had.

Redefine and Pad Risk

Every entrepreneurship book talks about risk, a word that sends scads of people hiding back under the covers. "Risk" remains a concept authority figures taught us to avoid, something scary, bad and dangerous. But in reality, we forget that the real risk lies in standing still and doing nothing. Stagnating in the status quo equals standing on a frozen lake in the spring: Sure, the ice propped you up fine all winter, but if you don't change course right now, your future will be wet and cold.

Ecopreneurs realize the best insurance is embracing change and newness, equating "risk" and "change" with the glass half-full scenario: I have an opportunity to protect myself, my family and my future by thinking, planning and working with tomorrow in mind. Such a mindset perhaps comes more naturally to the ecopreneur, who by definition possesses a deeper awareness and passion for the state of the world. With looming issues like peak oil and global warming — problems that ecopreneurs see erupting in the near versus distant future — we realize we need to instigate and lead change.

Don't look for ecopreneurs jumping off the high-dive without testing the water's depth first. Pad risk through research in various forms: books, resources on the Internet, visiting places, talking to people who have achieved noteworthy success like the ecopreneurs profiled in this book, Renewing the Countryside's website (renewingthecountryside.org) and on our ECOpreneuring website.

Use the two most important risk padding tools: the knife and the pillow. Use the knife to remember to chop up risk into manageable slices. Under the diversification theme, taking several smaller risks lessens your fear and gamble quotient, plus it increases the odds of success that one of the ideas will work. Why the pillow? Remember to sleep on it, take the time to mull on the idea and let it sit in your gut for a while. Which way does your intuition lead? Do you wake up feeling a sick-to-your-stomach dread, or do you feel a tinge of excited butterflies? Ecopreneurs learn to use the pillow, understanding how to read their raw intuitions and assess risk realistically.

Stay Flexible

Ecopreneurs balance a plan with serendipity. You may start out with a well-researched course leading from point A to B, but remember things change, evolve and, at times, erupt. Road construction prompts detours, a flat tire causes delay. Ecopreneurs remain flexible, agile and open to alternative routes and options not in the initial plan but that may prove even more beneficial to progressing toward the goal. In this Anthropocene period we live in, managing and adapting to increased vulnerability to unpredictable variability and instability is where ecopreneurs excel.

Passionate and Personal

Time and time again, the happiest and most prosperous people tend to be those who discovered their unique talents, skills and passions then, when applying their values, transformed their purposeful dreams into reality. Some even became famous or financially rich, but more less well-known people basked in the good life they created for themselves by being the best they could be.

Becoming the best you can be in whatever business you pursue is an expression of your soul, a visible manifestation of your calling. Within 15 years of our exit from corporate America, we've created the award-winning Inn Serendipity, authored numerous books that reached millions of readers, including several award-winning children's books, began the restoration and healing process of our land and have raised our own son, ourselves.

When you love what you do, you will discover the power in what it means to do it well. Before you know it, people will seek you out, share in your dream and help you in ways you never imagined.

The next section of this book will delve into the nuts and bolts of launching your business, helping you secure your green dream with an unaccredited degree in Green Business Administration (GBA).

Part Two

Green Business Administration

Chapter 6

Eco-business Basics

YOUR PARENTS OR CO-WORKERS ARE RIGHT, to a degree. If owning your own business is so easy, then five out of every ten new businesses wouldn't fail in the first year, according to some researchers, like Edward Frank claims in his book *The Real World of Small Business*. Eighty percent supposedly fail within the first five years. Some research pegs the failure rates even higher.

But as we discovered over the years — and it's echoed by most entrepreneurs or in the plethora of start-your-own-business books — failure is as fundamental to the entrepreneur's learning process as customers are to whatever product or service you are selling. While our culture tends to indoctrinate most people to choose a safe, secure path, with little downside, risk or chance of failure, it destroys our ability to be creative, be innovative and live our life's calling, our Earth Mission.

Thomas Edison is famously known for referring to his failed light bulb experiments not as failures, but learning opportunities. So rather than look at glasses half empty, realize that you might not get the business exactly right from the get-go. If you're flexible, adaptable and innovative, you might discover a breakthrough business idea. The growth of lifestyle and personal businesses, which often fly under the radar of most statisticians, may also overstate failure rates. When another B & B in our county closes their doors because of a divorce, what failed, their business or their marriage? The National Federation of Independent Business (nfib.com), the nation's leading small-business advocacy association, found that many businesses that closed did so for other reasons than lack of profitability.

Despite small businesses coming and going, their growth has exploded over the last decade by about 550,000 per month, according to the Ewing Marian Kauffman Foundation. This non-profit foundation is dedicated to promoting entrepreneurship and fostering a society of economically independent individuals who are engaged citizens, contributing to the improvement of their communities (kauffman.org).

This is matched by the rapid growth in non-profit, or independent sector, organizations, doubling in the last 25 years, according to the Independent Sector (independentsector.org). This is a non-profit, non-partisan coalition of approximately 600 charities, foundations and corporate philanthropy programs with a mission to advance the common good by leading, strengthening and mobilizing the charitable community. In the last decade, the number of charitable organizations registering with the Internal Revenue Service (IRS) has grown at double

Intelligent Fast Failure and Green Biodiesel

Civil and environmental professor and ecopreneur-inventor Jack V. Matson, PhD dedicates his life to practicing "intelligent fast failure," an expression he coined to capture the essence of innovation. It's captured in his irreverently titled book, *Innovate or Die: A Personal Perspective on the Art of Innovation.* As an ecopreneur, he started an environmental design firm, Matson & Associates Inc., housed in a green office building and personally holds two patents on water purification products.

In *Innovate or Die,* Matson suggests that the goal with intelligent fast failure is to move as quickly as possible from new ideas to new knowledge by making small and manageable mistakes — intelligent failures. By moving quickly, we can determine what works, and what doesn't, without draining the bank account and energy devoted to developing the idea. With the increasing variability in climate and rapidly changing global marketplace and social fabric, ecopreneurs are creating new business models, products and services that defy common conventions. Some will fail. The key is to keep learning and try to avoid letting your intelligent failures negatively influence your emotions and self-esteem. And by all means, fail falling forward.

Given the widespread interest in producing biodiesel domestically, Matson launched the Green Biodiesel, LLC, a spinoff venture of Matson & Associates Inc., seeking to develop a new biofuel production process that relies entirely on non-toxic materials to produce a clean-burning alternative fuel from renewable resources in the US. One of the problems facing biodiesel producers and users is that the conventional biodiesel production process uses a number of toxic chemicals to convert vegetable oil feedstocks into a usable fuel. Methanol and sodium hydroxide, two toxic industrial chemicals widely used in the transesterfication process to produce biodiesel, are potentially dangerous to humans and the environment. In order for biodiesel to be a truly environmentally friendly fuel, current and future producers need an alternative process that does not use toxic chemicals or produce significant waste products.

the rate of the business sector. These days there might well be more people launching their own business or starting a non-profit organization than interviewing for jobs. Some are deciding that there's more to retirement than hitting a ball around the golf course. Others embrace meaning and savor greater security by creating their own business or doing some good with their non-profit rather than selling more goods.

Our educational system, well-meaning parents, government and even companies for which we might work tease us into believing that failure is bad. Regurgitate the correct answers back to the teacher. Don't rock the boat in the office. Our

Green Biodiesel's new process settled on the use of solid metal oxide catalysts in a continuous flow process, discovered through various tests and experimentation using the Intelligent Fast Failure process. Green Biodiesel solves many problems associated with the present processing of biodiesel, including the ability to use plant and animal feedstocks and a stable, non-toxic catalyst, plus increased purity of the end product reducing the need for "washing" the biodiesel. "In less than a year, we've gone from an idea on paper related to a chemical process to turning out small batches of biodiesel in the lab," winks Matson, recognizing America's love of the automobile won't change fast. "We tried out a lot of ideas with a nominal investment and found a process that works incredibly well. Instead of making a product better, we've made a better product with an entirely different process."

Besides having a comprehensive business plan, Green Biodiesel works in collaboration with the Biofuels Center at Pennsylvania State University, with the Green Biodiesel process protected by a patent applied for by Penn State University and licensed to Matson & Associates Inc. Various options for the full patent among the collaborators are available to secure control over the licensing of the technology, while grant proposals have been submitted for initial research and development, including to the Environmental Protection Agency SBIR Grant Program and Department of Energy SBIR/STTR Program. Numerous strategic partnerships are being entertained, while funds are being sought totaling $1 million for various phases of start-up that include business plan development, proof of concept, design of pilot plant, design of commercial Green Biodiesel reactor and commercialization and marketing of the technology. Adds Matson: "It's a breakthrough innovation inspired by how elements in nature chemically interact with each other to produce a fuel that does not add to global warming. We just add the know-how, the creativity to make it happen."

school system served the United States well when it needed to build its armed forces (now the most powerful in the world) and national economy. Workers were needed who were educated in the ways of becoming mannered employees or soldiers who followed orders well. Parents reinforced the myth that they themselves believed in: go to school to get a good job — even though it has increasingly entrapped them in mortgages, car payments and credit card debt. But we're not Clone Troopers.

Bill Gates, Steven Jobs, Henry Ford and Richard Branson have something in common: They never finished school. In fact, a growing number of entrepreneurs believe there no such thing as graduation day. Entrepreneurs embrace lifelong learning where every day is a school day. For ecopreneurs, every day is also Earth Day. Learning throughout life, regardless of age, is what keeps us sharp, creative and alive.

Getting a high-school and college education can play an important role in our development, not to mention provide access to networks of friends and colleagues who may support your business in various ways. But when school becomes more about getting a job and promoting the consumption culture without considering the planet and its inhabitants, there's something out of place. We've yet to find a truly carbon neutral university, yet professors lecture about threats posed by global warming brought on by fossil fuel consumption. Schools teach about solar energy but use electricity from coal-fired power plants to power their lights and computers.

Learning about entrepreneurship and business, not to mention life, must take place outside the classroom more than it does now, though more universities are awakening to the opportunities to better serve entrepreneurs with new programs and classes. We need to trust our personal experiences and intuition more while embracing failure as an integral part of the learning process. Harnessing failure can improve your business. As it turns out, nature is most innovative when under stress and must adapt.

Businesses fail for lots of reasons. New products or services take off for little apparent reason, like the ludicrous pet rock or invisible dog on a leash — neither of which are socially or environmentally responsible. Sometimes a business has the right idea at the wrong time, structures its operation in a way that cannot keep up with demand or grows too fast — or not fast enough — to sustain itself. Perhaps the most common reason is lack of cash flow. Just because we opened the doors of our Inn Serendipity doesn't mean customers lined up to stay here. Patience, perseverance, marketing and a long-term vision for the business must be matched by cash flow and debt control to keep things afloat.

There are hundreds of small business start-up books. Consultants and websites abound, eager to help you set up shop, whether a storefront on the Internet or helping you incorporate your business. In fact, among our diversification moves as ecopreneurs was using our talents as marketing and public relations people to serve non-profit organizations or businesses that shared similar values.

Starting a business on solid footing improves the likelihood of a surviving business. Yet millions of businesses fail because of poor management, lack of a compelling product or service — perhaps launched before the market was ready to embrace it — or, simply, a lack of a good business plan. It's amazing to us how many small businesses and non-profit organizations don't even have a business (or strategic) plan; we've consulted for a few. For a business plan to be an effective guide for your business or non-profit organization, the number of pages doesn't matter; the ideas, processes, organization and marketing do. When you fail to plan, you plan to fail.

Structuring Your Business

There are various approaches to business ownership:

- a self-employed sole owner or sole proprietorship
- a partnership with two individuals
- a team, typically three or more owners, usually with different skill sets, talents and knowledge
- a cooperative, a group of people who share ownership of a business that provides them with products or services
- a worker-owned cooperative corporation, in which employees are extended the privilege to voluntarily choose to become an owner of the corporation

A Cooperative Economy

There's a growing interest in cooperatively owned businesses, as demonstrated by the financially, ecologically and socially prosperous farmer-owned Cooperative Regions of Organic Producer Pools (CROPP), marketing numerous products under the nationally recognized Organic Valley Family of Farms brand name. The International Co-operative Alliance (ICA) Statement on the Co-operative Identity defines the cooperative business as "an autonomous association of persons united voluntarily to meet their common economic, social and cultural needs and aspirations through a jointly owned and democratically controlled enterprise." Cooperatives come in numerous forms, including farmers, utility, food, banking and housing. According to ICA, cooperatives "are based on the values of self-help, self-responsibility, democracy, equality, equity and solidarity. In the tradition of their founders, cooperative members believe in the ethical values of honesty, openness, social responsibility and caring for others."

‣ an employee ownership arrangement by which your employees
become owners of your business through an Employee Stock
Ownership Plan (ESOP), the most common.

Each of the above approaches fosters, to varying degrees, more democratic, fair, transparent and responsible business practices. Instead of being wage earners, owners of the business can control their business while benefiting from the profits that their work contributed to generating.

Most writers, bookkeepers, independent truckers, plumbers and computer consultants are sole proprietors. Many family businesses that operate retail stores, bed and breakfasts and farms are husband and wife partnerships, sometimes employing their children. Often, for reasons of complexity, access to capital or legal demands, a team approach to business tends to dictate how founders collaborate in the start-up of manufacturing businesses or high-technology firms.

All of the above approaches to business, however, can be structured in many ways, each with advantages and disadvantages, too numerous to address in this book. These details and specifics are best left for CPA or business attorney professionals to address. Ecopreneurs must evaluate their own situation and business to determine which works best for them. While all business structures require governmental record keeping and forms to be filed, corporations and Limited Liability Companies (LLCs) involve additional legal and accounting requirements.

Franchising

Owning a business that's based on someone else's ideas, called a franchise, can fast-track your business launch since most of its systems, products or services, legal and accounting, marketing and other start-up aspects have been taken care of. In a franchise a parent company sells the license to a franchisee for a fee plus a continuing royalty based on a percentage of sales. It usually offers the franchisee a lower-risk business opportunity, since its model has been developed and includes the name, logo, business systems, products or services, marketing materials, goodwill and the like. A franchise business is a hybrid, since you work for yourself yet you share some of your revenues with the parent company that specifies how and in what ways you must operate the franchised business, usually right down to the shirt you wear on your back. Franchises account for more than 35 percent of all retail sales in the US. If you're the owner of a business that's ripe for franchising, it can be a profitable way to expand the reach of your business and Earth Mission.

If entrepreneurial freedom is your calling, buying into a franchised business may feel like imprisonment since the parent company often encumbers your zest for

Below are several common forms of business structure, broken down by the most recognized reason for choosing one over another: personal liability protection, a shield that prevents anyone with a court judgment against the business to touch anything other than the assets of the corporation. In other words, certain business structures protect the personal assets of the officers, stockholders and employees of the business, reducing the risk that your house, personal property or bank accounts will be taken as a part of a settlement.

No Personal Liability Protection

Sole Proprietorship

Many business owners who are self-employed — often working as free agents, freelancers, construction contractors or nannies — set up their enterprise as a sole proprietorship, with few special requirements and no legal paperwork. This one person is responsible for the liabilities and debt of the business. If your business is sued, everything you own could be threatened by the lawsuit. Income from the business is reported as a part of the owner's personal income using the IRS Schedule C, and you pay self-employment taxes of 15.3 percent.

General Partnership

When two or more individuals who are owners of a for-profit business, typically operating under a written Partnership Agreement, the business is a general

creativity or innovation with the protocols, regulations and policies established by the franchise agreement. One notable exception to this might be the Great Harvest Bread Company (greatharvest.com/franchise/franchise.html) that franchises bakeries that feature high-quality breads. Its more responsible approach to business allows locally owned franchisees to operate in ways that foster innovation, creativity and operator freedom. The only requirements of their so-called freedom franchisees are that franchisees purchase wheat from parent company-approved sources and grind it fresh daily. Unlike other franchises with lots of downwardly exerted control, Great Harvest Bread Company prides itself on not having recipe standards or store design requirements. It also leverages the power of technology to create an internal network for storeowners to converse, collaborate and innovate while doing the unthinkable, decreasing the royalties that the franchisee must pay to the parent company every five years since its more seasoned operators need fewer support services.

partnership. All partners are responsible for the liabilities and debts of the business. Income is reported on the IRS Schedule K-1 and may be subject to 15.3 percent self-employment tax. The partnership must file an annual return, Form 1065, with the federal government and possibly a state return.

Distinct Legal Entity Offering Personal Liability Protection to Shareholders

C Corporation

The most expensive and complex of business structures, C Corporations are legal entities set up within a given state and owned by shareholders of its issued stock. The corporation, not the shareholders or directors, is responsible for the debt and liabilities of the C Corporation. Most multinational corporations and many multimillionaires preserve and build their wealth by setting up a C Corporation that provides numerous opportunities to generate income and incur expenses that enrich its owners and shareholders while reducing the net income (and, therefore, reducing the tax burden). C Corporations must file articles of incorporation, hold director and shareholder meetings, file an annual corporation tax return, keep corporate minutes and vote on corporate decisions. Income from C Corporations, after expenses have been deducted, is taxed both at the corporate level and at the individual level, on wages and dividends paid to shareholders.

S Corporation, or Sub-chapter S Corporation

Essentially a tax accounting classification, an S Corporation is a common stock-issuing, legal entity, income from which is taxed only once when it passes through to the employees or shareholders of the corporation on their personal income tax return. Like C Corporations, S Corporations must file articles of incorporation,

Officers, Shareholders and Taking Stock

Unlike a sole proprietorship, a corporation or LLC is a distinct legal entity, with a corporate formality that separates the owners of the company, the shareholders and its advisory body, the Board of Directors and its officers (President, Secretary, Treasurer) and managerial body, the Chief Executive Officer (CEO) and Chief Financial Officer (CFO).

By law, a corporation must maintain a registered office and agent within the state where it is formed, to respond to legal and official matters of the corporation. If your corporation is in the same state as your residence, you can be your own resident agent. A one-person or family corporation must still follow the formality of corporate procedures related to decision-making and meetings. Document the hold director and shareholder meetings, file an annual corporation tax return, keep corporate minutes and vote on corporate decisions. Most S Corporations can use the more straightforward cash method of accounting whereby income is taxed when received and expenses are deductible when paid. Unlike C Corporations, S Corporations are limited to the number of shareholders it can have.

Limited Liability Company

The Limited Liability Company (LLC) is a separate legal entity established by filing articles of LLC formulation or a similar document in the state where it was formed. The number of LLC members, various classes of stock and tax accounting selection determine a diversity of avenues to properly meet tax liabilities, whether the LLC is treated as a partnership, C or S Corporation.

Non-profit Corporation (Non-profit Organization)

Businesses that wish to generate revenues to make the world a better place through charitable, educational, scientific or literary activities can establish a non-profit organization that is tax exempt, provides personal liability protection for its governing board of directors and allows the charity to apply for funding from governmental and private charitable foundations. The most common non-profit designation by the IRS is the 501(c)3 organization. While some non-profit organizations pride themselves on being volunteer-based, many can and do offer salaries and fringe benefits to staff who serve the mission of the organization.

Business Deductions and the IRS

There are many financial benefits of becoming a business, depending on how you structure it. Not only are businesses taxed after their expenses have been deducted,

"meeting" with Corporate Minutes, even if that means you write down your decisions if you're the only board member, CEO, President, Secretary and Treasurer in a one-person-owned corporation.

Ownership of the company is signified by receipt of stock certificates reflecting financial, property or service contributions to the business; shares can be voting or non-voting, common or preferred; the latter acts similarly to a bond in terms of its value. Shareholders taking stock usually have voting rights, financial distribution rights to dividends if declared by the Board of Directors and proportionate rights to assets should the corporation be dissolved.

but many legitimate deductions are available to a small business that reduce its reported earnings. The IRS tax code specifies the following related to business expenses:

> IRS Code Section 162(a), Trade or business expenses: "There shall be allowed as a deduction all the ordinary and necessary expenses paid or incurred during the taxable year in carrying on any trade or business."
>
> IRS Code Section 212, Expenses for production of income: "In the case of an individual, there shall be allowed as a deduction all the ordinary and necessary expenses paid or incurred during the taxable year."

Some of the more common tax deductible business expenses include the following:

Home Office and Use of Premise for Business Purposes Only

As long as your home office and other portions of your premise are used exclusively for business, you can deduct the corresponding portion of the square footage of the property as a business rental expense, plus the corresponding portion of utilities, insurance, repairs and taxes.

Based on the fair market value of a local rental property for office space or manufacturing space, you can establish the rental rate for the use of your personal property (i.e., room in your home for a home office) and pay yourself rent for such use by the business. You need to set up a simple rental agreement

Who's Watching Me Now, the IRS?

The US Internal Revenue Service is the federal agency designated with the daunting task of monitoring and enforcing the collection of legally mandated taxes. Daunting, because the thousands of pages of tax code is enough to give even specialized certified public accountants a headache in trying to correctly interpret the laws — which change every year. Perhaps a sign of the times, the US tax code is several times the number of pages of the Bible. It's the IRS that describes or defines what constitutes an expense, business and employee. In truth, we live in the most business-friendly country in the world. Follow the rules, be fair and reasonable in your interpretation of them and document everything.

For our hospitality business, Inn Serendipity, the IRS is the agency that cares what we did, for whom and for how much. Of course, our state department of revenue between you as the homeowner or property owner and the business. In our case, about 24 percent of our home is used for a home office and two guest rooms (and bathrooms) for the bed and breakfast, translating to $2,400 in annual rent, a business expense and personal income for us. Rent is passive income, however, not subject to Social Security and Medicare payroll taxes. We're also personally reimbursed for a percentage of utilities and related costs associated with using the portion of the house for business.

Office Supplies

From staples to postage stamps on our holiday newsletter to customers across the country, any out-of-pocket expenses associated with how we do business can be deducted.

Use of Your Personal Vehicle for the Business

Owners of vehicles that are used for business purposes can deduct those miles associated with business use and be reimbursed for mileage by the business. For example, when we drive to speak at a conference or to visit a client, we reimburse ourselves at the IRS specified rate. Make sure to maintain a vehicle travel mileage log for each vehicle used for business purposes.

Meals and Entertainment

Many of us have had an expense account with an employer, perhaps when attending a trade show or entertaining a prospective client. The exact same thing holds true for your own business, so long as verifiable business as been transacted during the occasion. By choosing to work with people and clients who you care

also requires a tax return (and the state in which you formed it, if different, also has requirements that must be met to maintain your business "in good standing"). Our business generates revenues from overnight stays by B & B guests and incurs business expenses related to our guests' stays. The IRS tries to be very clear on what is an acceptable business expense and what's not. Rather than conduct under-the-counter cash business deals (like some contractors do) or ignore our responsibility to document cash tips (from our guests), we make sure to capture every last cent that our business earns. The same holds true for our writing endeavors. Visit the IRS website (irs.gov) for the latest updates and changes to the tax code and consider contracting the services of a Certified Public Accountant who specializes in small business returns. As a bonus, the CPA fee is a tax-deductible business expense.

about and share common interests with — perhaps like local, seasonal, organic food — business meal deductions take on a bizarre reality that many millionaires (and many politicians) have enjoyed for years.

Business Travel

As freelance writers, photographers, artists or consultants will attest, why not travel for work? If you love what you do, following your Earth Mission, you can deduct your airline, train, car rental and just about every other cost related to your business trip, so long as it's for business, and not just lying around on a beach. It's no coincidence that Las Vegas and Orlando are among the top US destinations for trade shows.

Equipment and Capital Expenses

Some investments in your business, like equipment or improvements that are usually quite large, are considered capital expenses and reflected as assets on your balance sheet. Rather than deducting them, you must capitalize them as long-term investments. Assets, however, can be depreciated, reducing reported earnings. A new metal roof on a rental property is a capital expense, requiring a depreciation schedule to be created (keep in mind that a quality metal roof will last longer than you will). A ream of recycled paper is not a capital expense; it's recorded simply as "supplies" and deducted in the year you purchased it.

Make Money off Your Used, Fuel-efficient Car

Every year, the IRS sets the reimbursable rate for the business use of your vehicle, based on national fleet repair and maintenance averages and fuel costs, both of which are rising. We get the same rate whether we drive a super-fuel-efficient Toyota Prius or Volkswagen Jetta TDI (diesel) versus a low-mileage Hummer. It turns out we've managed to make money off each business mile we put on our Volkswagen Jetta TDI because the cost of operating and fueling it is less than for other new and less fuel-efficient vehicles. How? First, we only buy used vehicles because as soon as most new vehicles are driven off the dealer's lot, they lose about 25 percent of their value. Second, by the time we might sell our used vehicle with years of reimbursed business miles paid to us as owners, the cost of the vehicle would have broken even. For example, one year we might have 7,193 business-related miles put on our VW Jetta, multiplied by the IRS designated rate of $.445/mile, resulting in the business reimbursing us for the business use of the car to the tune of $3,200. Keep in mind that this expense item reduces the reported earnings of the business by $3,200 as well.

Depreciation

Business assets wear out, break down and become obsolete, especially with the rapid advancements in technology. The IRS allows a non-cash deductible business expense of depreciation to account for the loss of value over time for assets owned by the business. Depreciation reduces the reported earnings of the business. The amount of depreciation and its duration varies by the type of asset.

Health Insurance

Depending on the structure of the business, health insurance and healthcare expenses may be deducted for employees or owners of the business.

Children or Family Members as Employees

As long as you are offering fair and reasonable compensation for your children or family members working for the business, there is nothing inappropriate with hiring and paying them for the work. When hiring a family member, however, the business may not need to pay Social Security and Medicare taxes (FICA) and federal unemployment taxes (FUTA). You may also be exempted from maintaining Unemployment Compensation insurance if there are only two or fewer owners of the business you own. You'll need to comply with child labor laws, however, if your children are minors.

Employees, Contractors and Subcontractors

In small businesses, your payments for services are generally made to employees in the form of wages or to contractors and subcontractors as fees. Contractors provide services for a set fee and time period for a particular client. Subcontracting refers to someone who has a contract to provide services for a contractor, for example, a plumber working for a building contractor. Often operating as a subcontractor proves logistically easier than as a contractor since the latter typically manages the whole project, including all planning and communications with the client. If the contract is government- or grant-based, this can often mean the subcontractor avoiding mounds of administrative paperwork.

Business Accounting and Bookkeeping

Keep detailed file folders by month for every invoice, receipt, payment and any other financial transaction related to the business. Most of this information can also be entered on a computer using the Quicken bookkeeping software, so that you have easy access to records of sales and business expenses related to each month of the business year.

While viable business ideas lead to new products or services for ecopreneurs, many businesses still fail in the marketplace because they did not have

Contractor or Employee?

The IRS provides detailed explanations of the differences between employees and contractors/subcontractors. The important difference isn't so much between contractors and subcontractors — we bounce between those roles ourselves — but distinguishing between contractors/subcontractors and employees. While no single factor provides an answer to determining employee versus contractor/subcontractor status, there are a few general differences.

- *Form 1099 versus a W-2.* If someone works for you as a contractor/subcontractor, you must complete a Form 1099-MISC for each one earning $600 or more. If someone is an employee, the employer is responsible for withholding and paying the employment-related taxes and other state paperwork (referred to as W-2). Contractors/subcontractors are responsible for keeping records and paying income or self-employment taxes. Contractors/subcontractors receive no employee benefits from their clients (i.e., healthcare, retirement).
- *Amount of training and instructions.* Contractors and subcontractors usually work independently on projects. Few need or receive detailed instructions or training such as you would give an employee.
- *Expense reimbursement.* Typically contractors and subcontractors pay for their own business expenses, equipment and tools and deduct these expenses.
- *Contracts.* Contracts form the basis of relationships between contractor and subcontractors and their respective clients, detailing the services to be performed, payment structures and timeline. Employees are hired to fulfill responsibilities outlined in a job description.

More than just buying another office desk, hiring employees — even just one — means opening up a perpetual Pandora's Box of federal and state labor laws requiring compliance. As an employer, you are now responsible for paying half of your employees' Social Security and Medicare taxes as part of the Federal Insurance Contributions Act (FICA). You also need to pay state and Federal Unemployment Tax Act (FUTA) taxes in addition to workers' compensation fees, which vary by state, kind of work, and wages. Employers must also coordinate calculation of employees' payroll deductions, which can get complicated if this includes alimony or child support payments. Additionally, if you have a retirement plan or benefits for yourself, you must also offer these programs to your employees. The list goes on and on, which is why more and more small businesses seek to keep their scale on a family level.

Small Business Tool Kit

- Nolo Press Books and website (nolo.com)

  Deduct It! Lower Your Small Business Taxes, Stephen Fishman

  Working for Yourself, Law & Taxes for Independent Contractors, Freelancers & Consultants, Stephen Fishman

  The Corporate Minutes Book, Anthony Mancuso

  Every Landlord's Tax Deduction Guide, Stephen Fishman

  Inc. & Grow Rich: How to Cut Taxes by 70% and Protect Your Assets Forever, C. W. Allen, Cheri Hill, Diane Kennedy and Garrett Sutton (Sage International)

- Business Plan Template

  Don't bother typing in your business plan; download (for free) the easy-to-use one from the Small Business Advice Service. While based in the United Kingdom and requiring a little adjustment to the margins, this business plan template guides you through the business plan writing process.

  www.smallbusinessadvice.org.uk/busplan/bpdownloads.asp

- Quicken

  Numerous bookkeeping software packages exist, but Quicken from Intuit ranks as the best-known, reliable and easy to use for small business. There is also Quicken Rental Property, Medical Expense and Home Inventory Managers.

  quicken.intuit.com

the business systems in place to grow to the scale they desired. Some get big too fast while others collapse under the burden of orders. If products are sold, like books or antiques, an inventory system must be devised, bookkeeping system set up and warehousing needs planned. Thanks to affordable software packages that include widely available spreadsheets for bookkeeping and financial records, database programs to keep track of your customers and word processing and graphic design programs for correspondence and communications, just about every aspect of a small business can be managed from a home office, in an urban studio space, suburban ranch or farmhouse.

Two methods can be used for accounting, the process by which financial information is recorded, summarized and interpreted. The more commonly used and straightforward "cash basis" of accounting establishes that income is taxable when received and expenses are deductible when paid. The more complex "accrual basis" method records payments or expenses when they're agreed upon but which may take place at some future date; cash may not have been received or spent by the business.

The business is summarized by an income statement reflecting revenues and expenses, also called a Profit and Loss Statement (P&L), as well as by a balance sheet reflecting the assets and liabilities (and equity) of the business. The difference between assets and liabilities is the net worth of the business. Most small businesses are set up to have a calendar year, rather than a fiscal year that is a period of 12 months starting at some date during a current year.

While income and balance sheets are important to your understanding of how your business functions and are required for federal and state tax filing if

Purposeful Profits

The following simplified samples of an Income Statement and Balance Sheet are based on a typical year of our business, JDI Enterprises, Inc. (DBA Inn Serendipity).

Sample Income Statement

Revenues	$54,430
Expenses	
Compensation of officers	$4,000
Repairs and maintenance	$1,834
Rents	$12,300
Taxes and licenses	$4,714
Interest (on loan to us personally)	$320
Depreciation	$3,712
Advertising	$946
Other itemized deductions	
Government filing fees	$311
Legal and accounting	$750
Mileage	$4,771
Telephone/Internet	$1,619
Photo shoot expenses	$421
Memberships	$441
Food for B & B	$747
Credit card fees	$760
Meals & entertainment	$683
Subcontractors	$940
Supplies	$894
Office expenses	$922

your business is formed as a corporation or LLC, cash flow is one of the more challenging aspects of getting a new business going. Too often, not enough cash is kept in reserve or there's limited access to additional capital, forcing the business to close before the product or service is effectively marketed. At least three to four years should be anticipated as the start-up phase for many businesses, so financing and cash flow considerations should be paramount during this period. Developing a diversified portfolio of enterprises or business activities — with a varied customer base or clientele — helps maintain sufficient cash flow until the

Miscellaneous	$1,057
Travel	$1,326
Utilities	$514
Insurance	$471
Total Expenses	$44,453
Net Revenues (profit)	$9,977 (pass through income from S corporation to owners)

Balance Sheet

Assets		Liabilities	
Cash	$7,663	Loans from shareholders	$18,889
Inventory (i.e., books, mugs)	$3,683		
Buildings (less depreciation)	$11,944		
		Retained Earnings	$4,401
Total Assets	$22,736	Total Liabilities and Shareholder's Equity	$22,736

As evidenced above, our business makes some profit, but not much, largely due to our focus on living systems — clean air, safe water and healthy soil — and maintaining a healthy quality of life rather than super-sizing our bank account. Keep in mind, the more money you earn, the more you pay in taxes. And the bigger the operation, the more complex and involved your income and balance sheet might become.

business has developed an adequate market to support itself and generate consistent profits.

Integrated Profit Management

The shelves are stacked deep with management how-to books, usually from a perspective of top-down tactics on employee control. How to get someone to do something for you. How to dominate and manipulate the process and outcomes. From *Swim with the Sharks Without Being Eating Alive* to *The No Asshole Rule* to *Death by Meeting*, these books focus on a strategic line of attack to controlling others to turn a buck.

Ecopreneurs take a different approach to management. Think round versus linear. Holistic versus purely strategic, equating "management" with how we intentionally treat all aspects of our life. From our relationships to our living and work environment, it all interrelates under the umbrella of purposeful management. For the keen observer of nature and how it functions in a healthy ecosystem, it's all about relationships and interrelationships.

Having purpose and doing something with intention goes against the reactive management mode: When a problem occurs, then react to solve it. Some automakers wait until global warming directly impacts millions of people and wildlife before redesigning cars. The decisions we make in both our business and personal lives dig deeper than the bottom line. Ecopreneurs realize business does more than produce a great product or service that doesn't destroy or exploit the planet. Ecopreneurs operate in ways that value people and relationships.

Law of Unintended Consequences

As humans, we're imperfect. So are tomatoes. Conservationist Aldo Leopold once wrote that the rule of creative tinkering is to keep all the parts. He, like we, recognized that sometimes in the world of creativity and innovation things don't turn out the way you hoped.

The more we learn, the more we realize just how much we don't know. The financial corollary is the more we earn, the greater we spend. It's a relationship with money that defies a more conservative side of our nature that suggests caution and prudence, to save the surplus cash for a rainy day or when you need it for an emergency. A growing number of Americans no longer have a stash of cash. As small business owners, having a little money in reserve for tough times can make the difference between shuttering your enterprise or allowing it time enough to prosper. Cash flow kills many small businesses that did not project enough time to become established. Don't let it happen to you.

Rather than putting out fires, how can we reimagine businesses that don't have them?

Practice Integrated Profit Management (IPM), reflecting a holistic lifestyle that stems from a core entrepreneurial passion about meaningful work. It blends work — positively and legally — with leisure, family and relationships. An eco-preneurial business achieves a rate of return that maximizes long-term social and environmental benefits — for example, cleaning up rivers, improving the health of the soil, offering experiential education for guests — rather than externalizes social or ecological costs in order to maximize shareholder return, like most major corporations do. So while income statements and balance sheets are valuable tools for understanding how well your business is operating from a financial perspective, it falls way short in capturing how well the business serves the greater good.

Cash Flow

Cash flow is simply the cash received and spent by the business over a specific period of time, usually a year. Worth mentioning again, don't run out of money while waiting for customers to discover your business. We almost did, until we realized our Diversified Income-producing Portfolio of Work model that shifted seasonally with variations in projects to accommodate the natural fall-off in hospitality business during the winter (our cabin is completely closed for the season). Often, much of the work related to our writing and photography, along with consulting projects, takes place during the winter. Payment for freelance writing or book projects, however, can be received months later at the time of publication.

The diversity of enterprises and activities supports our stable year-round cash flow, especially when we most need it in January when many governmental fees and filings are due. A cash flow projection includes both anticipated cash receipts from sales (or loans) on a monthly, quarterly or annual basis and cash disbursements for cost of goods sold (direct costs related to your products), selling, general and administrative (indirect expenses related to your products) expenses, taxes (sales) and equipment. The goal is to avoid or minimize any periods where you have a net negative cash balance.

We're increasingly selective about the companies or organizations we work for, since we've written pieces for magazines that folded and some companies have lost photographs we've sent them. We gravitate away from clients who don't promptly pay for photography, writing or other services, while we constantly seek out new potential clients — often when on trips or at conferences. Working on projects that don't require us to jump through hoops to get paid makes managing cash flow easier.

Sample Seasonal Cash Flow for JDI Enterprises, Inc. ($)

Business Components	Jan.	Feb.	March	Apr.	May
Bed & Breakfast	375	963	845	1285	1986
Cabin rental *		200	200	445	650
Writing & Photography **	1330	375	1259	389	175
Speaking & Workshops	150	375	400	1441	335
Marketing Consulting	1800	2135	1790	1253	
Special Projects	1876	1387	1489	630	
Authoring Books			175		311
Retail Store/Book Sales	80	289	287	247	301
Direct Sales Ag Products					15
Cash Recipts ($)====>	5611	5724	6445	5690	3773
Cash Disbursements =>	4872	4356	4100	5360	3521
Net Cash Flow ($)	739	1368	2345	330	252

* Cabin is closed from mid-September through Memorial Day (late May), but reservations taken year-round.

** Writing/photography typically in late fall, winter and early spring even though often paid upon publication.

Insurance

In an age of more violent storms, hurricanes, downpours and forest fires, not to mention a possible lawsuit over accidents or incidents beyond our control, insurance coverage is a necessary part of helping manage the risks associated with operating our business. While policies are written based on your industry, some insurers recognize that less-voluminous, human-scaled small businesses are less risky and less likely to encounter problems, passing along lower premiums to its customers. Discussed in chapter 7, maintaining excellent credit — translating to a high (good) credit score — also has a direct bearing on reducing our premiums. For microcorporations, purchasing a $1 million umbrella policy on top of an existing homeowners and vehicle policy might meet your insurance needs. Additionally, microbusiness owners may be exempted from maintaining state-mandated Unemployment Compensation insurance if they are the sole owners of the business.

June	July	Aug.	Sept.	Oct.	Nov.	Dec.	TOTAL	Percent
1735	1893	1788	1522	793	495	389	14069	29%
883	795	785	375				4333	9%
250	450		1235	230	970	150	6813	14%
				600	450		3751	8%
			980	592	260	188	8998	18%
						497	5879	12%
202			170		386	235	1479	3%
324	388	370	380	353	487	198	3704	8%
25	75	125	20	10			270	1%
3419	3601	3068	4682	2578	3048	1657	49296	
3380	3790	2990	4616	1800	2920	1435	43140	
39	-189	78	66	778	128	222	6156	

NOTE:
B&B, cabin rental, retail/book sales, authoring books, speaking, and sales of ag products are directly inter-linked.
Marketing and special projects are often indirectly linked with other aspects of our livelihood.

Depending on how you structure your business, you may be able to deduct your health insurance premiums, if not all your healthcare costs as the owner and employee of your business. The laws related to this keep changing and are complex, so consulting a CPA or financial advisor is a must. For example, S Corporations are prevented from having business-sponsored healthcare for owner-employees. However, the State Children's Health Insurance Program (SCHIP) is available nationally to working families (with children) based on household earned income; Insure Kids Now (insurekidsnow.gov) links the nation's children to affordable health insurance that often includes doctor visits, medication coverage and even checkup cleaning at the dentist for the whole family once a year; Cover the Uninsured was created to do the same thing (covertheuninsured.org). The state-sponsored healthcare program for working families is one way that being your own small business owner actually helps you secure better, more affordable healthcare coverage. Several states, like Wisconsin and

Illinois, are also demonstrating leadership related to healthcare for their residents and may soon offer state-sponsored healthcare for all residents in need, whether or not they have children.

Legal Issues

We live in a litigious society, where misapplication of common sense can result in business-destroying lawsuits. Accidents and miscalculations have made attorneys

Diversified Income-producing Portfolio of Work

The more income-producing and complementary projects we have, the more stable and secure we feel, careful to not let work override quality of life considerations. In any given year, we receive mini-paychecks from about 50 businesses including publishers and non-profit organizations, plus thousands of dollars from individuals who stay at Inn Serendipity, order products from our website or buy books at our speaking events. What we work on changes or adapts to new opportunities, interests, passions and our evolving Earth Mission.

a) **Inn Serendipity Bed & Breakfast (29%):** We manage all facets of this two bedroom bed and breakfast, sharing cleaning, breakfast preparations and hosting guests.

b) **Consulting (18%):** Because of our varied backgrounds and educational experiences, we've consulted on projects including database management, public relations, advertising and marketing endeavors.

c) **Freelance writing and photography (14%):** Among our passions is the need to express in words or photographs how we interpret the world. John's photography and writing clients are varied and international, with a focus on tourism, environmental issues and sustainable development.

d) **Special projects (12%):** Sometimes one-time opportunities offer the ability to generate our electricity or work on specially funded projects. This is the most serendipitous aspect of our income.

e) **Inn Serendipity Woods cabin rental (9%):** We manage cabin rental contracts, website marketing and guest relations, while also maintaining the cabin and property.

f) **Workshop facilitation and speaking (8%):** Conferences and fairs allow us to share our perspectives while learning about the many inspiring ways others have embarked on similar journeys. From the renewable energy and sustainable living fairs to the Green Festival, our presentations or workshops hopefully jumpstart others into action and reinvigorate our commitment.

wealthy while bankrupting businesses or individuals (if they were structured as a sole proprietorship).

From time to time, we hire an attorney to guide us through possible sticky spots related to legal issues we might face, or other concerns that might arise as a part of our business. While small-sizing our operations can minimize our exposure to risk — we can talk with all of the guests who rent the cabin or visit the bed and breakfast before they arrive — we still engaged an attorney to assess

g) **Cottage retail store and book sales (8%):** We sell our books, photography prints and handmade mugs to B & B guests.

h) **Authoring books (3%):** Much more involved than writing for magazines or newspapers, authoring books provides an avenue to address in a comprehensive and artistic way those issues closest to our hearts. Income varies greatly from nothing in one year to several thousand dollars in another.

i) **Farm-direct agricultural products (1%):** We sell super-energy-efficient LED lights for greenhouses, surplus flowers, vegetables, fruits and herbs grown on the farm, and eventually, unique, niche agricultural crops grown in the strawbale greenhouse.

We search for synergistic business activities that cross over from one project to the next, or help lead to new opportunities. While hired to complete a business and marketing plan for one non-profit organization, for example, we prepared a sample three-page feature article for a major statewide magazine and submitted it on spec (non-assigned) as a part of the public relations plan. It was accepted, helping position the organization as a conservation leader in the state. We synergistically cultivated both our PR skills and writing abilities to produce a better result for the client and possibly lead to future freelance writing projects for a statewide magazine. As knowledge workers with varied skill sets, we seek a natural balance of interrelated projects that challenge us while also helping us achieve our overarching Earth Mission.

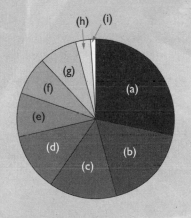

Diversified Income Pie Chart

JDI ENTERPRISES, INC.

potential legal or liability issues. Reflecting the spirit of sustainable business-to-business relationships, we chose one of our B & B guests, an attorney who shared our values and understood our concerns. He advised us on both our rental contract and liability release form that we have cabin rental guests sign before their stay.

Corporate Charter

Every state has various regulations and requirements for starting a new business. For simplicity purposes, we will only discuss starting a sub-chapter S Corporation, though many other options are possible and should be selected based on your situation and advice from professional counsel. Most states provide a checklist to new business owners that will walk you through the requirements for operating your business.

To start a sub-chapter S Corporation, you file the articles of incorporation or a similarly worded corporate charter. Our corporation was started in one state, then moved and now operates in a different state as a "foreign corporation." A registered agent (and office) is maintained in the original state as required. Stockholders are the owners of the corporation with the board of directors directing the actions of the corporation and officers and employees executing these actions. At the present time, we're the shareholders, officers and sole employees of our S Corporation.

Naming the Business and Trademarks or Servicemarks

A DBA refers to "doing business as" and establishes the name of your business. Our sub-chapter S Corporation serves as the legal business while we hold a

Piercing the Corporate Veil

The limited liability advantage offered to a corporation or limited liability company (LLC) is only as good as your ability to operate as a business in good standing, treating the corporation or LLC as a separate entity and apart from you personally, and to abide by the legal requirements, even if they seem trivial in the case of a one-person S corporation. Operating your corporation as a corporation helps minimize the chances that you will personally be held liable for something that happens as a part of the business (unless by clear negligence on your part).

You can avoid the courts "piercing the corporate veil" by maintaining, among many things, excellent records, never commingling business and personal money, adhering to corporate formalities, signing as Officer of the Corporation, using your corporate name in correspondence, and filing all required paperwork with the federal and state governments, including annual corporate returns. A little bit of busywork can insure the viability and soundness of your business.

DBA, Inn Serendipity®. Often, many DBAs can be created within one umbrella business name. Increasingly, many businesses choose to create an authentic connection to a real place, like their farm that sells honey, by branding themselves and using their personal name in the business name. There is no correct business name. But whatever name you select must not be used by any other business, otherwise you might find yourself in a legal dispute.

Naming your business is fulfilling and should be a meaningfully creative process. While possibly requiring the services of an attorney, establishing the name of your business and registering its trademark or service mark with the US Patent and Trademark Office can be done with the forms provided on their website (uspto.gov). Protecting your business name insures that no other business will usurp your reputation and borrow your identity for their profit, not yours. The small "TM" refers to a registration mark waiting for approval by the US Trademark and Patent Office. Once approved, the "®" replaces the TM. It's important to use these marks to protect the reputation of your business and reaffirm that you are pursuing business in earnest, not as a hobby.

Inn Serendipity logo with ®

Patents and Copyrights

Protecting your ideas is important. Patents, usually lasting up to 20 years, are offered by the US Patent and Trademark Office for intellectual property that is unique in design, utility (a process or machine) or plant. Copyrights apply to "original works of authorship" and include literary, musical and other artistic forms of expression; the length of a copyright depends on when it is created, how many individuals may be involved and various other factors. Our books are copyrighted. If we invented a new wind turbine that mounts on our roof, it'd be patented. The bigger or more complex the idea, the more you might consider hiring an attorney to assist you in protecting your interests.

Building a Business Plan

A business plan is a simple to read document that guides your business and sets forth the mission, objectives, management, marketing, strategy and implementation, financial profit and loss statements and sales projections. The approach to the plan is based on whether you're starting a company, raising funds, trying to secure a business loan or expanding your operations. A sample of our Inn Serendipity business plan is available on the *ECOpreneuring* website (ecopreneuring.biz).

Concept Testing or Feasibility Studies

Just because you have a great idea for a product or service — a toilet that does-n't require water or socially responsible eldercare service — you need to ascertain its viability in the marketplace and determine the best means by which to mar-ket it, and to whom. Safety, reliability, durability and ability to meet needs of your potential customers without producing waste, damaging the environment or requiring cheap exploitative labor to make it affordable to enough customers to make it viable are all facets of the business to be evaluated.

Operating your business, perhaps as a corporation or LLC, is one of the quickest ways to allow you to focus on your Earth Mission and achieve the qual-ity of life you desire. As ecopreneurs, we have priorities, like caring for the planet and community, that internalize what many other businesses externalize. By operating effectively within the entrepreneur-friendly legal and tax system in the US, your business can prosper while you leave a lasting living legacy.

The next chapter will examine money matters, including personal finance and securing financial capital. Like any business owners, ecopreneurs need some money to get started.

Chapter 7

Money Matters

It is well enough that people of the nation do not understand our banking and monetary system, for if they did, I believe there would be a revolution before tomorrow morning.

— Henry Ford

MANY OF US DON'T LIKE TALKING ABOUT MONEY, especially amongst the family. Nor do most people enjoy fundraising for charity, though some people excel at it. We learned early on, while in our mid-twenties, just how much money matters had taken over our lives, in part, because we were earning income to pay taxes and buy lots of stuff; we had unwittingly joined the earn-and-spend consumption culture, heading toward the American Debt Trap. Ironically, most business schools and colleges don't even offer courses about investing in your own home — or personal finance in general. In high school we read classic novels but fail to learn how to balance a checkbook.

We all need money to meet our basic needs, pay the bills and pay for the financial responsibilities we accept in our country, based on increasingly complex laws and regulations. There are licenses and fees for just about everything these days, from owning a pet, putting up a wind turbine, launching a business or passing through airport security. America's household dis-savings rate — we're spending more than we earn, based on abundantly available credit — hovers around what it was during the Great Depression. It's matched by underfunded or debt-laden governmental and big business commitments. This cannot continue indefinitely. As we and many other lifestyle ecopreneurs have discovered, you don't need hundreds of thousands of dollars to enjoy the good life, if you can work smartly about it. It's how you approach your personal finances in a more sane and sustainable way while letting your business work for you in ways to achieve your Earth Mission.

American Debt Trap

The American Debt Trap: Buying something when we don't have money, in the bank account or otherwise. It has never been easier to do. In fact, one mortgage company is offering us $162,098 cash in a "new fast-track loan program" to "pay off higher interest-rate credit card and loan balances, make home improvements or start a new business," despite the fact that our average annual adjusted gross income is less than $20,000. Not to be outdone, our credit card company just enrolled us in a new credit card without a spending limit. For those who fall into the American Debt Trap, it consumes your life energy by forcing you to earn income to pay interest, installments or minimum payments on vehicle loans, mortgages and credit cards. Many people struggle to keep up, even when the overall economy is supposedly prospering.

Thriving in an Age of Social (and Economic) Insecurity

Especially over the last three decades, we've entrusted our nation's expanding economy to fill up our homes with goods or contract out for a dizzying array of services — from lawn care to daycare. Not only is spending on goods or services — being a consumer — important to our economy since it represents two-thirds of our GNP, it's portrayed as our civic duty. While we're out spending like never before, much of what we're buying is rarely made by our neighbors or fellow Americans any more. Global capitalism and trade have spread and seemingly erased boundaries (and, in many cases, the effectiveness of national laws and regulations), and it's devastating the planet.

Refinancing our house or putting it on plastic has become an easy way to get what we want. For the US government, taking the easy way out is as simple as rolling the printing press to produce more greenbacks or borrowing more money. It won't be long before half of the US Treasury Bonds are owned by Chinese businesses and foreign governments' central banks. In America's drive to emerge as a global leader and economic powerhouse, we've succumbed to an addiction of credit, borrowing from future generations and living and spending beyond our means.

As discussed earlier, the odds are against most of us ending up as the senior partners at a big company, retiring on a fat nest egg, and good-enough health to play that never-ending game of golf. If you're young, you've already meditated on the disclaimer in big print on the front of your US government Social Security Administration Statement, the one that forecasts what you might not receive at retirement age after religiously paying into the federal system:

> Social Security retirement benefits are funded by today's
> workers and their employers who jointly pay Social Security
> taxes .... In 2017, we will begin paying more in benefits than
> we collect in taxes. Without changes, by 2041 the Social
> Security Trust Fund will be exhausted.
>
> — Excerpted from July 24, 2007 and July 21, 2006 Social Security
> Administration Statements sent to US citizens

Instead of setting aside the Social Security taxes collected, perhaps investing it for our retirement, the federal government has spent the current Social Security receipts to meet current liabilities of retirees. Ditto for Medicare expenses. About 20 percent of the annual federal spending is devoted to paying out Social Security benefits for retirees, with an additional 15 percent of the budget devoted to Medicare health benefits. Amazingly, about 58 percent of the entire budget involves payments made to individuals as "entitlements," about double what they were in the 1960s and happening regardless of which political party is at the helm. Of course, the Social Security and Medicare problems could possibly be solved by removing the payroll tax cap of around $90,000, forcing the big earners to pay more. But what's the chance of that happening? Instead of looking to the government to take care of us in our old age, we can reclaim responsibility, through our business, for managing our own finances. We envision a nation of fiscally responsible proprietors and ecopreneurs.

Those Taxing Taxes

Federal and state laws require us to pay our proportion of taxes, according to the respective tax codes. However, we do not need to overpay or increase our contribution to the national or state treasury, unless we're inclined to do so voluntarily; that's a big reason why some wealthier Americans choose to live where they do or form their own corporations in Delaware or Nevada (where corporations pay no state income taxes). For many of us, as much as 60 or 70 percent of our annual earned income is consumed by taxes. As much as 75 percent of taxpayers pay more in Social Security and Medicare payroll taxes than they do in income taxes according to the Center on Budget and Policy Priorities, a non-partisan research and policy institute (cbpp.org). It's no wonder we're spending money as quickly as we earn it.

Here's what many of us face by way of taxes:

+ Federal income taxes: 10 to 39 percent, averaging 28 to 39 percent
+ Social Security and Medicare payroll taxes (FICA): 15.3 percent, including what your employer must also pay for employing you (self-employment: 15.3 percent)

- State income taxes: as much as 12 percent, though the states of Alaska, Florida, Nevada, South Dakota, Texas, Washington and Wyoming have none. The states of New Hampshire and Tennessee tax only interest and dividend income.
- State sales tax: as much as 7 percent or more, but not in the states of Alaska, Delaware, Montana, New Hampshire and Oregon where there is none.
- County and city taxes: maybe a half percent or so, and one of the reasons more Americans are leaving the cities.
- State and local property taxes: highly variable, ranging from hundreds to thousands of dollars per year. Again, much higher in some urban and suburban areas.
- Embedded taxes: on gasoline, utilities, lodging accommodations and telephone service.
- User fees and registrations: cars, businesses, airports and animals. Is the Internet next?

Interestingly, what's not taxed yet are various forms of pollution, waste or other ecologically damaging practices — a future revenue stream likely tapped by governments seeking to clean up their communities while raising revenues from people or companies polluting it. From taxes on greenhouse gas emissions to gallons of wastewater, ecopreneurs will hold another competitive advantage should the "green taxes" suggested by Paul Hawken in *The Ecology of Commerce* and many others actually become law. Increasingly, the politicians are feeling the heat in more ways than one.

As discussed previously, passive and investment portfolio income derived from capital gains and dividends are taxed at lower rates than salaries and wages. Therefore, if most of your income is from portfolio and passive income, perhaps in the form of a rental property, your tax burden is much less than someone who earns a lot more in a big salary. Obviously, there's no payroll tax on rental income. Given this, it should be no surprise that from lakefront homes to rustic cabins, in any given year as much as a third of all residential property sold in the US has been in the form of second homes, according to the National Association of Realtors.

If you rent out your second home, using it yourself for less than 15 days a year, your property can be considered an investment. Depreciation, a non-cash allowance for wear, tear and obsolescence — or "paper loss" — can account for a portion of the expenses associated with an investment property, resulting in the investment property to have a loss. If you "materially participate" in managing the property — marketing rentals, cleaning, maintaining the grounds, repairing furnishings and the like — you can deduct up to $25,000 of your investment property losses against your earned income, assuming your adjusted gross income is less than $100,000. Another approach is to offer a triple net lease to a tenant. Triple net leases mean that the tenant is financially responsible for the insurance, taxes, repairs and maintenance associated with the building rented.

Inn Serendipity Woods is our investment property with a recreational cabin on 30 mostly wooded acres nestled in the coulees of west central Wisconsin. We rent the rustic A-frame cabin seasonally, while enrolling a few acres in the Continuous Reserve Program (CRP) as a riparian buffer. We also rent about 3 tillable acres to an Amish farmer down the road who grows organic corn for his organic dairy operation. Income from our cabin guests allows us to pursue our reforestation and conservation priorities, while they might enjoy gathering wild mushrooms or spending an afternoon floating on an inner tube in the pond, counting dragonflies overhead. The cabin provides both a Return on Investment and Return on Environment.

Many financially wealthy Americans take advantage of trading up in investment real estate property ownership and avoid paying any capital gains taxes on

Inn Serendipity Woods recreational cabin, a property that incorporates sustainable forestry and agriculture practices.

lucrative real estate deals. Instead of paying capital gains tax on profit of $10,000 from an investment property that is sold, you can place this money in an IRS Code 1031 tax-deferred exchange, also called Starker exchange, at a third-party intermediary to be held until it's used for a new investment property. Such new property must be purchased within 180 days of the closing of the sold property. This process is how many property investors keep building wealth in assets without necessarily having to be big wage earners. If one of your new exchanges is a rental property then all the better. For ecopreneurs, their rental properties might offer affordable housing in areas where there is none or "green leases" that provide discounts to renters if they practice conservation measures.

Corporations can, likewise, be used to help reduce tax burdens since they generate revenues, deduct expenses before being taxed (reducing their tax burden) and then are taxed only on net revenues. The main point is that corporations and LLCs are taxed only after expenses are deducted. For many ecopreneurs, various facets of our business and our "below our means" lifestyle are unable to be taxed, such as growing our own food or generating our own electricity, like we do.

Since we operate an S Corporation, we must file our annual corporate return every March. Because of the complexity of the tax code, and constant changes made to it, we hire a local CPA firm to help us properly complete our corporate return and personal income tax returns. In this way, our CPA advises us on the proper interpretation of IRS tax code and alerts us to anything that may be incorrect, or suspect. Again worth reiterating, America is genuinely business-friendly as dictated by the IRS tax code.

In part due to our focus on living below our means and intentionally staying small in our business activities, we find that by running our own business as an S Corporation, we join big companies like AT&T and The Walt Disney Corporation in paying little or no taxes at all. Unlike our S Corporation, however, these large profitable corporations take advantage of even more tax advantages that come with operating as a C Corporation.

Borrowing Future Hope and Income

According to Thornton Parker in *What if Boomers Can't Retire: How to Build Real Security, Not Phantom Wealth*, the inflated corporate stock prices (and home values) are creating the illusion of a phantom wealth, a mere illusion of real wealth. We're counting our chickens before they've hatched every time we price a stock based on future earnings projections — on what we hope might happen based on what is going on behind closed doors in boardrooms. When investors purchase stocks at prices that are 44 times the company's earnings, referred to as the PE ratio, they're doing just that — like stockowners of the Internet darling, Google. Despite this, more and more of us are looking to their stock portfolios and appreciated home values — through reverse mortgages and home equity loans — to fund retirement or a dream vacation. This makes sense only when there are more stock investors and more homeowners. If, however, the US decides to severely limit immigration or if other stock markets (and currencies) around the world appear more attractive than in the United States, what then?

By focusing on your personal finances and household economy mentioned in chapter 1, those who are wise related to their personal finances can build up their assets to support their quality of life while minimizing their liabilities, as depicted below.

Rather than from wages, our income is derived mostly from passive investments or, nominally, from investment portfolios, reducing our expenses and liabilities. Expenses are minimal, in part due to the realities of thriving in a more

Personal Finances

Income
>   Wages
>   Passive (rent, royalties, interest income from Certificates of Deposit [CDs] or bank accounts)
>   Portfolio (stocks, bonds, partnerships, capital gains from sales of appreciated investments)

Expenses
>   Payroll tax (Social Security and Medicare)
>   Income tax
>   Utilities
>   Property taxes
>   Housing
>   Insurance
>   Food
>   Clothing
>   Transportation

Assets	**Liabilities**
Stocks, bonds, mutual funds (socially responsible)	Mortgage and house
Cash	Property taxes
Real estate (investment)	Car loan and car
Intellectual property (patents, copyrighted materials)	Credit cards
House as primary residence	
(only if used partially for business)	

self-reliant Household Economy and other non-market-based economies. For people who do not use their home partially for business, it's likely that, after deducting various expenses associated with its ownership (especially the mortgage), it may be considered more of a liability than asset, as explained later in this chapter. Despite the widespread home-is-great-investment myth, the primary purpose of a home for the vast majority of homeowners is the shelter it provides.

Caring Capitalism

Most Americans today have at least some savings invested in the stock market through Individual Retirement Accounts (IRAs), employer-sponsored retirement plans (401(k) plans) or, if self-employed already, through a Keogh retirement plan. Some investors own individual stocks or bonds while others invest in mutual funds offered by various investment firms. Facilitating investments that are consistent with social and ecological values, the socially responsible investment (SRI) movement has emerged, offering ways to invest in stocks, bonds and mutual funds that are screened on various criteria, including ecological impacts, workplace diversity and social responsibility. There can be either positive screens, rewarding progressive companies, for example, like those committed to offering solar electric systems, or negative screens whereby you can avoid companies that are known polluters, have exploitative labor practices or manufacture bombs. Two other aspects of SRI include shareholder activism, whereby you express your voice as a shareholder on key operational issues of the company, and community investing that support local investments, often in underserved areas of the country. Like voting with your purchase dollar, investing responsibly and actively can create positive changes and influence companies.

Most of our investments are in tangible property where we can invest in our Earth Mission: our organic farm and sustainably managed forest with a rental cabin. Some of our minimal savings are invested to create an SRI stock portfolio that yields dividend and capital gains income. Our financial wealth is based largely on the health of our property investments, used also for business purposes. We do not envision our so-called retirement as too different from our present life — except for a smaller garden.

Corporate scandals are commonplace today, with the demise of the Enron Corporation the most famous. It's hard to keep track of which company owns what. Thanks to scale and complexity, the larger the corporation, the more unlikely it can operate in ways that don't exploit people and nature. Besides the single-minded profit-maximization targets for shareholders, there's a growing trend of many large corporations to underfund their pension and healthcare accounts for their employees. Some corporations are using bankruptcy laws to absolve themselves (remember, in America a corporation is treated as a person)

Socially Responsible Investing Resources:

Investing with Your Values: Making Money and Making a Difference, Hal Brill, Jack A. Brill and Cliff Feigenbaum

Green Money Journal
Educating and empowering individuals and businesses to make informed financial decisions through aligning their personal, corporate and financial principles.
www.greenmoney.com

Sustainable Business.com
Providing global news and networking services to help green business grow. Rather than covering a slice of the industry, they offer a unique lens on the field as a whole, covering all sectors that impact sustainability: renewable energy and efficiency, green building, green investing and organics.
www.sustainablebusiness.com

from meeting pension and healthcare obligations, deferring such promises to the Pension Benefit Guarantee Corporation, a US government agency that insures private retirement accounts — which is likewise underfunded. These concerns and trends are buttressing the growth in socially responsible investing, since returns on investments are increasingly and positively correlated with returns on the environment and society.

Back to Small Business

Reacting to the above trends, more Americans are getting into business than ever before. Given the uncertainty and lack of transparency among corporations, social insecurity of Social Security and questionable long-term viability of Medicare, in addition to increased variability and unpredictability of climate change and other impacts wrought by ecosystem collapse and peak oil, the ecopreneurs we've talked with over the past decade are plotting a different course. We're weaving a new story, reinventing community and redefining wealth, basing it less on financial aspects and more on the intangibles and quality of life that matter most. Operating an ecopreneurial business becomes the puzzle piece that allows your personal finances and Household Economy to operate effectively in a state of balanced equilibrium, much like in a stable, balanced ecosystem.

A business needs some money to make money. For ecopreneurs, money is a tool to serve their Earth Mission. Many have discovered how little they need, balanced by how creative they are in their approach to financing start-up. Profits can be plowed back into the business to grow and enhance the enterprise or be reduced by expenses associated with offsetting carbon emissions, restoring the land or compensating vendors or employees beyond the "free market price" established for their services or products.

Financing Your Business

How much money you need to start your business depends on what type of business it is, how well you save money prior to launching it, how creative you are when incurring start-up expenses or your ability to tap funds from family members, a bank or the investment community. Hundreds of thousands of businesses can be started for less than $500; Apple Computer was started with less than $2,000. Select a business where you can use your knowledge, experiences, personal talents and, perhaps most important of all, your passions. The growing service sector — demanding far less investment than manufacturing that requires equipment — offers clear advantages to an upstart business offering services as opposed to making products. But outsourcing to specialty manufacturing or processing facilities is one way some companies avoid owning lots of equipment at first.

Most small businesses invest an immense amount of sweat equity — personal labor without pay — when launching the business. Instead of hiring painters for remodeling or contracting for Internet design services, ecopreneurs do it themselves, even if it takes a bit longer. Self-reliance and an agile do-it-yourself attitude, perhaps matched by an openness to working with mentors or other colleagues, goes a long way to balance the competitive playing field of the marketplace.

When funds are needed, some owners cash out of the stock market or sell off a few bonds. Others might spend several years of simple living and aggressive saving from an existing job to amass a down payment for a commercial building or funds for starting inventory in a retail store. Depending on your scale and scope of your operations, the following are several financing options.

Saving Up

The vast majority of small businesses start by drawing financial resources from owners' savings accounts or investments. For many early retirees or individuals who have started businesses later in life, most of their down payment or funds for merchandise come this way. In essence, the business owner acts like a bank by personally making a loan to the business. For example, we might loan our business about $20,000 at four percent interest to purchase various renewable energy systems and make capital improvements to one building used for business purposes. Every year, the business pays interest to us personally on that loan. Many of the ecopreneurs we've talked with are creative in how they choose to secure the necessary funds to launch their business, often in phases or while one person in the household maintains a steady job (and household cash flow) and the other devotes time and energy to start up the business.

Having just turned 30, we used our available savings when starting Inn Serendipity, accumulated from years of not frequenting fancy restaurants or bars with our friends. We started small with only two guest rooms in our bed and breakfast, setting aside one additional room in the farmhouse for the home office. Additionally, we selected a part of the country that offered affordable real estate (our $123,000 5.5 acre farmstead would have likely cost over a $1 million in California), which we bought with more than 20 percent down to avoid paying private mortgage insurance. Then we committed ourselves to several years of lean living, plowing any revenues back into building the business. Besides the mortgage — on which we aggressively pay down principal — and the loan to our business, we live debt free.

Borrowing from Family and Friends

While parents might seem like the best route for financing, approaching them can strain family relationships, not to mention the reality that one or more parent may not share the same enthusiasm for your enterprise. A parent can be a great source for a low-cost loan, but evaluate what would happen if the business falls behind on the loan payments. Consider going outside of your immediate family to more distant cousins or, better yet, friends who share your passion and interest in your business.

Leveraging Personal Assets: Refinancing, Home Equity and Credit Cards

In these credit card crazed days, many business owners finance their inventory or other expenses with their credit cards — in part, because it's so easy to do. Other ambitious entrepreneurs have refinanced their homes or took out a home equity loan. Consider these options for financing carefully, since doing so creates the same financial situation you were trying to escape from when earning income; this time your business is earning money for the banks.

Caring Customers

When your customers care about what you do and how you do it, sometimes they may even front you the money to make it happen. That's the wildly successful model of Community Supported Agriculture, or CSA (csacenter.org). Customers who are looking for healthy, fresh and seasonal fruits, vegetables and other agricultural products pay a fee to farmers in their area before the growing season begins. In return, the CSA subscriber receives a share of the harvest; a box, jam-packed with produce each week during the growing season, delivered to various drop-off points within the customer's community. Many established businesses are increasingly using their customer base, inviting them to reinvest in their expansion or help them develop a new product line. Angelic Organics (angelicorganics.com), among the nation's largest CSAs, invited their customers to become financial owners of the farm so the farmers can operate under a long-term farm-friendly lease and not be tied down as landowners. Other CSAs are set up as non-profit land conservation organizations, allowing foundations to support the work of the business. It's not unusual for professionals like marketing consultants, writers or attorneys to secure partial advance fees for work to be completed in the future. The completion of *ECOpreneuring* is based, in part, on an advance forwarded to us as authors by New Society Publishers, based on royalties to be earned after the book is published.

Vendors or Suppliers

Time can be used to your advantage if your vendors or suppliers might offer your business flexible terms for retail inventory or raw materials. Every time we accept a writing assignment but don't get paid until the article is printed, we are in essence making an interest-free loan to a magazine, which usually has already received partial or complete payment for advertising in the particular issue that includes our article. If you can secure terms that allow you to pay for inventory a month or two after you receive it, you are using the vendor as a bank. That's often why small businesses complete rather detailed credit application forms when

Capitalizing on Social Capitalism and Environmental Stewardship

Socially responsible venture capital firms or non-profit organizations serving the social VC market are growing throughout the country, many focusing on their bioregion. Below are a few of the more popular ones.

Good Capital

Good Capital is an investment firm that accelerates the flow of capital to innovative ventures and initiatives that harness the power of the market to create sustainable solutions to some of society's most challenging problems. Their initiatives and funds address a wide range of social issues including social enterprise financing, community and economic development, brownfield development and healthcare financing. These solutions include service businesses that hire and train disconnected youth, healthcare delivery systems that provide medical benefits to at-risk populations and they first form business-to-business relationships. Another approach, especially if you operate an Internet-based business, is to explore "drop-shipping" terms — heavily used by non-profit organizations with fundraising arms. The organization prints a catalog or places it online, accepts an order from their membership or supporters, then places the order with the vendor or supplier with the product shipped directly from the supplier. In many cases, customers don't realize that the organization or business never even took ownership of the item that was sold.

Bank Loans

Too often, entrepreneurs turn to the bank when in need of funds. Most banks require lots of documentation, collateral and can charge significant interest rates. Specialized community banks like credit unions or the ShoreBank based in Chicago might be able to offer more competitive loans. While there is a place for bank financing, circumnavigate the paperwork and process and avoid strapping your business with debt by exploring other less intrusive and formal forms of financing.

Angels and Venture Capital

Big ideas sometimes require funding beyond what you have in the bank account or are prepared to leverage with your home equity or value in your IRA. Attending conferences like the Business Alliance for Local Living Economies

Fair Trade coffee companies that provide access to US markets for marginalized farmers throughout the developing world. www.goodcap.net

Investors' Circle
A network of angel investors who seek financial, social and environmental returns on their investments. The Investors' Circle mission is to galvanize the flow of capital to entrepreneurial companies that enhance bioregional, cultural and economic health and diversity. www.investorscircle.net

Social Venture Network
This non-profit organization transforms the way the world does business by connecting, leveraging and promoting a global community of leaders for a more just and sustainable economy. www.svn.org

(livingeconomies.org) or Co-op America's Green Business Conference (coopamerica.org) might provide access to potential "angel investors," astute business people who thrive on helping companies start up. If your vision tends toward larger enterprises requiring millions of dollars, explore various venture capital (VC) forums for socially responsible investing. Sometimes it takes borrowed money to make money; try to secure this "good debt" from capitalists with a conscience.

Strategies of Abundance for Ecopreneurs

Nature tends to undergo the greatest innovation and breakthroughs when the greatest pressures or challenges impose themselves. The 21st century is posing numerous global and local issues, challenging the very premises upon which the free market economy is based. The following are business strategies for prospering during the storm of changes already emerging in the global and local marketplace. Since ecopreneurs often search for balance and meaning in their livelihood, expressed through their business, these strategies will be naturally paired with personal and household money matters.

Thrive on Natural Capital

Healthy soil provides our daily meals. Winds will blow, regardless of the raging political debate on the pros and cons of renewable energy. Ecopreneurs, by their very focus on enhancing, restoring or preserving natural and social capital through their business operations, will prosper in the emerging living economy. Implement The Natural Step framework, or use the Ecological Footprint analysis to guide

Lifestyle Migrating Ecopreneurs

Place-based enterprises thrive on creating a livelihood centered on where we want to live. Many ecopreneurs are becoming "lifestyle migrants," selecting areas of the country (or planet) best suited to providing or fostering a sustainable quality of life, healthy community and viable local economy rooted in restoring, preserving and enhancing nature. From eco-villages and cohousing to conservation developments, new approaches to living together in harmony with nature and each other are emerging. These include EcoVillage in Ithaca, New York, the Stelle community or Prairie Crossing in Illinois and Village Homes in Davis, California. Some of these forward-thinking communities are captured in the pages of *Finding Community* by Diana Leafe Christian or *EcoVillage at Ithaca* by Liz Walker.

   While some ecopreneurs are focusing on preserving places, others are leading the urban renewal movements in decaying cities or declining neighborhoods.

how, what, and where your business (and life) ebbs and flows. At Inn Serendipity, the more energy prices rise, the quicker our investments in renewable energy pay off. The more guests who experience a shower with solar-heated water, the more people who realize that a break from fossil fuel is not only possible, it's pleasurable.

KISS Principle: Keep It Small Stupid

While the mantra today might be get big or get out, be a millionnaire or — for the more socially responsible — "getting to scale" without losing the values the business was founded upon, we've discovered the more human-scaled our operations and practices, the more we can accomplish in terms of reaching our Earth Mission. Size matters not. It's what and how we operate. Do the best we can in whatever our priorities and live without regrets. It's a qualitative measure of success, not a quantitative one. Not bigger, but better. There's a small mart revolution going on, proclaims Michael Shuman in *The Small Mart Revolution*. It echoes the "power of one" worldview; we are the world. We don't underestimate what a nation of ecopreneurial proprietors might collectively accomplish. We also respect the decision of those ecopreneurs whose fire in their belly lead them to become household names or lead to the sustainable transformation of their communities.

Leverage the Local

A theme runs throughout this book: there's a lot to be said for a local economy that's largely about goods and services being exchanged among neighbors. A strong local economy can reduce shipping costs, exert fewer ecological impacts, offer greater social and community cohesion, result in more money circulated

Whether your business locates where there's a thriving art and culture scene or a college town boasting high-tech connectivity, a small town with abundant natural resources with community support to protect them or an urban neighborhood that is more self-reliant and green, ecopreneurs evaluate the long-term prospect that their business will provide a livelihood that enhances their community life and restores natural balance and health. To research how your property might be impacted by climate change and other environmental risks, you can plug in your address on Climate Appraisal's website (climateappraisal.com). Search NeighborhoodScout's website (neighborhoodscout.com) to locate more affordable areas less populated with McMansions and over-priced coffee.

within the community rather than being siphoned off to some distant place, provide a more stable economy with jobs less dependent on distant decision makers and therefore more secure, and provide a genuine ability to build mutual trust among community business owners.

> *Of three precious resources in life — time, money and creativity —*
> *the only unlimited one is your creativity. Make creativity your number one resource, and time and money won't be as scarce.*
>
> — Ernie J. Zelinski, *The Joy of Not Working*

Enough Is Enough

A key facet for many small business ecopreneurs is the recognition of living within our ecological and financial means. By exiting the rat race and crafting our own business at a level we can manage, we can commit ourselves to our Earth Mission. A key step, however, is to let go of the idea that we must own a new car or new stereo, go on lavish vacations or in myriad ways keep up with the fictional Joneses. Many Europeans have known this for years.

Real Wealth, Not Play Money

Appreciated assets like stocks or home value do not equal savings. As every investment prospectus states: Past performance may not be indicative of future returns. Money in the stock market is based on the wildly exuberant belief that the market will keep growing and that someone will want to buy your shares at roughly the price you want in the future. But stock shares are only worth the price of the last trade.

The same holds true when you consider your home as an investment. In reality, unless you're operating your own business from a home office or otherwise use your personal property for business purposes, most homes incur numerous expenses — like a new roof, repairing a leaky basement and property taxes — little or no positive cash flow and rather high transaction fees, assuming you sell when the housing market is up and use a real estate agent. Residential homes may not even offer good returns on your investment after the cost of the principal and interest of a mortgage, insurance, adjustment for inflation and other expenses are factored in, according to the Standard and Poor National Home Price Index that represents actual appreciation of the same house over time. Unless you're using your home in part for business, its key value is as a dwelling. As for stock market appreciation, your bet is as good as ours when the market tops out.

Many ecopreneurs we know measure net worth by their health, quality of life and in various other non-financial ways, though they comply with the IRS and pay other financial obligations. Many things in life can't be purchased, no matter how much money you have: good health, friends, family and community.

Opting Out of the Credit and Debt Economy

The home mortgage is the largest single debt for most people. A mortgage is a legal document in the form of a secured loan; the bank offers money at a specified interest rate for a property, and if the homeowner defaults on repaying the loan, the bank has the right to foreclose on the property. The mortgage creates a claim, or lien, on your property until you pay it off. Often, what we can afford for a property is confused by what our monthly mortgage payment is versus what we should actually be able to afford, based on our livelihood and lifestyle. It's easy to get in over your head, or become entrapped for 30 years, working to pay the bank.

But why pay double what something is worth? That's what we do when we buy a home and finance it with a mortgage. The true cost of our $123,000 farmstead — with 20 percent down to avoid having to pay private mortgage insurance and $98,200 in a 30-year fixed-rate mortgage at 8.55 percent — is a staggering $272,368, of which $174,168 is in interest (finance charges). If you think your house is such a great investment, try selling it for more than what you paid in principal and interest, plus taxes, maintenance and repair expenses.

Stop Paying the Banker

The longer you hold a mortgage, the more you work for the bank and the more profitable you make them. For comparison, below is a chart reflecting how interest can pile up on a $100,000 mortgage at 7 percent interest for terms of 15 and 30 years. While the monthly payment is less for the 30-year mortgage (the primary reason many of us choose it), we end up paying more than double for the use of the same pot of money.

By accelerating our mortgage payments on our 30-year fixed mortgage by paying down the principal when we could, we have the ability to earn less income

The True Cost of Money: Mortgage Term Comparison

	15-Year Mortgage	30-Year Mortgage
Monthly payment	$899	$665
Number of payments	180	360
Total paid during mortgage term	$161,820	$239,400
Principal paid	$100,000	$100,000
Interest paid	$61,820	$139,400

to pay the bank than if we did otherwise over the long-term. Prepayment on principal is usually acceptable and completely legal. Every time you pay down the principal, the remaining interest and balance is recalculated, meaning that more of your regular monthly payments go to the principal and not interest payments.

For example, in our very first homeowner mortgage payment of $722, only $7 went to principal and the remaining $715 went to finance charges. After the interest rates plummeted in the early 2000s, we refinanced the 30-year mortgage when we were able to secure a significantly lower interest rate, reducing the monthly payment to $653. Ten years later, after we realized just how much we were working for the bank and were well into our accelerated paydown of the principal, $610 of our monthly mortgage payment went to principal and $45 to interest. We paid off our farmhouse mortgage about two decades early, saving the need to earn about $95,000 in future income and freeing us to focus on the issues we cared about most, not making already profitable bankers wealthier.

Below is a simple, abbreviated amortization schedule that makes it compellingly clear that the bank owns your house for many years before you have much equity (paid-off principal). By the end of this mortgage, your $100,000 actually ends up costing you $239,508.

As Rob Roy, author of *Mortgage Free: Radical Strategies for Home Ownership*, says, "If there is any question as to who owns your house, stop making your mortgage payment." He, and we, suggests owning the house without the bank owning it for you. After all, the word "mortgage" is from the Old French, *mort gage*, or "death pledge." We agree with Roy that prepayment of your mortgage is among the best investments you can make, the quicker the better.

Mortgage amount: $100,000
Monthly payment: $665.30
30-year fixed-rate mortgage at 7 percent
(12 payments/year x 30 years = 360 payments)

	Principal	Interest	Remaining Balance
Payment 1	$81.97	$583.33	$99,918.03
Payment 2	$82.45	$582.86	$99,835.58
...			
Payment 242	$332.32	$332.98	$56,301.12
			(Break-even point, after 21 years.)
...			
Payment 360	$3.86	$661.44	$0

Source: www.calculator-loan.info

Those who argue for the mortgage interest deduction benefit of holding a mortgage, they must regularly itemize their federal income tax return. If, on the other hand, you do not itemize deductions and take the standard deduction on your federal income tax return, having a mortgage serves no taxation benefit. For most Americans, you will come out ahead paying off the mortgage rather than saving a few dollars on your federal income taxes. Mortgage interest, however, may help reduce your taxable burden on investment property where you have rental income. A CPA and tax advisor can offer professional guidance.

Dumping debt also applies to credit cards, college or car loans and other consumer loans. Just one credit card debt with a balance of $15,000 and a monthly minimum payment of $300 based on an interest rate of 13 percent would take nearly 20 years to pay off, amounting to nearly $9,000 in interest, according to the website Cardweb.com. What good are contributions to a 401(k) with a stock portfolio earning 10 percent a year when you're paying credit card debt at 16 percent? The same holds true for vehicle financing, especially if the financing offered is stretched over six years. Recent college grads don't set out to be poor savers. On average, they're saddled with a median undergraduate student loan debt of over $19,000.

Take Your Business Deductions

Mind your business and take all the deductible business expenses permissible by law and tax code, as discussed in chapter 6.

Credit Worthiness

Know your personal FICO credit score, typically between 300 and 850. This credit score determined by Fair Isaac Corporation (FICO) largely determines how much money your credit card company will extend as credit, the interest rate at which you can lock in your mortgage, what rate you receive for home and vehicle insurance and other variables that can increase or decrease your expenses. The FICO score is based on statistical analysis of your credit history, kept by three very large corporations, Equifax, TransUnion and Experian. Make sure this score is calculated on accurate information by requesting a free credit report, based on the federal Fair and Accurate Credit Transactions Act, from these three companies through annualcreditreport.com. Call 877-322-8228 or mail a standardized form to Annual Credit Report Request Service, PO Box 105281, Atlanta, GA 30348-5281. Build good credit by never missing a mortgage or credit card payment and paying off your credit card balance every month.

> *Being frugal is the cornerstone of wealth-building.*
>
> — Thomas Stanley and William Danko,
> *The Millionnaire Next Door*

Green Fitness through Efficiency, Eco-effectiveness and Frugality

Efficiency, eco-effectiveness and frugality are like muscles needing constant training to be strong and fit. Creativity fosters green frugality. This muscle needs to be strong since it's continually tested by outside forces, including mainstream media (Buy this!) and even members of your family who fail to recognize the significance of today's pressing and interconnected issues. Many Americans have succumbed to attention deficit disorder every time we complain about rising energy prices, broken families and poor health. Those businesses that pay attention are reaping financial and ecological benefits, while other businesses are forced to shutter their doors.

> *The greatest security is not in having the most, but in needing the least.*
>
> — Charles Long, *How to Survive Without a Salary*

An Affordable, Purpose-Driven Life

In chapter 4, we presented a table summarizing why an average American cannot keep up with the bills. The Average Household Expenses table reflects what an average America household might spend in a given year, including food, transportation and healthcare, compared to a small household minding their own business. It's no wonder that about 40 percent of Americans spend more than they earn each year, according to the Motley Fool Credit Center, American Consumer Credit Counseling, Bankrate.com and Debtsmart.com. Owning your own business and living below your means might be a better way to live.

In an average year, we sock away about $5,000 and use those funds to pay down our mortgages, invest in income-producing assets or make property improvements that immediately save us money, like energy conservation measures. We don't save for the future. Rather, our net savings are invested for the future. We do not set aside money for our son's college in a 529 Plan or a special tax deferred educational IRA because it'd be invested in the stock market. First, we do not know if he'll even want to go to college. Secondly, we're uncertain as to the long-term reliability of the stock market in meeting his or our needs when we can no longer enjoy our livelihood for whatever reasons. So for our retirement, we tend to see leveraging the equity that we've built up in our two properties if we haven't invested sufficiently enough in other projects that generate passive income, possibly taking out a reverse mortgage where a bank pays us for a portion of the equity we've built up in our home.

Many ecopreneurs, largely due to their human-scaled enterprises, are keen observers, innovative problem-solvers and holistic and systematic in their approach to operating their business. They're also wise with their personal finances, giving

Average Household Expenses

Household Expenses	Est. Avg. US HH Annual Expenses ($)	"Living within Means" HH Annual Expenses ($) and Rationale	
Federal income taxes	16,000	82	own small business
State income taxes	1,500	0	better, not bigger
Avg. min. balance on credit card to Bank 1	300	0	worse than death pledge
Mortgage payment to Bank 2	10,000	7,844	try to pay it off
Private mortgage insurance (PMI)	840	0	profits for BIG insurance
Car loan payment to Bank 3	5,748	0	buy used
Property taxes	2,385	3,000	variable by locale
Car insurance	847	589	metro areas cost more
House or property insurance	481	674	size and location
Healthcare (premiums and uncovered)	10,880	1,393	explore working family policy
Food			
At home	3,297	400	grow your own
Away from home	2,634	35	eat only when for business
Apparel and services	1,886	300	gift, thrift, second-hand
Transportation	8,344	400	stop driving; buy used
Entertainment	2,388	200	sunsets are free
Personal insurance and pension	5,204	0	why retire?
Other expenditures	4,823	500	needs, not wants
Total expenses	77,557	15,417	
Average US salary	58,712	20,000	rent & passive income
Net savings	(18,845)	5,417	

Source: Adapted from US Department of Labor Consumer Expenditures 2005; 2005/2006 data found on Bankrate.com, Edmunds.com, Insurance Information Institute, Mortgage Insurance Companies of America, Center on Budget and Policies Priorities, 2006 Parade magazine.

them the freedom, flexibility and financial resources to make their dreams come true.

Financial aspects of business, while essential to master, are not the focus for most ecopreneurs, many of whom determine that lifestyle, ecological or social issues override the profit motive that dominates other businesses. Ironically, the marketplace is beginning to recognize green businesses that operate more efficiently, adapt more quickly to change, approach customers and vendors more cooperatively and fairly end up earning a greater return for both the environment and investment made.

The next chapter will explore new realities of marketing your ecopreneurial business to values-driven customers.

Chapter 8

Purpose-based Marketing

Selling your products or services to the surging green marketplace starts with an understanding that people are not merely "consumers" — they're conserving customers, people with shared values, citizens who care about and accept responsibility for the state of the Earth. This growing global awareness has spawned companies and citizens searching for ways to exist without destroying the very life-support systems on which we all depend. Marketing for ecopreneurs has roots in creative and fresh approaches to communicating values, far beyond brand and image. As an example, the triple bottom line business T-shirt maker T. S. Designs lets you wear your values on your sleeve with a tangible product that reflects these values.

Value-based marketing aligns with our innate yearning to educate ourselves and feel positive about our contribution to society. Ecopreneurs strive to openly communicate information and educate people about their product or services, making connections that help their customers grow as individuals. Contrary to standard marketing tactics of driving people to feel inadequate or deficient, or spur purchases out of fear, angst or guilt, marketing for ecopreneurial businesses is about communicating abundance, clean air and water and Fair Trade products that help people, not exploit them. Marketing is about weaving authentic positive stories about positive futures, providing products or services that serve customers and help restore, enhance, protect or in myriad other ways make the world a better place.

There's no escaping it, being in business means you're selling something. But when your business and your customers share values and passions, the whole "selling" process takes on a different meaning. "Selling" transforms into "communicating," an exchange of information with a product or service that helps meet their needs without destroying or exploiting the planet in the process. Ecopreneurial businesses tell their story. Instead of hiding behind board room doors like leaders of many multinational corporations, small business owners put their whole life story on the Internet and invite customers to strike up conversations. By focusing on this rapidly growing green marketplace, marketing morphs into meaningful relationships with conserving customers who care as much about the planet as you do. This marketing is accomplished with refreshing transparency that would make most Fortune 500 board of directors balk in disbelief and apprehension.

Two key terms often pop up to describe this emerging green market: Cultural Creatives, your core customers, and Lifestyles of Health and Sustainability (LOHAS), the segment of the broader marketplace that reflects the values and priorities that foster a healthy, sustainable planet. After all, you don't need to sell to every person on the planet to be profitable. Many buy-local ecopreneurs have discovered it is immensely satisfying and profitable enough to offer goods or services to their neighbors.

Cultural Creatives

Coined by sociologist Paul H. Ray and psychologist Sherry Ruth Anderson and presented in their book, *The Cultural Creatives: How 50 Million People Are Changing the World* (culturalcreatives.org), the term Cultural Creatives describes a large segment of adult Americans — slightly over one quarter of the adult population — disenchanted with materialism and the status quo. The name "Cultural Creative" evolved because this group of people is creating a new culture and crafting fresh approaches to living a more sustainable lifestyle. Cultural Creatives defy demographics and instead are best reflected by their values, beliefs and behaviors.

Ray and Anderson point out that Cultural Creatives were once largely invisible to mainstream media, which tended to focus on the worldview reflected by the dominant culture of the Moderns, around since the Renaissance. The Moderns are keen on reshaping the environment through science and technology and increasingly using financial wealth and materialistic consumption as a way of defining success in the increasingly urban and industrialized society. If former President Bill Clinton were more of a Cultural Creative and less of a Modern, he would most likely have quipped: "It's the environment, stupid." Instead, he focused on the economy. In addition to the Cultural Creatives and the Moderns, the third cultural segment of our society, say Ray and Anderson, are the Traditionals. With numbers dwindling, the Traditionals often live in rural areas and focus on family, church and community.

The Lifestyles of Health and Sustainability Marketplace

Cultural Creatives continue to increase in economic power and impact, resulting in the industry-dubbed Lifestyles of Health and Sustainability (LOHAS), estimated at over \$227 billion in the United States alone. Stemming from their Cultural Creative roots, LOHAS customers are passionate about making our world a better place, focusing on health, the environment, social justice, personal development and sustainable living. We first described the LOHAS marketplace in chapter 3 when discussing sustainable businesses, exploring the types of enterprises best suited to serve these conserving customers. A detailed analysis of several groups of this segment can be found in Harvey Hartman and David Wright's *Marketing to the New Natural Consumer*, which summarizes research conducted by The Hartman Group.

According to The Natural Marketing Institute, the LOHAS marketplace includes goods and services that fall into five key market segments, ranked by size of the LOHAS market: ecological lifestyles (35 percent); sustainable economy (33 percent); alternative healthcare (13 percent); healthy lifestyles (13 percent); personal development (5 percent).

With a general understanding of trends and a rapidly growing LOHAS marketplace, next we'll address how to communicate with your most promising customers by examining the 7 Ps of marketing.

The 7 Ps of Marketing

Most marketing textbooks usually harp on 4 Ps of marketing: Product, Price, Place (distribution) and Promotion (advertising and public relations). An ecopreneurial approach to marketing adds 3 Ps: People, Partnerships and Purpose. The intersection of the 7 Ps determines your target market, reaching the customers most likely to purchase your goods or services in a large enough quantity at the price you've determined will allow your business to prosper.

A marketing plan that addresses the 7 Ps, usually including financial investments, is encapsulated as a section of your business plan. After determining your 7 Ps, create an umbrella mission statement that guides all marketing related to the business, typically followed by clearly defined objectives with a variety of measures, the most obvious one being sales. When developing your marketing mix and making decisions related to your 7 Ps, keep in mind your values and explain your product or service in language that you, yourself, respond to — your voice, so to speak. From your customers' perspectives, what are your product's benefits to them, not just the features of what you have to sell? Avoid being everything to everyone. We often redirect potential guests who are not in our target market because we're not offering the experience they're looking for. You won't find us freelancing writing about the benefits of "clean coal" or photographing a NASCAR race. We're not about heads on beds any more than we are about new client acquisitions. Know your limits, talents and skills and market those. Honest marketers. Imagine that?

We often do marketing consulting for various clients, including non-profit organizations. Although often overlooked, this is just as important for non-profit organizations as it is for other businesses. Having a great mission and purpose means little if you fail to market the services your organization provides or explain what problems it solves — and why it matters. That's one reason why you hear national charitable foundations sponsoring National Public Radio — they're sharing their story.

Product (or Service)

What makes your product or service unique and how does it relate to customer needs? Product quality, functionality, brand name, style and warranty are among the issues you might consider. Ecopreneurs also pay particular attention to products that don't harm the environment in their manufacture or use. Besides repairs or the ability to be recycled or recharged, how the product is disposed of at the end of its lifespan is a key variable. For the best green products, there is no waste or disposal.

Many products may serve multiple needs. A product or service may make a public statement on that person's values and priorities, often going beyond function, form or features. A quality product may represent how it contributes to the quality of life for all life. Purchasing Fair Trade certified, organic shade-grown coffee fulfills a much different need than instant coffee in a metal can for someone seeking a caffeinated beverage to start the day. The customer drinking shade-grown coffee wants to feel good about their choice, knowing their purchase dollar respected the environment where the coffee was grown, workers were treated fairly and equitably and the harvests didn't adversely affect populations of songbirds that might frequent the forests under which the coffee plants thrive.

For Cultural Creatives, no detail is too small to question. For example, excessive or obnoxious packaging — gratuitous marketing that possibly scores points amongst other target groups — may work against you in attracting ecologically minded customers. It provides creative opportunity to craft an eye-catching and unique package using recycled content, but few resources. Products come out daily that are biologically based and decompose naturally, like corn-based disposable dishware and utensils. We seek out stores, services, vendors or suppliers that echo our values and can provide products that are consistent with our marketing image.

Price

How do you price your product or service? With their growing understanding of the ecological impacts of certain products and the processes that go into more sustainably made products, customers stand willing to pay a premium for products like organic food, sustainably harvested FSC-certified hardwood flooring or Fair Trade certified chocolate. Travelers choose lodging based on the value reflected by the business's commitment to the environment. As discussed previously, sales are growing by double digits for organic foods, green building products, renewable energy and ecotourism, just to name a few industries.

Rather than discounting or competing on price with the mainstream market, it often proves more beneficial to add on a little extra to build customer loyalty. Many ecopreneurs allocate a portion of profits, typically ten percent, as donations to non-profit causes or purchasing carbon offsets to operate carbon neutral, explaining their practices on their website, product packaging or in other communications with their customers. Pricing decisions are determined by how you sell your products, retail or wholesale, which is related to the next P, Place. Pricing can include discounts of various kinds. At Inn Serendipity, for example, we welcome families with young children (a bit unusual for B & Bs). To make it more affordable to parents, we offer a discounted family rate for the whole second floor.

Place (Distribution)

Place refers to how you get your product or service to your customers. From distribution channels (direct, wholesale, retail and distributor) and order processing to inventory management and transportation, place considerations can play a big role in ecopreneurial businesses if they leverage the power of the increased interest in buying local or sourcing from the bioregion. How can these products or services be offered that serve the needs of our community, instead of things shipped from halfway around the world? Aware of global issues, many ecopreneurs localize their operations while restoring the planet. A resurgence in homegrown foods, fuel and even construction materials offers direct marketing opportunities for ecopreneurs, often leveraging the Internet and making more profit by eliminating an intermediary distributor.

Joel Salatin, an innovative and renowned Virginia farmer, broke conventional distribution rules. His goal for his business, Polyface, Inc., was not to get his sustainably raised chicken and meats into the coveted East Coast retail market. Instead, he self-proclaimed a local focus on building personal relationships, selling direct to customers from his farm through buying clubs, bypassing traditional wholesale distribution and pricing. "The buying clubs," Salatin tells us, "are really nothing more than refinements of the mushrooming Community Supported Agriculture (CSA) movement. The clubs make transportation — a real challenge for farmers to get their product to market — pay for itself through the volume of sales." Buying clubs are groups of customers in a specific geographic location who pool their retail orders into one order every couple months. Polyface's customer base includes about 400 individuals, 30 restaurants, 7 drop points for buyer clubs, and 5 stands at farmers' markets in Washington DC and Arlington, Virginia.

When acclaimed writer Michael Pollan asked Salatin to send him samples of his products for a book he was researching, Joel stuck to his local commitment and flat out said no — hardly following standard practice of schmoozing up to media requests on the hope of good, free PR. Per Salatin, Polyface just sells local; if Pollan wanted to sample some of their wares he would have to visit the farm. And so Pollan did, resulting in a lengthy and personable section in his acclaimed book, *The Omnivore's Dilemma: A Natural History of Four Meals*, and generating a wealth of positive PR for Salatin's family business.

Promotion (Advertising and Public Relations)

Promotion is what most of us think about as marketing, the applied art form of persuasive communication by graphics, words and such to help sell products. Creative, innovative thinking thrives through your approach to promotion, communicating information — telling the story about your business — that leads to customers patronizing your business. Marketers often refer to brand as the embodiment of your product or service in the form of your name, logo, slogan and other design aspects. The goal, of course, is to devise communications that help your customers understand and remember what your business is about. While multinational corporations spend millions on developing their brand, you can do it with almost no money at all — by harnessing the power of the Internet and a home computer along with your own creativity.

Included in promotion is both purchased advertising and solicited or unsolicited free publicity related to public relations (PR) efforts. The smaller the business, the less you'll need to focus on paying for traditional advertising in media like magazines or newspapers and the more you might want to focus on public relations efforts since PR involves time more than money. Promotion decisions include developing a sense of what your company offers with words, graphics and other communicative elements that reinforce what your business offers. These elements often include your logo, product slogan and unifying colors, styles, themes and images expressing what you do, for whom and why it matters. They position you in the marketplace and define how your marketing efforts unfold.

In the spirit of the barter economy, exchanging your goods or services for an advertising opportunity proves to be a double win — garnering exposure while promoting your business. Publications, particularly regional or non-profit newsletters, can be open to creating a giveaway of your product or services (perhaps as an incentive for renewals) in exchange for a "free" publication advertisement, garnering conventional advertising exposure through an unconventional means.

Public relations represents your reputation, what you and the public say about your business. The growing interest in the green arena provides a double-edged sword for ecopreneur upstarts. On one level, snowballing interest in sustainable business and environmental issues means the media is more educated and savvy on green. However, simply the fact that your business is powered by renewable energy is no longer enough. When we first started over a decade ago, we garnered media interest because we uniquely focused on natural building and energy conservation. Then the local television news crew came to film the commissioning of our residential wind turbine. That event alone may not warrant interest today, unless we add a fresh angle to the story.

Some tips for generating media interest include:

Determine your media goals. While the adage of "There's no such thing as bad publicity" genuinely remains true, think strategically about what audience you want to attract, based on your business needs.

- *Local:* Attract customers from your immediate area. Business examples include retail stores and restaurants.
- *Regional:* Attract customers from accessible driving distance. Business examples include B & Bs and seasonal recreation.
- *National/international:* Attract customers purchasing your product nationally or globally. Business examples include mail-order online businesses or freelance writing or consulting.

While public relations goals can overlap — a local-food-based restaurant can evolve into a regional tourist destination — think of your goals so that you can best target the publication or media outlet relevant to your business and the message you're trying to convey. When *Newsweek* magazine included Inn Serendipity in an article profiling people who ditched lucrative corporate careers for more fulfilling livelihoods, the piece generated only a night stay by only one reader. But after we were mentioned in the newsletter of an area retail food cooperative, a targeted group of people interested in sustainable living and eating healthy, our phone started ringing. No complaints on the *Newsweek* piece; it helped establish us as a business since we could use the line, "As featured in *Newsweek*." But regional, targeted efforts in media that are read by Cultural Creatives brought more business. To be an effective marketer, you need to know what you are and who you want to reach.

Tie into a national story or event. While the green story angle alone is no longer novel, tying into a national current issue promotes your business while staying relevant to the media. With rising oil prices, issue a press release on the amount of fossil fuel your business saves by running on renewable energy. On Earth Day (April 22) — a day the media looks for environmental stories — provide your list of the top ten ways you help the planet. We garnered media interest playing off the Independence Day idea by demonstrating how we live largely fossil fuel free, a fresh approach to the Fourth of July when the media feels obligated to cover the holiday but are searching for new twists to the usual picnic and fireworks story.

Create a press room. Make it easy for the media to access your story by creating a "press room," easily identifiable on your website, creating one-stop shopping for potential media. Include a basic fact sheet, archived press releases or previous articles and contact information. Add a message stating "photos available" and have an inventory of high-resolution digital photos you can email to interested media to use for free.

Through our partnership with Renewing the Countryside, we created a jam-packed public relations resource kit available for free download through our ECOpreneuring website (ecopreneuring.biz); while the PR resource kit is designed for rural entrepreneurs, the ideas are relevant for any business anywhere.

People

Products and services are for people. Examined by the marketing research firm Strategic Horizons, founded by Joe Pine and Jim Gilmore, and captured in their book, *The Experience Economy: Work Is Theatre and Every Business Is a Stage*, "experiences are as distinct from services as services are from goods." It's this trust and respect earned from your business as it contributes to restoration while prospering in a living economy that will allow it to differentiate itself from the competition. You and your employees, if you have them, determine the experience your customers may have. Interactions with customers move beyond "transaction" relationships, seeking to establish unique, emotional and uncommon experiences on the part of individual customers. Hands-on workshops, learning or service holidays like Elderhostel or spa retreats all tap this transformational marketing trend. Next time you visit a farmers' market, you'll notice the relationships and bonds between farmers and their customers who will eat the food they grew. Many who frequent farmers' markets are getting their fill of friendship, ecological connections to the land and a sense of hope and optimism for the future — far more than potatoes and peapods.

From the first telephone call to the delivery of a product or service, how ecoprenuerial businesses interact and form relationships with their customers solidify their position in the market. Many companies or organizations we've consulted for or interviewed use the 80-20 rule to help prioritize their marketing efforts and focus on building long-term relationships and loyalty among a select group of customers. Practical experience has led many ecopreneurs to observe that about 80 percent of their sales come from only 20 percent of their customers. Covet the 20 percent, doing everything possible to keep them happy, since they're the ones that are repeat customers, big on referrals or ordering gift certificates for friends and family.

Ecopreneurs, in part due to their relationships with their customers, can let their customers do the selling through unpaid, impartial third-party endorsements. Customer referrals remain the most powerful form of unpaid advertising. While not an expense line item on your marketing budget spreadsheet, the believability of the words of a satisfied customer crafts a long-lasting message about you and your business's reputation. Ask enthusiastic customers for an endorsement quote to use on your brochure or website; don't be surprised when many blog about you. One of ours created an online photo scrapbook from their stay at Inn Serendipity. Handwriting a thank-you note to a customer who referred a friend adds a lasting impact for the price of a stamp. In our world of rapid technology, a personal touch goes a long way. Think of your customers who make referrals or recommendations as your zero-emissions advertising agency.

Provide opportunities for your customers to involve their friends and colleagues through second-tier educational referrals, with one caveat: You may need to magnify the education you provide to this group of people. Often, your loyal customers will use a second-tier educational referral as a gift to get a family member or associate exposed to and onto the green bandwagon. A thoughtful gesture, but this group may not have the same education and enthusiasm as your core customers. For example, we've sold a number of B & B gift certificates to adult children as gifts for their more elderly parents, with the aim of getting their parents introduced to a more sustainable lifestyle. Many times this may be the parents' first exposure to a B & B or renewable energy systems, so we've learned

Second-tier Educational Referral

What happens when one of your customers feels so loyal and passionate about your business and shares your values that they stand moved to purchase products or services for gifts or silent auction donations to the non-profit groups they support? These second-tier purchases represent the customer's desire to educate, to use your business as a platform for reaching out with your message. This represents a highly lucrative form of advertising, providing both immediate financial support and long-term advertising for your business.

to provide lots of additional information during our discussions over the phone prior to their arrival, since we do not have in-room TVs or air conditioning.

Relationship and experiential marketing with conserving customers may not appeal to a segment of the population that has yet to understand the magnitude of the changes taking place across our culture. They may not respond to the culture of agriculture found at farmers' markets, or at Inn Serendipity, for example. We need to carefully craft our story to reach those who most likely share our values and concerns, otherwise a transaction might occur that leaves both parties drained or disappointed.

Partnerships (Networking) and Cause-related Marketing

Partnerships and synergistic relationships — ecological and social networks and connections among like-minded businesses — are magnified by ecopreneurs. By steering away from traditional paid advertising outlets — and thereby saving money — you form strategic partnerships that open new doors to connect with your target audience. When dollars do exchange, like when your business makes a donation or takes out a membership with a non-profit organization — the money goes directly to furthering your shared mission.

Ecopreneurs thrive on connections with like-minded organizations, sending customers to each other. For example, Inn Serendipity often refers guests to Co-op America as a great starter resource for green living information. Co-op America featured our small Inn in their quarterly newsletter. By joining with non-profit organizations or various causes to help advertise a product or service, businesses participate in what is now called cause-related marketing, benefiting both the charity or organization and your business. You cultivate relationships that echo your values, reinforce your business's commitment to social or environmental issues and connect with people who share your interests, passions and sense of purpose. Rather than making donations, with cause-related marketing you create meaningful relationships that help serve the organization with which you partner. This mutually beneficial relationship is particularly salient to the nanocorp or micro-enterprise, since it offers the ability to comingle with much larger businesses that might be trying to improve their brand image.

Whatever your focus, there's a non-profit group out there with like-minded members. These groups often seek speakers for various events. Why not let it be you. Be sure to ask if they have an honorarium for speakers or are able to cover mileage and travel expenses. We donated use of the farm for our local women's club fundraiser garden walk and for the Midwest Renewable Energy Association's (MREA) education workshops. This latter involvement provided in-kind labor for renewable energy systems such as our wind turbine (we still paid for the equipment), offered a needed service to the MREA, garnered local media interest (we hosted an educational open house during the workshop) and attracted new people to the farm through these events.

In part because of their social or ecological approach, small businesses are continually hit up for donations to various non-profit silent auctions. Rather than contribute only to then be lost on a list of donors, seek out donation opportunities where you have a visible presence. We limit our donations to events where we present a workshop or have an informational booth. By explaining this approach to groups soliciting donations in this manner, we often generate future invitations to speak, balanced by our need to decide which donation requests to accommodate, since we can't give to them all. Ecopreneurs still need to make some money, too.

Purpose (and Passion)

An ecopreneur's purpose and passion for a sustainable enterprise does what the multinational corporations can never do to the same degree: Communicate honestly, openly and authentically. Everything is personal. When you buy something from a small business, you are often buying it from a friend, neighbor or community member. Consequences for the planet and the seventh generation guide decisions, not quarterly shareholder earnings statements. Capitalize on this idea, wear your business heart on your sleeve and feel satisfied at the end of the day.

Purpose-based marketing provides the ultimate in competitive advantage for small businesses; the bigger the operation, the less likely it can maintain its values throughout the company or organization. Only the most forward-thinking ecopreneurial companies, those that view their employees as family, grow larger without losing the ability to capture the sense of purpose and passion throughout the company.

Tips on nurturing purpose and passion in business include:

Know your elevator pitch

An elevator pitch consists of a brief "speech" that succinctly describes your business, something you might say to a stranger chatting with you in an elevator. The most successful ecopreneurs are those who conceived an idea and could express their passion for their product or service in a way that others could readily understand and support. The elevator pitch is both the "what" you do and the "why," as shown in the sample elevator pitch below.

> All in Play creates software that empowers the blind and visually impaired to socialize with their friends and loved ones: unhandicapped and as equals. Imagine how your life might become suddenly different if you or a loved one went blind tomorrow. The vast majority of social and recreational activities

Purpose-based Marketing

The ecopreneur marketing core, Purpose-based Marketing (PBM), fosters the idea that when you pursue a livelihood and business that reflect your values of wanting to change the world your enthusiasm and passion will prove to be your most compelling message. Most advertising we helped create over a decade ago sold the sizzle, not the steak. We sometimes dazzled with lots of information in the ads, but they lacked meaning. Other times, we tore at emotions with barely a glimpse of what we were actually selling. When was the last time you watched a TV ad that left you wondering what, exactly, was for sale? PBM seeks to clarify, crystallize and authenticate. For example, if you're selling organic food raised humanely by family farmers, ads would feature the actual family farmers who produced it. Bet you can name the brand.

Marketing plans need updates. So does PBM. Reinvigorating your PBM comes from keeping up your own energy and enthusiasm for your livelihood. Methods include networking with like-minded people, organizations or businesses. Find places where you can meet and interact with similarly spirited souls. Contagious enthusiasm blended with new insights will prove to be inspiring. This situation regularly erupts at Inn Serendipity while hanging out with our B & B guests. Their vocal

that we take for granted every day would become difficult or impossible. Since 2002 All in Play's website and suite of online games have allowed the blind to reconnect with their friends and loved ones in such a way that no one can even tell who's blind and who's sighted.

— www.allinplay.com

Get naked

Ecopreneurs necessitate transparency, a level of personal exposure and scrutiny not present in mainstream business. Ecopreneurs cannot live one set of green values during working hours and power down at fast-food joints off the clock. The green lifestyle pulses with your purpose and passion; it's not a burden but a blessing as we write about in *Rural Renaissance*. Everything is interconnected. This is one reason why more and more ecopreneurs are thriving as lifestyle entrepreneurs. This lifestyle creates a mentality of daily mindfulness: How energy efficient is your home? What did you eat for lunch? Where did your children's toys come from? The goal remains in the journey, continually questioning ourselves and challenging us to stretch out of our comfort zones and improve, while living our dream rather than just dreaming about it.

support of what we're doing — along with sharing their experiences on anything from making biodiesel to basil recipes — keeps our passion stoked. The feeling is mutual. Many of our guests depart with new ideas or next steps for securing their own grant for a solar electric system. For one couple, we helped set them up with a used solar thermal system.

Travel and getting away take on new meaning for the passion-fueled ecopreneur. Back in our corporate days, we scurried away vacation days and counted the hours till we could check out on holiday, desperate to veg out on the beach with no thought of work. But when passion and livelihood blend, there is less of a need to check out. When you love what you do, why leave it? Still, travel plays a role in providing new experiences to keep our passions stimulated. Options for such travel open up, involving off-the-beaten-path spots like small-town cafés, hiking paths and family-owned ethnic restaurants sizzling in flavors. Test drive your dream job through Vocation Vacations (vocationvacations.com), go on a volunteer vacation with EarthWatch (earthwatch.org) or Global Volunteers (globalvolunteers.org) or apprentice with a business that is operating in ways you'd like to emulate.

Question each other

Like a ping-pong ball, challenging questions should banter back and forth between ecopreneurs and their customers. Positive in nature, such exchanges stem from the idea that passion should never stagnate. We encourage this when we give B & B guests a farm tour. Likewise, guests open up to us, questioning our decisions and asking our perspective on theirs. Could I trade in my SUV for a hybrid car? Is there a CSA near me? The key to questioning each other remains an accepting, open exchange between two sides hungry for knowledge.

With an innovative tool kit of approaches, ecopreneuring moves marketing into new realms, forging passion with purpose — resulting in business as unusual. In chapter 9, we explore more in detail technology's effect on and potential for your business.

Part Three

Web of Relationships

Chapter 9

Technology, Information and the New Global Commons

WANDER THROUGH JUST ABOUT ANY RETAILER, and while you may not see it sitting on the shelf, the key commodity for sale is oil. From producing the raw materials to manufacturing the actual product to shipping it cross-country or around the world, we live in a marketplace based on fossil fuel consumption. But do the math: relying on economic systems addicted to something that is in increasingly short supply will not work long-term. Eventually, supplies will dry up or be so expensive that this model will collapse. Just about every form of non-renewable energy (oil, natural gas, electricity from coal-fired power plants) is getting more expensive. While we're not going to run out tomorrow, we're paying for it at the pump.

Free market capitalism's substitution effect when supplies run low fails to account for the invaluable ecological services now impacted by climate change and unwise land use. Fuel cells and the hydrogen economy remain elusive technologies, unlikely to solve pressing energy demands. Using one fossil fuel, like coal, to produce an oil substitute, like the gasification of coal into gasoline, creates other problems for global climate change, following, once again, the Law of Unintended Consequences. Making fuels like ethanol from corn or biodiesel from soybeans may not only transform the food system, it may also create an even greater risk of uncertainty by linking energy to increasingly unpredictable, variable and more extreme weather.

Information: Abundant Fuel

Ecopreneurs hold an opportunistic key to launching a new perspective on this matter: information. Through use of technology — from blogs to personal computers — information can be cost-effectively shared and distributed. Think of information exchange as the new fossil fuel, with infinite reserves and potential: The more you use, the more you have. The more information is shared and distributed, the greater the impact.

This information revolution contrasts sharply to the industrial version of the 19th century. A hundred years ago, machines improved labor productivity by as much as 40 times, replacing much physical labor. Today, because they accomplish more with fewer inputs, computers replace these traditional machines. While there exists a balance between use of technology and human hands-on interaction, use of computers does considerably lessen oil dependency. In addition to requiring fuel, machines inherently degrade with use, operating under the maxim "The more you use, the less you have."

Today the information era operates on the opposite principle, The more you use, the more you have. Like the natural world, information evolves, recreates itself in new forms and regenerates. Never complete, information improves with use and input from people — a polar opposite to the life cycle of fossil-fuel-based industrial machines.

With the Internet connecting and informing hundreds of millions of people — and growing — we sit on the cusp of the information era. As conversations and spontaneous organizing ignite between diverse peoples and cultures through the vast buffet of electronic interchange options, a new community commons forms. Akin to the historic commons where neighbors gathered on central green space, this new global commons takes place in cyberspace, where few boundaries, baggage or barriers exist — at least not yet.

Why is this movement toward the global commons key for ecopreneurs? The following aspects of the information and technological revolution serve ecopreneurs striving to do more with less.

Educational Opportunities

A mission-driven business and the Internet go hand in hand. While communicating product specs, pricing and other details remains an obvious necessity, the Internet provides a platform to educate, to supply seekers with answers and perspectives stemming from your values. People may find our Inn Serendipity website while initially looking for lodging but find themselves intrigued by our wind turbine or strawbale greenhouse and keep clicking and reading for further information and resources, or vice versa. Many guests arrive planning to learn more about how we make our own liquid fuel (biodiesel) or generate electricity in excess of our needs.

Dock in Any Port

Technology lifts you out of a traditional notion of a four-walled "office" and puts you on the beach, in the mountains, at the local coffeehouse — wherever you want to be, especially with the increasing availability of high-speed wireless access. Regardless of your location, your community, customers, clients and network follow you.

User-friendly for Non-techies

If you have memories of muddling through trying to put up a basic Web page a decade ago — or still cringe at the price tag of hiring your last Web designer — think again. Today's Web-based technologies offer user-friendly appeal, with nominal technical knowledge needed. Such access and simplicity fuels the growth of blogs (Web-based journals), where one can be up and running in a few quick steps.

Reaching Millions with E-commerce and eBay

A vast, and growing, audience of 152 million Internet users, so-called unique visitors 15 and older, exists in the US, accounting for about 25 percent of all Internet users in the world, according to comScore (comscore.com). Online retail portal eBay, for example, boasts of 147 million unique eBay customers, offering the ability to market a product-based business with a nominal investment. With PayPal and other Internet-based transaction processing tools, many businesses can open a storefront in a matter of days. Yahoo offers Yahoo Small Business (smallbusiness.yahoo.com), and eBay features their ProStores (prostores.com).

Lower Cost

Marketing budgets take on new meaning when focused on information sharing. Gone are the days of limited and expensive advertising options consisting primarily of purchasing printed ad space in publications or radio and TV spots. The financial commitment to use technology for information dissemination is low — often free. Your own domain name may be secured for less than $2 from GoDaddy.com when you sign up for their rather affordable website hosting plan; for $10 more, you can add your own online store. Your marketing and advertising dollars can go farther projected into cyberspace. An online press kit with readily accessible information for writers and the media, including high-resolution downloadable photography, tremendously increases opportunity for media interest.

No Paper, No Problem

Technology virtually eliminates the need to distribute printed material. We see our Inn Serendipity website as basically an extensive brochure, more personal and fresh than had we printed formal brochures. Saving more than the trees to make the paper, virtual information exchange significantly cuts back on fossil fuel consumption — from the mail trucks delivering the paper to the paper-making and printing machinery. For conferences and events where we need an informational handout, we photocopy a simple quarter-page black-and-white handout listing our seasonal calendar (open house and workshops), pointing folks to our website for more information.

Technology remains a constant anchor of any business plan, leaving us to question what role it should play and how much to invest in time and money. Thanks to Web technology, new business starts-ups — including those with green intentions — can quickly get up and running with global marketing potential for a relatively small investment. Yet when business — and, as a result, our lives — revolves too much online, technology can suck our time, money and focus in a flurry of mindless multitasking fog.

Like a teeter-totter, technology entails a dash of experimentation and risk. Sometimes you're high on the extreme end, while at others you rest safely on the ground. Outside factors play into your ride experience, including the mass of whomever you are riding with. Using technology, like riding the teeter-totter, we relish and thrive being in a constant state of flux and change.

Identify Your NIR: Needs, Interests, Resources

What's the key with managing technology? Find your NIR intersection, the place your needs, interests and resources cross.

Needs

What type of technology infrastructure does your business need? While new start-ups clearly stand deeply rooted in technology, there's still a wide range as to what level of techno-structure your venture truly needs. Look at technology and your business like managing a garden: everything works together. Not enough rain, plants dry up. Too much rain, the garden floods and nothing grows. Same concept with technology; getting just the right mix helps our businesses bloom, while an overdose stymies success.

Note that the question isn't if you need technology, but what kind and how much. Gone are the days when business books proffered the suggested "start a website" verbiage. Today it's assumed businesses have websites. The question now involves assessing what you need beyond general information, such as video downloads, blogs or podcasts.

Interests

Some of us are more technically inclined — and thereby technically interested — than others. While some of this may be based on training and education, there seems to be a proclivity by some to technical process and hardware while others effortlessly paint canvas or garden with abundance. This personal passion can drive directions, which isn't necessarily a negative thing. When you are passionate about something, you learn, process and complete projects more quickly.

Resources

How much money and time do you have for technology ventures? There's a consultant or designer available for just about any technology-related project. The question remains: How much cash do you have, and want, to invest? Time also forms a tangible resource in the technology equation. How much time can you invest? Is adding fresh content to a blog something you can reasonably do everyday, in addition to replying to customer e-mail inquiries?

Access to resources evolves with time. When we first moved to our rural setting a decade ago, Internet access recently became available with the local telephone utility charging five cents per minute. Now we have a high-speed connection that costs much less. Still, to wash away any illusions that we humans call all the shots, Mother Nature throws technology a curve ball. When a seasonal Florida hurricane wiped out our hosting site, our main website was down for a couple days, resulting in unpredicted business loss.

Web 2.0: Inert to Interactive

Nature hardly sits still. Ever changing, from the ebb and flow of the annual seasons to more dramatic disruptions like earthquakes and floods, nature continues to evolve. Same principle with technology and information exchange. The Internet evolves from "Web 1.0" to the next generation, affectionately dubbed by the industry as "Web 2.0." Web 1.0 refers to primarily static and passive aspects of websites that first and foremost communicate one-sided information coming from the company. Akin to online brochures, these websites evolved into accepted and sought-after venues for one-sided information.

We're entering the next generation: Web 2.0, involving various tools and features to make websites more dynamic and interactive. The growth of high-speed access and ease of use for these features bring blogs, wikis, social networks and video uploads into everyday life. Interaction rules in Web 2.0. Instead of you being the sole provider of content as in Web 1.0, these new features allow and encourage online communities to form and interact around your postings. This fundamentally shifts control to customers and the general public, something ecopreneurs can capitalize on to develop openness, trust and transparency.

Another key difference between Web 2.0 and its 1.0 predecessor is that you don't need to be a tech geek to navigate the possibilities of this new generation of technology. Designed to be user-friendly and available at no or low cost, Web 2.0 should be evaluated based on your NIR — needs, interests and resources. Be prudent and strategic in your return on investment decision: Will a particular investment in technology lead to more sales or market awareness? Be prudent in use of your time. While many of these new technologies like blogs are free or low-cost, evaluate the amount of time you may need to invest to get them up and running and keep content fresh.

Green Options

Founder & CEO: David Anderson
Place: Berkeley, CA, and the virtual global commons
Earth Mission: "Use the power of the emerging Internet technology to foster informational, economic and social relationships that encourage and enable true transformational change towards comprehensive sustainability."
Website: www.greenoptions.com

Green Options is not your father's business start-up. Then again, twentysomething founder David Anderson represents the millennial generation, people born after 1982 and into an era where the Internet reigned as a household staple next to peanut butter and jelly. David's technical knowledge, youthful zeal for environmental issues and skill set brought Green Options quickly to life at a time when the general public needed practical information about going green that was easy to relate to. The result is a venture snowballing, representing an inspiring example of how technology and the Internet can create an equalizing playing field for new ecopreneurs.

An internship while at the University of California gave David the inspiration for Green Options. "My experience in the green non-profit world of Washington DC convinced me that real change can only come through the for-profit market," David explains. "I saw many talented, dedicated people frustrated by the fixed game of the Washington status quo, convincing me that market solutions coming from the business world are what create effective change."

After graduating in 2005 and a brief stint as a technical writer, David left to focus on what eventually became Green Options, a green media portal launched in 2007 that focuses on engaging and informing people new to the green movement, taking advantage of the most useful and accessible formats that Web 2.0 has to offer. "Green Options is in the business of persuasion by providing information and connecting that information to our readers' own lives without being preachy," explains David. "We describe our niche not in terms of the 15 percent of people who consider themselves part of the green movement, but in the many simple ways that average folks, the other 85 percent, can start looking at any aspect of life through a green lens."

David founded Green Options through a Web-linked network of partners and staff countrywide, many of whom haven't met face to face. "As a recent graduate, I had very few business contacts to lean on for advice so I started a blog examining energy and environmental issues to network," David explains, quick to solve problems by harnessing the power of the Internet. Through blogging, David met his two partners, Shea Gunter, an ecopreneur based in Maine, and Jeff McIntire-Strasburg, an environmental writer and English professor living in St. Louis, Missouri. Bringing seasoned experts on board as partners proved immediately beneficial: Gunter had the venture capital experience to quickly find an angel investor, while McIntire-Strasburg provided provocative editorial content.

"Being practically fresh out of college, I realized I had a lot to learn about business in general, so I realized the importance of working with smart people with different skill sets," advises David. "My lack of experience has helped, however, in that I'm able to make connections and innovative scenarios that might not automatically occur to someone boxed into a particular business world experience."

Today David and Green Options are officially based in Berkeley, California, while his nationwide staff grows — many blogging as independent contractors. David's challenge remains to keep connected, taking advantage of online workflow tools, many available at no or low cost, such as Skype for phone and video conferences and BasecampHQ and Google Docs for managing shared documents. "Efficient communication remains a challenge, and part of me misses the cubicle," David adds with a smile. "There's something to be said about poking your head over the cubicle wall to ask a quick question." Green Options pays independent contracts through PayPal, saving both paper and fuel costs by staff working from home remotely and not commuting.

Green Options thrives as a leading green information portal thanks to well-written, fresh material. "At Green Options, we say we are 'greening the good life,' focusing on engaging content from green experts and enthusiasts that we hope appeals to a broad range of readers who consider themselves normal consumers," David explains. "Our content is our marketing. We write about what people are searching for on Google, such as 'climate change solutions' or 'green building materials.' Once people find us for one green tip, trick or piece of information, we hope they'll come back to learn and share more. So far, they are." Their innovative "30 Days to a Greener You" is a free "e-course" newsletter that teaches subscribers how to lighten their environmental footprint, while still living a comfortable life, providing a month of step-by-step actions, from the simple and free (turning off the lights, recycling) to major investments in a greener lifestyle (greener cars, solar energy systems).

Future plans for Green Options include using Web 2.0 media, unveiling new Web properties, or portals, that address different niche markets within the green movement, some adding different revenue streams from advertisers. "We think we are seeing the emergence of a new kind of media, content seamlessly integrated with community functions that will take many forms, such as text, audio and video," sums up David. "Overhead will be much lower than traditional media, in part because technology enables people-powered dissemination of information. Green Options thrives on the challenge of using technology to bring sustainable living education to the masses and turning the tides of society for the better."

Menu of New Technology

The hype around Web 2.0 technologies may leave your head buzzing with new terminology overload. Here's an overview of general technology categories.

Blogs

Definition: Abbreviated word for weblog. A "blog" is a Web-based journal through which people can publish their opinions and thoughts on the Internet.

Important aspects:

- Straightforward to start and, in many cases, free to use. Its premade templates and push-button publishing doesn't require much technical know-how.
- Provides direct way to interact with customers and garner valuable feedback — including criticism — from those who know you best: your customers.
- Provides easy portal for information distribution.
- Establishes you as an expert by creating a clearinghouse of information and expertise.
- Referring and linking to other websites and bloggers creates buzz around your efforts, often increasing rank status for Web-trolling search engines like Google and, as a result, media interest.
- An RSS Feed, a mechanism to "syndicate" your blog content to people who subscribe, enables you to readily communicate with readers.

Remember:

- Blogs require time. In order to keep readers engaged, content needs to be fresh with recommended updates of two to three times a week; some blogging experts advise daily entries.
- Keep objectively evaluating how much business is being driven by your efforts.

Two of the more popular free blog-hosting sites:
www.blogger.com
www.wordpress.com

Wiki

Definition: A website that enables visitors to add, remove and edit content. The word "wiki" is Hawaiian for "quick" and originated from the wiki wiki shuttle bus at the Honolulu International Airport. Based on collaborative technology for organizing information on websites, wikis allow for linking among infinite pages. Wikipedia, an online encyclopedia, is one of the oldest and best-known wikis. Wikis are often used internally by companies to facilitate communication and collaboration, replacing static intranets.

Important aspects:

- Builds community around your site.

+ Works well to show potential customers that there is a vibrant community of people using your products or services.

Remember:

+ Since the general public edits wikis, wikis have been criticized for their questionable accuracy of information.

Create a free wiki hosting site:
www.wetpaint.com

Virtual Communities and Social Networking

Definition: A group of people that primarily or at least initially communicates or interacts via the Internet, rather than face to face. Different from traditional communities within geographic entities (neighborhood, village), virtual and online communities are inherently dispersed geographically, bringing people together through common interests.

Important aspects:

+ Online community members increasingly serve as opinion leaders, with the potential to significantly impact an issue — and send a message quickly snowballing across the globe.

Free on-line communities:
www.zaadz.com (social)
www.myspace.com (social)
www.linkedin.com (professional networking)
www.flickr.com (for photo sharing)
www.youtube.com (for video sharing)

Support Your IT Department: You

No matter how you slice technology, as small business owners we are our own Information Technology (IT) department. When something goes wrong, when error messages blare across the screen, we ourselves are the first to troubleshoot. Given such realization, make things easier for yourself by safeguarding and protecting your system as best you can. Get into a routine of regularly backing up your hard drive and keeping up to date on virus and security protection software.

Better Off

To prove the point that technology should be in your court to manage and not the other way around, we confess to not having a cellphone. While we realize this fact quickly sends us into a minority in today's world, that choice is one we never question. We manage our phone calls — from B & B inquiries to writing projects to personal and social — with our main house landline and an answering machine. By choosing not to be accessible 24/7, we turn off ongoing distractions and clutter, enabling us to focus on our priorities. Cellphones exemplify how we have let technology seep into our lifestyles to the point that we no longer question routine actions: Watch at a restaurant how people will pick up a cell call while in the middle of a face-to-face conversation with someone without even questioning the situation. With every call having this "emergency urgency" status, we find ourselves in a tense state of being "on" all the time, someplace we don't want to perpetually be. By managing technology, versus technology controlling us, we find balance for ourselves.

That said, remain open to technology. We're first to admit we're on the lower end of the technology totem pole — based on all three factors of needs, interests and resources — we consider ourselves Submarine Techies. By remaining small, we don't need that much traffic and business to require us to be on the cutting edge of the latest, greatest technology. We can move slower, strategically, while keeping things green.

In the next chapter, we'll examine ways we can successfully — and happily — blend our work with our personal or private life and how this can support a richer quality of life.

Submarine Techie

Rather than jumping on — and paying for — every latest, greatest new technology phase, Submarine Techies quietly lurk for a while, observing what is going on above water. When the situation ripens and matures to the point that moving into a new technology area makes strategic sense, Submarine Techies go public and embrace it. This strategy of waiting and lurking often reduces the cost of entry, while educational resources increase.

Chapter 10

Blending Family, Friends and Fun

MOST BUSINESS HOW-TO BOOKS would have ended a few chapters ago. While *ECOpreneuring* covers many of the same topics albeit from a different perspective — corporate structure, marketing and finances — the idea of blending your personal life and business remains novel, even borderline unorthodox. Books tout creating definitive boundaries between "work and leisure" or "career and family." Yet many of the ecopreneurs we talked with aim to blend, rather than divide, synergize rather than suffocate. When we live passionately for our Earth Mission, it seasons and inspires every other aspect of our lives, and we're left with a richer, more meaningful end result. Some authors and academics refer to these proprietors as lifestyle entrepreneurs, crafting not only a business with a balance sheet but also one that provides a quality of life to its owners.

The idea that we need boundaries between work and leisure roots in the inherent notion that your "job" remains a means to an end: a nasty necessity of life that brings in cash to pay the bills or buy more stuff, and only then can you achieve happiness. But ecopreneuring involves more than a paycheck; we don't want to do "something" solely as a means to be able to do what "we really want to do." The blending of passions with livelihood cause us to think about and prioritize elements of our lifestyle in areas that normal work parameters fail to reach, like travel or caring for children or elderly parents. With some strategic thought, our lives can evolve into an active, engaging cocktail of fulfillment and fun; the key is identifying and acting on personal priorities. We don't seek to balance family life with work. We blend family into our workstyle and lifestyle, seeking to enhance our quality of life while restoring ecological viability.

Return to Cottage Industry

This blending approach reaches back to the cottage industry era during the 18th century when many workers produced items from their homes, typically part-time. Originally referring to homeworkers in Europe performing tasks like sewing or lacemaking, such cottage industries were common and popular when most people worked in agriculture since these venues provided income during the lean and less busy winter months. Such home-based industries often involved the whole family, with children helping with simple tasks and mom and dad in charge of taking the material to final form.

Experiencing a renaissance in its own right today, cottage industry shares the ecopreneuring priority of working from home on a flexible, often part-time, basis involving children and family. The online auction website company eBay, for example, has spawned a booming cottage industry where people can sell hand-made merchandise, collectibles or antiques — almost anything, paying only a nominal listing and transaction fee. If the item doesn't sell, you're only left paying for the listing fee and related costs. When parents run in-home businesses — from eBay to B & Bs — kids garner real-life, hands-on experience and feel part of the process, whether helping carry packages to the post office or prepping muffin batter.

It's important to strive for a healthy balance between involving family in the business and turning kids off. Ecopreneurs see their business as a chance to spend time together under the experiential learning umbrella. Our son's six-year-old skill set can't contribute much to B & B housecleaning or breakfast preparation yet, but he runs the campfire by gathering wood and roasting custom s'mores for guests. He doesn't get an allowance but earns spending money by selling "crazy crayons," colorful crayon globs made from melted recycled crayons, and his name appears with ours as a co-author of our *Edible Earth* cookbook. He is encouraged to be an engaged, contributing member of our family's work, our family livelihood.

We agree with and draw inspiration from fellow ecopreneur and Virginia farmer Joel Salatin of Polyface, Inc., who once said about his kids' allowance: "I don't pay my kids just for breathing." Instead, Salatin's brood helps with the family business. Through the years, his kids have handled various aspects of the business — and the income generated. Today, they have fledged into young adults who have fully taken on running aspects of Polyface, Inc. (polyfacefarms.com).

A cottage industry mindset fosters interdependency — akin to what makes a thriving ecosystem prosperous. No longer an island, we rely on others to reach our potential and are eager to be mentored by those more knowledgeable. Mentors serve as the Obi-Wan Kenobis of the ecopreneur galaxy, those people who come into our lives and fundamentally alter our world for the better. Mentors advise and consult but also, if you are fortunate, push, challenge, question and lead you into new directions and arenas. Speaking from a "been there, done that" perspective, mentors provide us a safety net of sorts. By hearing stories of their experiences, our own confidence levels expand and bloom; we no longer feel alone in our venture.

While mentors may play an important role in developing your business, their impact typically extends beyond the balance sheet. A true mentor serves as a mirror, a person in which you see — or want to see — yourself. They exude the qualities or lifestyle characteristics that you admire, dream about and want in your own life. Sometimes such mentors pass through our lives briefly and rather serendipitously.

Our neighbors down the road, Phil and Judy Welty, drove up our driveway a few years after we moved to the farm. At first glance, they looked like typical senior retirees curious about the solar panels we recently installed on our roof. Little did we know at the time, this couple would evolve to be an integral part of our lives and business, mentoring us in everything from renewable energy systems (they ran a solar hot water heating business in the 1970s) to getting our electric CitiCar up and running, quickly earning them the honorary titles of "Uncle Phil and Aunt Judy." We dedicated *Rural Renaissance* to these two, a small token of appreciation for knowing we'd never be where we are today had they not reached out to us.

Priority Integration

Priority integration (PI) is the ability to schedule and organize one's life and livelihood around personal key priorities. It proffers a balance between life priorities and livelihood. You are not choosing one and forsaking the other; rather, you are aware of each at the start and aim for the best blend of various elements.

Ecopreneuring is grounded on the ability to "PI" the elements you find important to form a fundamental aspect of a value-based lifestyle. Your priorities may change and evolve at different stages in your life, often including the following two elements, children and elderly parents.

Children

Dual or single working parents struggle a lot these days. They try to blend the economic realities of needing income (in part because they've been entrapped by debt and garner income in the form of wages) with the desire to be there for their kids. Society sings refrains about how "expensive it is to have kids," and many parents become stuck in the earn-and-spend paycheck trap. If one spouse gets laid off, the situation gravely escalates. As the media debates the pros and cons of the "choice" between going to work and staying home, particularly for women, the ecopreneuring philosophy suggests crafting your own work-life blend, PI-ing children into your livelihood. The question no longer is either-or but how. Ecopreneuring can be the answer, providing parents with the following opportunities.

- *Tag-team parenting.* Setting one's own work schedule that reflects the independence factor behind ecopreneuring enables parents to PI children into a balanced daily workflow. Often this stems from having both

The Simplicity of Ecopreneuring

"Simple living" continues to garner much pop culture hype, sparking books, magazines and a slew of self-help opportunities to assist you to declutter, scale back and slow down. Environmentally conscious and sustainable living fall under the simple living radar, but where does ecopreneuring fit in?

We've incorporated numerous "simple living" strategies into our business over the years. While our lifestyle may exude quintessential simple living elements — from canning applesauce to crafting holiday gifts — there remains an inherently complex element to our ecopreneuring workstyle. Our calendar looks like a treasure hunt map of lines of travel, B & B guests arriving and departing, writing deadlines, family gatherings, cabin bookings and Liam's home-school group projects. We always juggle multiple unrelated projects. A better word than "simple" to describe our ecopreneuring approach is "focus." By consciously choosing to do certain things, we inherently simplify by prioritizing. We open more time to focus on what we really want to do by eliminating (or at least seriously reducing) time drains, including the following:

- *Daily commute.* With the average daily commute in the US now nearly a half-hour, by working from home, we save over seven days per year, not to mention the fossil fuel emissions of daily driving.

parents working together, usually from home, in the business. We call this "tag-team parenting," where one of us is "on the kids" as the other works in the home office or meets with a client.

With two parents around, minimal outside daycare assistance is needed. When we both occasionally need to be in work roles simultaneously, we access a network of local like-minded families who help each other out with babysitting. Grandparents nearby are often eager to step in for other stints.

- *Teaching green values.* When work and home values blend under the green umbrella, these practices become the norm for our children. Flash forward a couple of decades, and a fresh generation of children will be aware of and care for our planet. The public or private school system should not be the sole institution to teach our children how to recycle or plant trees; we'd argue we should be doing that as parents. Ecopreneuring provides ample educational opportunities to teach green values, from sharing your purchasing philosophy when shopping to taking kids along on business travel when appropriate.

- *Television.* Avoid the national average of watching three hours per day and — poof — add over 45 extra days to your year to do things more important to your family, community and environment. We still have a television, a classic 1979 RCA model, used primarily for watching movies in the winter, tucked away in the corner of an upstairs room. The passive entertainment garnered from most television programs adds up to wasted time. Try unplugging the TV and connecting with your priorities.

- *Communication and technology.* Technology can be a powerful, cost-effective ecopreneuring tool. Manage communication technologies selectively since it has the potential to turn every day into a perpetual 24-hour workday. Don't let it. By not using a cellphone or text-messaging, we carve out chunks of productive time to focus on our priorities.

- *Unlimited development potential.* Defining "success" by the size of your business and bank account will perpetually suck time as growth has limitless potential. You'll never be "finished" since the race to keep up with the Joneses, or be a "successful" business by mainstream standards, always kicks in one level higher. How big you want to grow your business remains up to you. But by setting growth limits, by defining wealth by factors other than financial, time opens up for other opportunities and priorities. We strive to build a better business, not a bigger one.

- *Reclaiming and redefining the family dinner.* While the majority of American families feel guilty about never gathering around the dinner table with any snippet of regularity, ecopreneuring families stockpile shared family time. But once again, ecopreneurs need to be open to tossing out society's expectation of what a "normal family" should do and make our decisions and priorities based on what works best for our lifestyle. Is gathering around a dinner table that important if we are spending time together in other ways? When we're in peak summer busy mode on the farm, we'll each grab a quick supper individually and then spend the early evening hours together working in the gardens, taking advantage of cooler temperatures. We're spending time together and talking as a family, just gathered around the tomato patch instead of the table.

- *Educational alternatives.* Once you've launched an ecopreneurial business, don't be surprised if this innovative attitude seeps into your approach to educating your children. Perhaps you don't agree with the schools' priorities of teaching for national standard tests or their blind acceptance of issues or behaviors that conflict with your own value system, from processed cafeteria food to pesticides on the playground. Fortunately, an increasing number of educational options exist today, both within and outside the public school system. Depending on where you live, there may be public charter schools, innovative, publicly funded schools that don't always adhere to general school norms of curriculum or organizational structure. Some charter schools are "virtual schools," providing free in-home computers and curriculum access for students to learn at their own pace, often targeting families who prioritize a flexible schedule and independent learning. Home-schooling continues to grow as parents look for more educational opportunities for their children, believing that their family's lifestyle can provide a creative educational backdrop, especially in work-at-home situations. Home-schooling provides opportunities to use your own blend of different educational philosophies, including Waldorf, Montessori and Charlotte Mason.

Resources for Alternative Education

www.homeschoolzone.com
General website for getting started with home-schooling.

www.nacol.org
North American Council for Online Learning promotes increasing opportunities for K-12 online teaching and learning.

www.uscharterschools.org
Resources on how to start and run a charter school, including school profiles.

Elderly Parents

While each family has different needs and resources, a desire to be there for one's parents and other relatives as they age remains strong for many of us. What exactly "be there" means is a personal question, but for many this involves wanting to spend time with and give care to our parents through their later years. Caring for elderly parents is increasingly emerging as a central consideration in our decision as to where we live and what we do.

Randomness remains a big piece of this eldercare puzzle. We don't know and can't predict how our parents' final years of life (or those of other seniors we are close to) will pan out. Caring for elderly parents demands flexibility and adaptability, not rigidity and schedules dictated by many large corporations. Having flexibility and independence in one's work structure can be a valuable variable in the elder-care puzzle. Often ecopreneurs have the opportunity to work remotely from various locations as needed. If parents live closer, you can better help with doctors' appointments and assist as needed during the day.

Aside from the ability to assist with eldercare, an ecopreneuring lifestyle gives us more opportunity to relish the moment, enjoy the quality time we do have with senior parents and relatives. As we did with childrearing, we want to live by a "no regrets" philosophy, the ability to look back at our days no matter what the outcome and sincerely feel we would have done little differently.

Customized Freedom

Opportunity to customize takes on deeper meaning for ecopreneurs as we sculpt our schedules to suit our natural tendencies. Freedom to control your schedule and be independent remains the quintessential entrepreneurial lifestyle perk. No longer tied to the cubicle or someone else's time schedule, you can work when, where and for whom you desire. Some of you may be drooling in desire at this description while others may be shaking their heads, knowing that there is a steep admission criteria to independence, including self-motivation, discipline and focus.

Pebble Publishing, Katy Trail Bed & Bikefest and Mighty Mo Canoe Rentals

Books, bikes, canoes. Publishing, tourism, outdoor recreation. Family, friends and fun. Like nature's diversified geography providing the Missouri River backdrop for the scenic town of Rocheport, Brett and Tawnee Dufur's ecopreneurial life reflects the strength in diversity. Despite the sleepy town with a population a dash over 200, 15 minutes outside of Columbia, Missouri, the thirtysomething husband-and-wife team has created a laboratory of innovative, ecopreneurial ventures that keep life and livelihood blended and blooming, locally focused, yet reaching audiences and customers well beyond the river's touch.

Brett's first venture started in 1995, when he wrote and self-published the first guidebook for the Katy Trail, the longest rails-to-trails project in the United States,

Co-Owners: Brett & Tawnee Dufur
Place: Rocheport, Missouri
Earth Mission: "Follow your dreams and do what you love, creating community wealth in a living economy. Explore, listen and share. Help others see the interconnections. Realize that all the solutions we need are here now, and do what we can to help others embrace the real life and what can be."
Websites: www.pebblepublishing.com; www.katytrailbb.com; www.mighty-mo.com

225 miles along the meandering and mighty Missouri River. It remains a best-seller to this day. "What I discovered is that people are hungry for the opportunity to connect with a sense of place, and that's what this guidebook is all about," explains Brett.

This guidebook introduced Brett to Rocheport and sparked his passion for local commitment. "With publishing I knew I could be based anywhere, thanks to the Internet and shipping options. Rocheport delivered such a strong sense of place blended with nature, a place where I could walk out the front door and just keep walking without worrying about fences or property lines. This place immediately felt like home."

Brett's Katy Trail guidebook, now in its ninth edition with over 35,000 copies sold, prompted him to officially start Pebble Publishing, nurturing the business into a leading purveyor of books exclusively about Missouri. "When I first started working out of a house on the bluff overlooking Rocheport, self-employment was like tumbling down a big hill," admits Brett. "I welcomed the challenges and recognized early on that no one else was doing what I was doing. Boxes of books lined the walls and served as chairs. I didn't even know what a P&L statement was until several years later."

Flash forward through the years and experience deepened while new ideas germinated. Brett's wife, Tawnee, joined him as a partner. Creating a business that enabled Tawnee to use her natural resources degree without needing to commute out of Rocheport, the couple purchased and renovated the Katy Trail Bed & Bikefest, blending green practices with hospitality. "At first, I admit the B & B business idea didn't appeal to me since B & Bs typically are such luxury resource and energy hogs," Brett comments. "Then Tawnee and I thought maybe we could create earth-friendly lodging that reflects our own low-impact lifestyle that still delivers a comfortable experience."

Doing the renovations on a lean budget, the Dufurs were pleasantly surprised to find that most of the energy-saving changes, such as compact fluorescent bulbs and calking around windows cost less than $15. "Our personal beliefs stood in sync with the bottom line, and we realized this is a no-brainer way to do business," Tawnee says. Today, the Dufurs have found that their B & B guests appreciate their green B & B initiatives. "It is one thing to talk about something, it's another to provide an experience where someone uses a low-flow showerhead for the first time and loves it. We think of our guests as being on a 'field trip' when they are here, taking ideas and new approaches for their lives back home."

Simultaneously Pebble Publishing grew to offering 12 titles plus others sold through Missouri Gold Booksellers, a distributor of over 500 Missouri books. Needing more space, the company transformed an old brick 1917 gas station building into an attractive retail store, publishing house and book warehouse. As with most ecopreneurial businesses, restoration provides a central framework for how businesses operate. "The retail storefront brought years of publishing work full circle and allowed us to directly connect with the people who enjoyed our books," explains Brett. Additionally Brett launched Mighty Mo Canoe Rentals. He offers guided interpretive floats by canoe or kayak on the Missouri River, tapping into the rapidly growing interest in experiential travel and ecotourism. "Mighty Mo is the only canoe rental on the Missouri River and the Lewis and Clark Trail this side of Montana."

These business ventures add up to a solid, diversified income mix, with 50 percent of their income stemming from their oldest, established venture of Pebble Publishing, about 30 percent from the B & B and 20 percent from the canoe business, getting away from lots of earned income and focusing instead on passive and royalty income. "Our diversified income mix is always in fluid change from year to year, especially as some of our newer ventures get established," explains Brett, with the B & B running at double the previous year's volume. Rather than playing the distant stock market, the Dufurs are building long-term equity locally by investing into fixer-upper properties they plan on using as rental income.

The Dufurs still keep open to new opportunities, particularly those that enhance and involve their local Rocheport community. "When I started the canoe business, I wanted a more earth-friendly shuttle vehicle option than a gas-sucking huge van. Then a friend suggested biodiesel," adds Brett. This idea evolved into a local cooperative of six, adding up to enough fuel for Brett to run the diesel shuttle van and heat his home.

Brett's passion for Rocheport prompted him to run for mayor, and he is now in his second term. Ever modest, he sees his all-volunteer role as mayor as a means to effect change, particularly in a small town like Rocheport. "Small towns are like balls of clay, where everyone can have an active role in shaping its destiny," Brett explains. His goal is to see Rocheport, recently voted "One of America's Top Ten Coolest Small Towns" by Frommer's Budget Travel, evolve into a top ten "greenest small town," starting with community programs to help residents with easy, efficient green changes, similar to what the Dufurs did at the B & B.

Never seeing money as a huge hurdle, Brett emphasizes the personal aspect of business loans. "We've done it all when it comes to raising money, from taking out Small Business Administration loans to maxing credit cards to borrowing from friends and family," explains Brett. "Remember the majority of our country is burdened with needing to turn a decent interest rate on their investments. When interest rates are down, it is easier to compel business associates or friends to loan our small business money rather than putting it into a faceless CD."

Sowing their passions into their businesses has been a lot like creating a garden for the Dufurs, a garden that now includes their young son and daughter, Everett and Naomi Jane. "We've been sowing seeds for a long time now, and our 'garden' is starting to create abundance both for us and this community," concludes Brett. "I look at success from the perspective of the three 'I's: identity, working on what you truly want to be; interactions, meeting lots of interesting people; and income, to pay the bills and provide enough to reinvest in my family and business. We're not business superheroes, we're simply being who we want to be, putting our heels down in this town where we want to live, work and raise our kids."

Biorhythm Balance

If you could only work three hours a day, which three hours would be your "Most Productive Time," your MPT? Everyone proffers a different perspective on this; don't be shy to think out of normal work hour boundaries. Lisa's MPT is 5 am to 8 am. An obvious morning person, she's learned that by tackling a priority project during the first three focused hours in the morning, before Liam wakes and the phone starts ringing, she sets a positive momentum to her whole day. If you're coming from an office environment, three hours probably doesn't seem like much. "I'm at the office closer to 12 hours a day," you say. But when you eliminate distractions, the office social scene, commuting time, latte runs and administrative meetings, how much of that time is truly productive? By focusing on your best, most creative and prolific productive time block, you open up your daily schedule to other possibilities, like training for a triathalon or just maintaining a regular workout routine at the gym. Ecopreneuring fosters a healthy lifestyle. What good is the touted company perk of "great healthcare" when what you're doing is making you sick?

Working with — not against — your biorhythms naturally takes on a seasonal ebb and flow. Granted we live on a farm where seasonal living is embedded in our business and daily routines. Plant in spring, harvest in fall. The B & B business bustles in the summer; we hibernate and recuperate a bit during winter, when we focus on writing, speaking and consulting and catch up on bookkeeping. But you don't need to live rural to appreciate the seasonal changes. Mother Nature provides us with an annual cyclical flow of themes that we can all tap into. Think of each season as a fresh chapter ushering in new opportunities to connect to the Earth thematically.

By listening to these biorhythms, we grow to know ourselves better and can fine-tune our focus. We garner deeper understanding of how we work, create and innovate. Yet we still find the need to continually work on focusing, reminding ourselves of our priorities. This process evolves in two directions. First, we keep communication between the two of us clear and open, starting every day with a "morning meeting." It varies in length but is always our time to mutually focus on myriad current issues and, importantly, to make sure we share a perspective on how our day will evolve. Second, we keep income generation a priority. When choosing between projects and opportunities, we focus on finishing the one bringing in income first, and then move on to others. This approach doesn't stem from a greed-and-growth motivation but rather from the realization that we need to generate income to be viable long-term. By keeping our income needs low — a theme discussed throughout this book — we can achieve our income goals quickly.

Working independently requires discipline and commitment to your goal. Motivation and procrastination issues face us at times, yet this ability to keep going and stay on track separates those who succeed as independent ecopreneurs from others who may have great ideas, talk a lot about their vision and plan but go nowhere. Take Yoda's advice to heart: Do or do not ... there is no try.

Travel

Our first agenda item after leaving the cubicle office scene was to gear up the backpack and hit the road. Travel can be a learning, engaging, inspiring experience that can help restore the planet and build peace, especially if approached as ecotourists. Between the two of us, we've visited 35 countries on six continents. Now the business we've created is used as a tool for change and a means by which we can restore the planet, including the carbon dioxide emissions we ended up emitting as a part of our travels.

Travel remains an important element of our lives and those of many ecopreneurs. But we have shifted from travel as vacation to merging work and travel. It makes smart business sense too. By writing off our expenses against associated business revenue related to writing and photography or to other speaking events, travel becomes both a strategic and profitable endeavor. What else can you do in the area you are traveling to that could be income-producing? We're always looking for freelance writing opportunities when we travel, often adding a few travel days outside the usually packed conference schedule to do interviews and research. If you sell products or services, is there a potential new client or retail outlet you could visit in the area?

One of the hot growth areas in travel is including the extended family. With our busy lifestyles and schedules today and an aging population — many of who are grandparents — such travel provides an ideal backdrop to both relax and share new experiences outside the customary holiday gatherings. There's something about getting away from our day-to-day routines and being together in a new place that fosters memories and the opportunity to see relatives in a whole different context. Besides your business bank account, there are memory banks worth filling too.

Traveling with extended family, we've learned, requires a bit more planning since you need to recognize and accommodate different travel needs, in our case from six- to eighty-five-year-olds. Still, we've found the results quite fulfilling as we encounter new experiences we would not normally have. And while there are perks to traveling with family, deducting everyone's expenses is not one of them. Your hotel room and mileage qualify as expenses; additional meals for family members do not.

Remember to keep good records of business travel. Not surprisingly, business travel often sends up red flags to the IRS, since there could be so many gray areas. Keep detailed records of meetings attended, who was at each business meal (even if it was just you and your partner), and an accurate mileage log. One approach to these records is to copy what the mainstream corporate system does: file an expense report after each trip, grouping your receipts and records for that trip in one batch.

What combination you concoct of business, family, friends and fun remains your choice, with elements and priorities varying at different life stages. Ecopreneuring describes this journey, a continual evolution toward putting purpose, passion and the planet before profit. It absorbs and thrives on diversity and change. Like nature, we adapt and evolve based on need and situations through

Travel Green

With increasing awareness of global warming, we can't ignore travel's huge impact on fossil fuel consumption and greenhouse gas emissions. The answer isn't don't travel — and miss out on such benefits as cultural awareness and inspirational new experiences — but travel as an ecotourist, someone visiting areas of cultural or natural interest with the purpose of observing, participating in and preserving the environment and local culture. Consider the following options for ecotourism.

- **Go fuel-efficient.** Consider traveling by train or bus, when possible. If you must drive, invest in a gas-electric hybrid car, diesel vehicle that you can run on biodiesel, an all-electric car or other gas-powered vehicles (perhaps used) that get better than average mileage. Check to make sure your tires are properly inflated, increasing your mileage and cutting gas costs by 15 percent. Try to buy gas from more environmentally responsible oil companies. While it's hard to argue the merits of oil companies, BP Amoco, Sunoco and Shell have consistently been recognized as being more progressive on environmental issues and renewable energy investment than their industry counterparts. If you have a diesel car like us, seek out the biodiesel cooperatives or stations that offer homegrown fuel options.

- **Offset emissions.** Consider neutralizing your greenhouse gas emissions associated with travel, particularly by air, through a nominal fee to a growing number of non-profit programs involved with carbon offsets. See chapter 2 for such options as The Better World Club's TravelCool program (betterworldclub.com).

- **Reuse on the road.** When on the road, apply the same recycling and reuse principles you practice at home. Pack a reusable travel mug for coffee rather than using disposable cups. Many hotels post signage asking if you would like to reuse your sheets and towels to reduce use of water, detergents and energy — or you can let the housekeeping department know to leave your room alone by notifying the front desk.

focusing on our strengths. Rather than molding to fit the norm, we strive to continually discover our true self, our Earth Mission. And, again like nature, diversity fosters strength. The webs of our lives can be complex, interdependent, evolving and strong.

So launch an enterprise. Have your own "eco-zip code." Garner independence and fulfillment through the multiple layers and flavors of your ecopreneuring ventures. As you set forth on your ecopreneuring next steps, may the perspectives, resources and information in these pages provide you with the tools and confidence to make your mark in leaving our world a better place.

- **Eat local.** Look for locally owned restaurants that support local, seasonal and organic cuisine. The Chef's Collaborative lists member restaurants across the country (chefscollaborative.org).
- **Research your options.** Green travel organizations are popping up to help you green your travels. Some sites to look into include:

  International Ecotourism Society (TIES)
  General information on ecotourism principles and travel options.
  www.ecotourism.org

  ECOCLUB: A Global Ecological Tourism Network
  International network of green lodging. www.ecoclub.com

  Green Vacation Hub
  International listing of green lodging. Travelers can read online how establishments self-scored on energy efficiency and other green practices. www.greenvacationhub.com

  Green Routes
  Minnesota-based green travel program of Renewing the Countryside that identifies locally owned establishments operating with sustainable practices. www.greenroutes.org

  Sustainable Travel International
  Provide educational services that help travelers and travel providers that support environmental conservation and protect cultural heritage while promoting cross-cultural understanding and economic development. www.sustainabletravelinternational.org

Epilogue: Legacy Living

LEAVE THE WORLD BETTER THAN WE FOUND IT. The power of an ecopreneurial business has emerged as an effective tool to accomplish social or ecological change at a pace rapid enough to influence the 24/7 world in which we now live. In minutes, the tragic September 11 terrorism acts become the crashes seen around the world. In real time, a Doppler map on our home computer, generated by orbiting satellites, bounces signals of Hurricane Katrina blowing ashore and laying waste to New Orleans in 2005.

Perhaps it's seeing so much more than we ever have before — and in such visceral detail — that inspires the humanist and survivalist instinct in us all to reach out, help heal and restore a planet signaling code red. Ecopreneurs, in whatever field, industry or geographic location, are embarking on a calling that can give no greater satisfaction, meaning or sense of purpose. Writes William James: "The great use of life is to spend it for something that will outlast us."

Our legacy, linked to our passions, beliefs and values, drives ecopreneurs to accept the authentic and bold challenge to our calling. At the end of life, it's not what we own or where we've worked that matters most. It's what we've managed to accomplish during our short time on Earth and the purposes we've devoted our life energy to that are bigger than ourselves and will live on long after we pass away.

"When you have completed 95 percent of your journey, you are only halfway there." This Japanese proverb sums up the ecopreneuring mindset: the journey propels innovation, inspires change, provides meaning and satisfies the soul. Ever evolving, this journey provides us with refreshment and renewal. When we truly feel passion and love for what we're doing, we can't keep away from it — we keep refining, improving and rebuilding.

The pages of ECOpreneuring serve as catalysts for change. These practical resources and philosophical inspiration now continue around the "water cooler of the global commons" on the Web. Join this movement as we ecopreneurs connect, share, inspire and support one other by visiting the following sites.

ECOpreneuring

www.ecopreneuring.biz
The hub of this book's online community, this site provides the core gathering point for ecopreneurs. From a sample business plan template for you to download and customize to our blog chronicling both our own personal experiences and those of ecopreneurs worldwide, this site complements this book as a next step to find support and resources for finding purpose, living well and restoring the Earth. You'll find various means to connect, from sharing your story to networking with like-minded potential partners and funders. Tell your story — share your dreams — together we are changing the way business is done. For correspondence, or to volunteer as a mentor or demonstration site, contact:

ECOpreneuring
PO Box 811
Monroe, WI 53566

Inn Serendipity Bed & Breakfast and Farm

www.innserendipity.com
As home page for our B & B and farm ventures, this site brings to life our own ecopreneuring voyage, from fact sheets on our renewable energy systems to updates on new ventures like the restoration of an all-electric CitiCar. If you're interested in a farm tour, check out the calendar section for annual free farm open house tour dates and workshops — or perhaps we'll see you around the campfire as a B & B guest sometime.

Renewing the Countryside and the Rural Renaissance Network

www.renewingthecountryside.org
www.ruralrenaissance.org
Inaugurated with the publication of our first joint book, *Rural Renaissance*, our partnership with the non-profit Renewing the Countryside now includes a variety of resources for rural-based entrepreneurial ventures, organized through the Rural Renaissance Network we co-founded. The database of case study profiles on the Renewing the Countryside website — some of which we've written — provide an online mentorship of small business experiences and success stories, paired with helpful resources. Your donations to the Rural Renaissance Network and Renewing the Countryside help continue these efforts toward sustainable rural revitalization.

To help fund the Rural Renaissance Network, contact:

Rural Renaissance Network
Renewing the Countryside, Inc.
2105 First Avenue, South
Minneapolis, MN 55404
Toll Free: 1-866-378-0587

Ten percent of the authors' proceeds from this book will be donated to the Rural Renaissance Network, a program of the non-profit organization Renewing the Countryside, providing educational resources to foster more creative, healthy and ecologically and economically viable rural communities. Visit the Rural Renaissance Network on the Internet at ruralrenaissance.org.

Selected Bibliography

Abrams, John. *The Company We Keep: Reinventing Small Business for People, Community and Place.* Chelsea Green, 2005.

Aburdene, Patricia. *Megatrends 2010: The Rise of Conscious Capitalism.* Hampton Roads, 2005.

Allen, C. W., Cheri Hill, Diane Kennedy, and Garrett Sutton. *Inc. & Grow Rich: How to Cut Taxes by 70% and Protect Your Assets Forever.* Sage International, 2000.

Anielski, Mark. *The Economics of Happiness.* New Society, 2007.

Anosike, Benji O. *The National Home Mortgage Reduction Kit: How to Cut Your Mortgage in Half and Own Your Home Free and Clear in Just a Few Short Years.* Do-It-Yourself Legal Publishers, 2000.

Bamburg, Jill. *Getting to Scale: Growing Your Business Without Selling Out.* Berrett-Koehler, 2006.

Banner, Bill and Addison Wiggen. *Empire of Debt: The Rise of an Epic Financial Crisis.* John Wiley, 2006.

Benyus, Jenine. *Biomimicry: Innovation Inspired by Nature.* Harper Perennial, 2002.

Berle, Gustav. *The Green Entrepreneur: Business Opportunities That Can Save the Earth and Make You Money.* Liberty Hall Press, 1991.

Bornstein, David. *How to Change the World: Social Entrepreneurs and the Power of New Ideas.* Oxford University Press, 2004.

Brende, Eric. *Better Off: Flipping the Switch on Technology.* Harper Perennial, 2005.

Brill, Hal, Jack A. Brill and Cliff Feigenbaum. *Investing with Your Values: Making Money and Making a Difference.* New Society, 2000.

Brooks, David. *Bobos in Paradise: The New Upper Class and How They Got There.* Simon & Schuster, 2000.

Brown, Lester R. *Eco-Economy: Building an Economy for the Earth.* W.W. Norton, 2001.

Carson, Rachel. *Silent Spring.* Mariner, 2002.

Castro, Elizabeth. *Publishing a Blog with Blogger.* Peachpit Press, 2005.

Chiras, Dan. *The Natural House: A Complete Guide to Healthy, Energy-Efficient, Environmental Homes.* Chelsea Green, 2000.

Chiras, Dan. *The Homeowner's Guide to Renewable Energy: Achieving Energy Independence Through Solar, Wind, Biomass and Hydropower.* New Society, 2006.

Christian, Diana Leafe. *Finding Community: How to Join an Ecovillage or Intentional Community.* New Society, 2007.

Clyatt, Bob. *Work Less, Live More: The New Way to Retire Early.* Nolo, 2005.

Corbett, David D. *Portfolio Life: The New Path to Work, Purpose, and Passion after 50.* Jossey-Bass, 2007.

Dacyczyn, Amy. *The Tightwad Gazette Book: Promoting Thrift as a Viable Alternative Lifestyle.* Villard-Random House, 1993.

de Graaf, John, ed. *Take Back Your Time: Fighting Overwork and Time Poverty in America.* Berret-Koehler, 2003.

de Graaf, John, David Wann and Thomas H. Naylor. *Affluenza: The All-consuming Epidemic.* Berret-Koehler, 2005.

Dominguez, Joe and Vicki Robin. *Your Money or Your Life: Transforming Your Relationship with Money and Achieving Financial Independence.* Penguin, 1999.

Dufur, Brett. *The Complete Katy Trail Guidebook.* Pebble Publishing, 2002.

Edwards, Paul and Sarah Edwards. *Working from Home: Everything You Need to Know about Living and Working under the Same Roof.* Tarcher/Putnam, 1999.

Elkington, John. *Cannibals with Forks: The Triple Bottom Line of the 21st Century.* Capstone, 1999.

Fishman, Stephen. *Deduct It! Lower Your Small Business Taxes.* Nolo, 2006.

Fishman, Stephen. *Every Landlord's Tax Deduction Guide.* Nolo, 2006.

Fishman, Stephen. *Working for Yourself: Law and Taxes for Independent Contractors, Freelancers and Consultants.* Nolo, 2006.

Florida, Richard. *The Rise of the Creative Class: And How It's Transforming Work, Leisure, Community and Everyday Life.* Basic Books, 2002.

Fodor, Eben. *Better Not Bigger: How to Take Control of Urban Growth and Improve Your Community.* New Society, 1999.

Frank, Edward F. *The Real World of Small Business: A Street Fighter's Guide to Success.* Liberty-Grant, 2001

Gabriel, Gwendolyn D. *Become Totally Debt-Free in Five Years or Less: Pay off Your Mortgage, Car, Credit Cards, and More!* Brown Bag Press, 2000.

Gardner, Susannah. *Buzz Marketing with Blogs for Dummies.* Wiley, 2005.

Glavin, Terry. *The Sixth Extinction: Journeys Among the Lost and left Behind.* Thomas Dunne Books, 2007.

Gore, Al. *An Inconvenient Truth: The Crisis of Global Warming.* Viking, 2007.

Handy, Charles. *The Hungry Spirit: Purpose in the Modern World.* Broadway, 1999.

Handy, Charles. *The Elephant and the Flea: Reflections of a Reluctant Capitalist.* Harvard Business School, 2003.

Hartman, Harvey and David Wright. *Marketing to the New Natural Consumer: Understanding Trends in Wellness.* Hartman Group, 1999.

Hawken, Paul. *Growing a Business.* Fireside, 1987.

Hawken, Paul. *The Ecology of Commerce: A Declaration of Sustainability.* Harper Collins, 1993.

Hawken, Paul. *Blessed Unrest: How the Largest Movement in the World Came into Being and No One Saw It Coming.* Viking, 2007.

Hawken, Paul, Amory Lovins and L. Hunter Lovins. *Natural Capitalism: Creating the Next Industrial Revolution.* Little, Brown, 1999.

Henderson, Hazel. *Ethical Markets: Growing the Green Economy.* Chelsea Green, 2006.

Hendricks, Mark. *Not Just A Living: The Complete Guide to Creating a Business That Gives You a Life.* Perseus, 2002.

Horn, Greg. *Living Green: A Practical Guide to Simple Sustainability.* Freedom Press, 2006.

Ivanko, John. *The Least Imperfect Path*. Paradigm Press, Ltd., 1996.

Ivanko, John and Lisa Kivirist. *Rural Renaissance: Renewing the Quest for the Good Life*. New Society, 2004.

Ivanko, John, Lisa Kivirist and Liam Kivirist. *Edible Earth: Savoring the Good Life with Vegetarian Recipes from Inn Serendipity*. Paradigm Press, Ltd., 2007.

Joannides, Jan. *Renewing the Countryside: Minnesota*. Renewing the Countryside, 2001.

Kamoroff, Bernard. *Small-Time Operator*. Bell Springs, 1991.

Kiuchi, Tachi, and William K.Shireman. *What We Learned in the Rainforest: Business Lessons from Nature*. Berret-Koehler, 2002.

Kivirist, Lisa. *Kiss Off Corporate America: A Young Professional's Guide to Independence*. Andrews McMeel, 1997.

Kiyosaki, Robert T. *Rich Dad, Poor Dad: What the Rich Teach Their Kids about Money That the Poor Do Not*. TechPress, 1998.

Kotlikoff, Laurence J. and Scott Burns. *The Coming Generational Storm: What You Need to Know About America's Economic Future*. MIT Press, 2004.

Korten, David. *When Corporations Rule the World*. Berrett-Koehler, 2001.

Kunstler, James H. *The Long Emergency: Surviving the Converging Catastrophes of the Twenty-first Century*. Atlantic Monthly Press, 2005.

Leopold, Aldo. *A Sand County Almanac*. Ballantine, 1986.

Long, Charles. *How to Survive Without a Salary: Learning How to Live the Conserver Lifestyle*. Warwick, 1996.

Luhrs, Janet. *The Simple Living Guide: A Sourcebook for Less Stressful, More Joyful Living*. Broadway Books, 1997.

Mancuso, Anthony. *The Corporate Minutes Book: A Legal Guide to Taking Care of Corporate Business*. Nolo, 1998.

Mason, Margaret. *No One Cares What You Had for Lunch: 100 Ideas for Your Blog*. Peachpit Press, 2007.

Matson, Jack V. *Innovate or Die: A Personal Perspective on the Art of Innovation*. Paradigm, 1996.

McDonough, William and Michael Braungart. *Cradle to Cradle: Remaking the Way We Make Things*. North Point Press, 2002.

McKibben, Bill. *Deep Economy: The Wealth of Communities and the Durable Future*. Times Books, 2007.

McMakin, Tom. *Bread and Butter: What a Bunch of Bakers Taught Me About Business and Happiness*. St. Martin's, 2001.

Nadeau, Robert. *The Wealth of Nature: How Mainstream Economics Has Failed the Environment*. Columbia University, 2003.

Parker, Thornton. *What If Boomers Can't Retire: How to Build Real Security, Not Phantom Wealth*. Berrett-Koehler, 2000.

Pernick, Ron and Clint Wilder. *The Clean Tech Revolution: The Next Big Growth and Investment Opportunity*. Collins, 2007.

Pine, Joe and Jim Gilmore. *The Experience Economy: Work Is Theatre and Every Business Is a Stage*. Harvard Business School, 1999.

Pink, Daniel H. *Free Agent Nation: How America's New Independent Workers Are Transforming the Way We Live*. Warner Business Books, 2001.

Pollan, Michael. *The Omnivore's Dilemma: A Natural History of Four Meals*. Penguin, 2006.

Putnam, Robert D. *Bowling Alone: The Collapse and Revival of American Community*. Simon & Schuster, 2001.

Quinn, Daniel. *Ishmael*. Bantam, 1991.

Ray, Paul and Sherry Ruth Anderson. *The Cultural Creatives: How 50 Million People Are Changing the World*. Harmony Books, 2000.

Roy, Robert L. *Mortgage Free!: Radical Strategies for Home Ownership*. Chelsea Green, 1998.

Salatin, Joel. *Everything I Want to Do Is Illegal: War Stories from the Local Food Front*. Polyface, 2007.

Savitz, Andrew and Karl Weber. *The Triple Bottom Line: How Today's Best-Run Companies Are Achieving Economic, Social and Environmental Success — and How You Can Too*. Jossey-Bass, 2006.

Schumacher, E. F. *Small Is Beautiful: Economics As If People Mattered*. Harper & Rowe, 1989.

Shuman, Michael H. *The Small Mart Revolution: How Local Businesses Are Beating the Global Competition*. Berret-Koehler, 2007.

Smith, Adam. *The Wealth of Nations*. Bantam Classics, 2003.

Stanley, Thomas and William Danko. *The Millionaire Next Door: The Surprising Secrets of America's Wealthy*. MJF Books, 2003.

Stauffer, Todd. *Blog On: The Essential Guide to Building Dynamic Weblogs*. McGraw-Hill/Osborne, 2002.

Stoyke, Godo. *The Carbon Buster's Home Energy Handbook: Slowing Climate Change and Saving Money*. New Society, 2007.

Teller-Elsberg, Johnathan. *Field Guide to the U.S. Economy: A Compact and Irreverent Guide to Economic Life in America*. New Press, 2006.

Thoreau, Henry David. *Walden*. Running Press, 1990.

Trask, Crissy. *It's Easy Being Green: A Handbook for Earth-friendly Living*. Gibbs Smith, 2006.

Uchitelle, Louis. *The Disposable American: Layoffs and Their Consequences*. Vintage, 2007.

United Nations. *Millennium Ecosystem Assessment*. UN, 2005.
www.millenniumassessment.org/en/index.aspx; www.greenfacts.org/en/ecosystems/#1

Urbanska, Wanda and Frank Levering. *Simple Living: One Couple's Search for a Better Life*. Viking, 1992.

Urbanska, Wanda and Frank Levering. *Moving to a Small Town: A Guidebook for Moving from Urban to Rural America*. Simon & Schuster, 1996.

Urbanska, Wanda and Frank Levering. *Nothing's Too Small to Make a Difference*. Blair, 2004.

Wackernagel, Mathis and William Rees. *Our Ecological Footprint: Reducing Human Impact on the Earth*. New Society, 1996.

Walker, Liz. *EcoVillage at Ithaca: Pioneering a Sustainable Culture*. New Society, 2005.

Walters, Jamie S. *Big Vision, Small Business: The Four Keys to Finding Success and Satisfaction as a Lifestyle Entrepreneur*. Ivy Sea, 2001.

Wibbels, Andy. *Blogwild! A Guide for Small Business Blogging*. Portfolio, 2006.

Wolf, Peter. *Hot Towns: The Future of the Fastest Growing Communities in America*. Rutgers University Press, 1999.

Zelinski, Ernie J. *The Joy of Not Working: A Book for the Retired, Employed, and Overworked*. Ten Speed, 2003.

Index

About the Authors

JOHN IVANKO AND LISA KIVIRIST are co-authors of *Rural Renaissance* and *Edible Earth*, innkeepers of the award-winning Inn Serendipity Bed & Breakfast, national speakers, freelance writers and co-partners in a marketing consulting company.

John Ivanko is also an award-winning photographer, freelance writer and author or co-author of numerous books, including the award-winning children's photobooks, *To Be a Kid*, *To Be an Artist*, *Be My Neighbor* and *Animal Friends*. Lisa Kivirist is a Food and Society Policy Fellow, author of *Kiss Off Corporate America* and freelance writer contributing to numerous magazines, including *Hobby Farm Home* and *Mother Earth News*.

Former advertising agency fast-trackers, the husband-and-wife duo are nationally recognized for their contemporary approach to ecopreneurship, homesteading, conservation and more sustainable living. Based in Browntown, Wisconsin, they share their farm and Inn Serendipity with their son, busy bees thriving in the honey bee economy, and millions of ladybugs.

If you have enjoyed *ECOpreneuring* you might also enjoy other

BOOKS TO BUILD A NEW SOCIETY

Our books provide positive solutions for people who want to
make a difference. We specialize in:

Natural Building & Appropriate Technology

Ecological Design and Planning • Sustainable Living

Conscientious Commerce • Environment and Justice

Educational and Parenting Resources • Nonviolence

Progressive Leadership • Resistance and Community

New Society Publishers

ENVIRONMENTAL BENEFITS STATEMENT

New Society Publishers has chosen to produce this book on recycled paper made with
100% post consumer waste, processed chlorine free, and old growth free.

For every 5,000 books printed, New Society saves the following resources:[1]

23	Trees
2,050	Pounds of Solid Waste
2,225	Gallons of Water
2,941	Kilowatt Hours of Electricity
3,726	Pounds of Greenhouse Gases
16	Pounds of HAPs, VOCs, and AOX Combined
6	Cubic Yards of Landfill Space

[1]Environmental benefits are calculated based on research done by the Environmental Defense Fund and
other members of the Paper Task Force who study the environmental impacts of the paper industry.

For a full list of NSP's titles, please call **1-800-567-6772** or check out our website at:

www.newsociety.com

NEW SOCIETY PUBLISHERS